For

Dr. & Mrs. John D. Sink
with appreciation and
best wishes from their
friend

[signature]

December 2, 1995.

Recovering the Sacred

Papers from the Sanctuary and the Academy

EARL G. HUNT, JR.

Recovering the Sacred

Papers from the Sanctuary and the Academy

EARL G. HUNT, JR.

JONATHAN CREEK PRESS

RECOVERING THE SACRED
Papers from the Sanctuary and the Academy

Scripture quotations not otherwise identified are from the authorized King James Version of the Bible.

Scripture quotations designated (NKJV) are from the Holy Bible, The New King James Version. Copyright 1972, 1984 by Thomas Nelson, Inc., Publishers.

Scripture quotations designated (RSV) are from the Holy Bible, Revised Standard Version, copyright 1946, 1952, 1971, 1973 by the Division of Christian Education, National Council of Churches of Christ in the United States of America.

The photograph of Pope John Paul II in the photo section is the courtesy of Arturo Mari, Servizio Fotografico, L'Osservatore Romano, 00120 Vatican City State.

Cover design: C. J. Helms
First printing: January, 1992 (3)
ISBN: 0-9631308-0-3

Published by Jonathan Creek Press, Lake Junaluska, N.C.

To

Members of the Council of Bishops

Living and Deceased

My Honored Colleagues and Treasured Friends
for Nearly Three Decades

and to

The Trustees of The Foundation for Evangelism

Whose Deep Commitment to Jesus Christ

and

Warm Friendship

Have Brightened My Latter Years

Table of Contents

Foreword

In preparation for writing the foreword to this book, I read twice the manuscript which Bishop Hunt sent me—first, as anyone would read a book, out of curiosity and general interest, entertainment, and in this case friendship for the author; and the second time studiously, analytically, even critically in order to be able properly to introduce the book to the reading public with an evaluation of its contents and its usefulness, remembering Francis Bacon's dictum that no pleasure is comparable to being able to stand on the vantage ground of truth. Both readings of the manuscript produced the same results: information, insight, intellectual stimulation, spiritual discernment, and inspiration. The book has the lilt of a song and at the same time the profundity of a comprehensive philosophy of life, both inviting and convincing. "Some books," wrote Bacon, "are to be tasted, others to be swallowed, and some few to be chewed and digested." This one is to be chewed and digested.

The first chapter of the book is an autobiographical prelude to all that is to follow. It is entitled "Purely Personal," which is an apt description; for a person's own view of his career, its purpose and goals, though comprised of the same facts, may be quite different from a biographer's. This author, out of modesty and self-effacement, tells the story of his life with British understatement, a healthy contrast to most of the autobiographies we read today. He places emphasis on the contribution others have made to his growth and development and little or no emphasis on his own creative initiative and originality. Nonetheless, the facts themselves bespeak his talent, industry, and even genius. There emerges the picture of a farsighted, practical, and successful church leader combined with a studious, reflective, and profound person—a classical scholar who has continued to read Latin all through his busy life. Even his chief hobby displays his intellectual predilection, for since an early date he has collected autographs of famous people, past and present. His collection before he disposed of it was one of the best and most extensive in the country. It was international in scope and consisted of persons in various walks of life over the entire world.

It is not without point that the minister who exerted the greatest influence on Earl as he was growing up was a person with an earned doctorate from Drew University who had previously been a Rhodes Scholar at Oxford. Under this minister, Earl received the call to preach. The tenderest and most moving part of this chapter, however, is the author's tribute to his wife and his parents, especially his father, who was the best person he has ever known. "Purely Personal" unveils the portrait, however reluctantly painted, of a most talented, charming, devoted, and pious man.

Except for the first chapter, this book is a miscellany of addresses and sermons given on special occasions over a period of thirty-three years by an eminent divine and ecclesiastical statesman to signalize important events. The first one was delivered in the spring of 1957, and the last in the fall of 1990. There are sixteen of them, seven sermons and nine addresses. The sermons, however, are not from the usual repertory of a preacher, even a famous one such as Phillips Brooks or Harry Emerson Fosdick, but rather from a special category of messages determined by the nature of the occasion for which each one was constructed. Before I received the manuscript, I asked Bishop Hunt if one of his best-known sermons, "Pilate's Washbowl," would be included in the book. He told me that it would not simply because it was not composed for some special occasion. Therefore, these addresses and sermons provide us with a precís of the Bishop's career.

Only one of the sixteen comes from the author's ministry prior to his election to the episcopacy, while two were written and delivered after his relinquishing the duties of a so-called "effective" bishop—that is, a bishop who presides over an episcopal area and is responsible for the ministerial appointments within that area. That one address was his inaugural address as president of Emory & Henry College. This does not mean that nothing significant happened in the author's career as a pastor and college president. In both fields he made signal achievements. Otherwise, he would never have been elected to the episcopacy. But as these achievements were marked by special occasions, someone else gave the address. The author established a new congregation and built a church to house it in Chattanooga, but a bishop dedicated it and preached the sermon on that occasion.

The same was true at the times when new buildings were dedicated and endowed lectureships were established at the college. The author gave many important addresses and preached innumerable sermons, many in preaching missions over the country, developing a national reputation as an orator; but these did not mark some special occasion or signalize some important event. After all, there was only one occasion for the Gettysburg Address. The failure of the author to include sermons and public discourses from his pre-episcopal years but emphasizes the nature of this collection and the purpose for which it was made—namely, to use some special occasion to think about what it represents to all of us and to draw from it lessons for the living of our lives.

The collection is focused on what the author styles the sanctuary and the academy—that is, religion and education. The title of the book is *Recovering the Sacred,* which can only be achieved by what society, at least in the West, seems once to have had but now has lost, namely Christian values and a Christian standard for life. The assumption of the book is that this recovery can take place only through a system of education the foundation of which is Christianity. Its aim is the wedding of knowledge and vital piety, for a society cannot be good unless it is populated with good people. For a state to be just and righteous, its citizens must be just and righteous. Laws are but the codification of the mores of the people who enact them. Thus the very first lecture in the book establishes the development of Christian character as one of the primary, if not the most essential, functions of a college. Though this applies specifically to a church college, which should be that institution's teaching wing, it must in the end characterize all educational institutions in a society motivated by Christian principles and shaped by Christian values.

The social ethics of the book reflects a combination of Plato's *Republic* and Augustine's *City of God,* for the civic principles of the Greek city-state as an organizational pattern are apparent, but the overmastering conviction is that these are just principles if divorced from the motivating power of divine grace which is operative in the personal lives of citizens. Plato's *Republic* was only an ideal, wonderful as it was; it never attained reality in any commonwealth. Augustine's *City of God* became the blueprint for the Christian commonwealth of the Middle Ages and the foundation of Western civilization.

Evangelization is the normal expression of Christian education, for if life is to be modeled on Christian principles, there must be the strength to utilize in deed and action what is believed to be true and right. This comes only through the transformation of heart and life by the grace of God, which is made so clear and convincing in the address delivered at the banquet for the Friends of the World Methodist Museum, entitled "John Wesley: Our Historical Contemporary." This address is really a portrayal of John Wesley as a preacher and through him an assertion of the power of preaching in the transformation of personal life and of society.

Very little has been done on Wesley as a preacher, and most of what has been done has been scant and inadequate. I am alleged to be a Wesleyan scholar, and I have tried to read everything John Wesley ever wrote and much that others have written about him. This address by Bishop Hunt is the best portrayal of Wesley as a preacher I have ever read. It far surpasses the long chapter of fifty-seven pages entitled "John Wesley as Preacher" in the theological biography of John Wesley by the German historian Martin Schmidt, which was published in German in 1966 and translated into English in 1973. The English biographers of Wesley, even Tyerman, the most thorough and dependable of the lot, neglect this subject altogether. Therefore, we are deeply in debt to Bishop Hunt for the research and thought he gave to this issue, his careful analysis of Wesley's homiletical method and manner of delivery and textual skills and use of illustrations, especially those drawn from his own experience. Evidently his messages delivered in the open air and in the few churches open to Wesley were quite different from his published sermons, though I was not aware of the great contrast between the two until I read Bishop Hunt's address. To a historian this is the most remarkable address in the collection.

The importance of theological, or doctrinal, preaching is emphasized in the address the Bishop gave during Ministers' Week at Emory University in 1978, entitled "Preaching Theology." This is an unusual address in that it does not deal with the explication of individual doctrines as such but rather with a basic theological understanding that should underlie and determine all sermonic utterances. The subtleties; delicate distinctions; and, more than all else, the implications of the message are quite remarkable. The Bishop gives us a concrete example of theological preaching in the two sermons "The Day of the Lord" and "In the House of the Lord Forever," the one as the keynote address of the World Methodist Conference in Dublin, Ireland, in 1976, and the other at the opening of the General Conference of The United Methodist Church in Saint Louis in 1988, which marked the conclusion of his term in office as president of the Council of Bishops.

The Bishop's ecumenical commitment is registered in an address he made in his own episcopal area in Charlotte, North Carolina, to a joint meeting of United Methodists and Roman Catholics. That address entitled "United Methodists and Roman Catholics: A Contemplation of Christian Unity" is complemented by a sermon, "Common Glory," preached to a Roman Catholic congregation at Saint Patrick's Cathedral in Charlotte. Both messages display the hungering heart of a shepherd for a sheepfold big enough and comfortable enough for his sheep and those of his Roman Catholic brother to dwell together in mutual understanding, support, confidence, and love. The United Methodist and Roman Catholic bishops during Bishop Hunt's and Bishop Michael Begley's time there together made Charlotte such a sheepfold.

The sermon "Toward a Recovery of the Sacred," given at an ecumenical colloquy at Notre Dame University, of which I was a participant, provided the idea for this collection and is contained in its title. It is placed not at the beginning but in the middle of the book. This, I am sure, is due more to the chronological sequence in which the addresses were delivered than to anything else. Though it is fortuitous, it is fortunate as well; for this sermon is the soul of the book, gathering, as it were in a centerpiece, what comes before and what follows after: argumentation and persuasive evidence that leads up to the establishment of a truth and then proof in pragmatic examples of its effectiveness and wholesome results.

The contention of this message is that God can and does disclose himself in our moment of history as he has in the past, and we can discern him in the lighted mind and in the recovery of the authentic character of the church if we will but open our eyes to his contemporary activity.

Here Bishop Hunt advances the idea that our acts of worship are not just to improve ourselves and win God's favor but that they actually have meaning for God himself. In other words, at public worship we—the people of God—are the actual actors on the stage and God is the audience. The role we play, which is the life we live, must be a life of holiness if it is to win God's approval. In another chapter of the book, he quotes Bishop Soderblom as saying that holiness is more essential to religion than even the notion of God. Notion, yes, but not the person of God, who alone can define holiness and provide the grace to attain it. The divine epiphany, which Bishop Hunt expects, won't, in my opinion, reveal a new set of values or even a different pattern of life but will merely be a disclosure of the worth we already have in Jesus Christ and the incentive to be more like him.

There is a strong prophetic ring to this book where the Bishop addresses such issues as marriage and the breakup of the family and permissiveness in morals and the eroding of the restraining influence of fixed ethical standards through situation ethics. During his tenure as president of the Council of Bishops he gave an address to the Council in which he pointed to racism and human sexuality as the two most serious social and moral problems facing the church. On the first of these issues there was general agreement with his point of view, but on the latter, in which he condemned overt homosexual behavior as altogether unacceptable behavior in Christians, there was some negative reaction even in the Council of Bishops itself. This negative reaction was minor in the Council, but his address was a red flag to advocates of the acceptance of homosexual behavior as an approved way of life for clergy as well as lay people in our denomination. This position has been condemned and the Bishop's position upheld by the last several general conferences, but the small minority in the church will not let it die, so that we continue to discuss and debate the issue regardless of the agitation is causes within the church.

In his address at the National Convocation on World Mission and Evangelism, Bishop Hunt in a remarkable way did a balancing act in which he delineated both the assets and liabilities in the contemporary United Methodist Church. He did this in sermonic form with a strong hortatory appeal to admit and correct our mistakes by abandoning a leadership of avoidance with its timidity and ambivalence and, as prophets, declare that the church is God's, not ours; and it is for us to obey God's will, not to foster and try to justify our pleasures and desires. This message is included under its title, "The Excellency of Carmel."

One receives a delightful and appealing picture of the author himself in his love of books, delight in reading, and devotional life in the two addresses "On Books and Values" and "A Devotional Odyssey," the charm of which is indescribable. His admiration and love for the churchman who exerted more influence on him than anyone else and helped to mold his ministerial and episcopal careers, Bishop Roy Hunter Short, is displayed in his tribute to the Bishop at the last session of the Louisville Annual Conference over which Short was to preside as its resident bishop. This sermon shows us the vitality and strength of our Methodist heritage by displaying how it has been used effectively and creatively in the contemporary church by one of the most distinguished and successful of our bishops, for Bishop Short's episcopate has already become a legend in our denomination.

The last sermon in the book is its climax, for it expresses the heart and soul of Bishop Hunt's ministry. Evangelism has been his love, as it has mine, since his ordination. This was the heartbeat of his pastoral ministry. This concern did not desert him during his years of college administration, and it was always the chief aim of his episcopate. Now in retirement he is devoting his full working days to the Foundation for Evangelism. It is therefore fitting and proper that he should in the last chapter of the book lay bare what he takes to be the basic principles of evangelism in order to win people in our contemporary secular society to Jesus Christ.

Recovering the Sacred is a compelling and motivating book, well conceived, thoroughly thought out, and admirably written. Its style is clear and convincing as well as elegant. In places it lapses into poetic prose. Despite his protests that he lacks a terminal degree—that is, an earned doctorate—and his complaints that heavy administrative duties have denied him the leisure to study, Bishop Hunt's book is an example of scholarly accomplishment and preaching and lecturing at their noblest and best. It shows him to be in our generation what Phillips Brooks, Harry Emerson Fosdick, Edwin Holt Hughes, and Arthur James Moore were in theirs. Bishop Hunt has one of the best furnished minds in the church. His reading is wide and extensive and his knowledge is almost encyclopedic in range. His mind is clear, incisive, and profound; and I would say of his style in writing what Walter Lippmann said of Fosdick's, that it is unsurpassed in contemporary English prose.

Everyone who has an interest in religion and literature should read this book.

+William R. Cannon
Atlanta

Preface

This is a portrait of my thought.

At the suggestion of friends, the addresses and sermons in this book have been chosen to convey some of the principal ideas and convictions which have motivated my ministry for nearly half a century.

Each chapter is set within its own time frame, its specific content being relevant to the particular period for which it was written. All of us have become progressively more sensitive to the use of inclusive language and certain adjustments in thought and expression in recent years. However, in order to preserve their historical flavor, the earlier documents in this volume have not always been edited to reflect later growth in understanding but are included for the most part as they were used originally.

Portions of the text in three or four addresses have appeared earlier in books I have written and are identified in the endnotes. I am grateful to my publishers, The Upper Room and Abingdon, for permission to use them in this volume. Other material, in a few instances, has been published elsewhere. This is noted, and reproduction here is by permission.

I am grateful to many who have helped with this task, and especially to Janice Grana, editor and publisher of *The Upper Room;* Dr. Lynne Deming, editor, Upper Room Books; Janet McNish and JoAnn Miller, editors for this volume; Dr. Webb Garrison, author, former college president and dear friend who made his Jonathan Creek Press available for this volume; and Dr. Harry Gilmer, former college president, now head of Scholars Press. In a very special way, my dear friend, colleague, and mentor, Bishop William Ragsdale Cannon, one of United Methodism's greatest minds and spirits in this century, has honored me by his willingness to write the Foreword. Finally, I wish to express appreciation to Mr. John H. Marshall, Jr., Chair of the Board of Trustees of The Foundation for Evangelism, and Mr. Phillip F.

Connolly, member of the Board, for their extraordinary assistance in making possible the publication of this book.

My special thanks are extended to my loyal and devoted secretary, Mrs. Joretta Caldwell, for patient and painstaking typing and retyping of the manuscript.

Earl G. Hunt, Jr.
Lent 1992

Purely Personal

The most obvious unifying theme for the various selections in this volume is my own life and faith. To use the figure of a circle, the circumference of my interests has been expansive and diverse, while the center has remained traditional, even orthodox. The essence of my religion has been devotional, a Bible-informed empiricism, the kind of warm, personal experience of Jesus Christ exalted so effectively in publications like *The Upper Room.* Like Dante so many years ago, I have come to see theology as God's poetry. My faith, although as carefully tutored as I could make it, has retained an elemental simplicity akin to childlike trust. I was trained in the principles of a religious liberalism now gone, but the flames upon the altar of my heart throughout my ministry have been those of a *classical* evangelicalism. What I have crafted into addresses and sermons through the years is a reflection of the religious content in my own soul.

A publisher urged me to write my autobiography at the time of my retirement from the effective episcopacy in 1988. My deferred response (amounting to a refusal) was based upon an experience I had just been through with the late Dr. James S. Stewart, famous Scottish scholar and preacher, one of the Queen's chaplains, who was our dear friend across many years. I had written Dr. Stewart proposing that I undertake to identify a biographer for him, either in Britain or the United States. I was not prepared for the vehemence of his reaction: "No, I could not countenance that!" he replied. "It would vex me to think of anyone undertaking that. I almost shudder at the very thought of it.... My life and ministry have been too ordinary altogether.... I should be quite definitely against it."[1]

If Dr. Stewart, authentically a twentieth-century "giant" in the world Christian community, could not "countenance" the story of his life being written, how presumptuous would be my undertaking to set to record the facts about my own career! And yet,

I have wanted to provide some sort of interpretative context for the following selections which articulate much of my life's thought and conviction. Hence, this chapter about backgrounds and influences.

Family

I was born in Johnson City, Tennessee, less than two months before the armistice at the close of World War I. A cousin of mine, a brave and independent woman who has endured much hardship in her life, says, "To me, family is everything." While I might not say "everything," I would never disagree with the spirit of her comment. Let me, therefore, write first about those who have been dearest to me.

My mother, quite beautiful as a young woman, was born on Pack Square in Asheville, North Carolina, in 1887. Her father, a pharmacist, died in the influenza epidemic of 1888. He is buried in an unmarked grave somewhere in "the Land of the Sky." Her mother took her as a baby back to her own native haunts near Jonesborough, Tennessee, and she went through the lower grades in a rural school nearby, moving then into the home of a relative in Jonesborough and completing her high school work there. She acquired modest social graces and refinement and became a lover of learning and culture, although her exposure to both was limited. She was a perfectionist, an excellent cook, and a housekeeper whose emphasis upon cleanliness approached the fanatical.

My mother married my father at the home of her aunt and uncle in Whitesburg, Tennessee, on October 12, 1912. I was an only child, and she was a faithful, understanding parent to me. After living with my wife and me for twenty years, she resided at the Wesley Nursing Center, a part of The Methodist Home in Charlotte, North Carolina, until we were moved to Nashville in 1976. She wanted to be where we were, and we took her by air-ambulance to McKendree Manor near Nashville in early autumn of that year. The trauma of the move proved too much for her, and she survived only a month.

My father was the best man I have ever known. He was born in the Sulphur Springs community near Jonesborough in 1886 and went only as far as the eighth grade in his formal education. While a young man, he began forty years of association with

Summers Hardware and Supply Company in Johnson City as an old-fashioned "drummer" in the Western North Carolina territory.

Dad was unostentatious about his religion, but he went to church regularly and supported the church as generously as his limited income allowed. He lost all his meager savings during the Depression but refused to take bankruptcy (which friends had advised him to do) and paid off every penny of his indebtedness before suffering a heart attack.

In all the years I knew him, I never heard him tell an off-color joke, use profanity, or speak unkindly to my mother. As a parent, he was a strict disciplinarian but always kind and generous.

Dad was known for his integrity and his capacity to form friendships. These characteristics lingered to bless me during the early years of my episcopacy when I was assigned to serve as bishop over the very Western North Carolina territory where he had sold hardware for four decades and where many old-timers still remembered him affectionately. I have sought unsuccessfully to become as good a person as my father.

During the last eight years of his life, because of shattered health and straitened economic circumstances, my father and mother had to accept our invitation to live in our parsonage homes in Chattanooga and Morristown. My father faced the loss of his own independent pattern of life with quiet dignity, good-natured patience, and gentle gratitude to my wife for making room for her husband's parents in our little family circle. He never lost his care for his appearance, his regal gentlemanliness, or his pride in his children's ministry. As his health began to deteriorate, he became a serious craftsman in wood and leather, and we still have in our home beautiful products of his skill. Among all the positive influences I have known, none is greater than the strong example of my father's life.

My earliest years were happy, despite the loneliness of being an only child. My father, constantly struggling to make ends meet, somehow found fifty cents a week for my allowance. I spent it on books, an incongruous mixture of Tom Swift, Charles Dickens, the Rover Boys and Mark Twain! Some lovely memories persist from those childhood years: summer picnics, on one of which I was permitted the luxury of my first Coca-Cola; afternoons at Redpath Chautauqua matinees with my mother; two alarming bouts with pneumonia before the days of antibiotics with nurses around the clock at an expense which even my childhood awareness knew was far beyond my parents' means. I remember fourteen years of fun with my little fox-terrier "Blackie"; going after the cows at early dusk on my grandfather's farm; eating delicious country dishes like stuffed peppers and homemade *Schmierkäse* in the cool screened-in summer dining room of the old farmhouse; and making the rounds of neighborhood cottages and apartment houses peddling flowers from my mother's garden to add a few dollars to our grocery fund. Those were rich, satisfying years during which I never sensed any disadvantage because our family lacked the financial bounty others had.

On the afternoon of June 15, 1943, Mary Ann Kyker and Earl Gladstone Hunt, Jr., were united in holy matrimony before the altar of First Methodist Church in Johnson City, Tennessee. She is the daughter of Dr. and Mrs. Charles Hartsell Kyker, both deceased, and was my childhood sweetheart from the fifth grade through college. Her father was a beloved physician and her mother a registered nurse; both were highly respected local citizens and faithful members of our home church. They died prematurely, Mrs. Kyker in 1933 and Dr. Kyker in 1942.

As a girl and young lady, Mary Ann loved life and laughter and people. She began quite early her steady but always private devotion to Jesus Christ and her daily study of the Scriptures. She has always abhorred piosity and ostentation in religious expression, but I have never known a person able to discern more quickly genuine depth in Christian commitment. Throughout our ministry together in pastorates, on a college campus, and across more than a quarter of a century in the episcopacy, she has drawn folk, both plain and famous, to herself by her unfailing gifts of friendliness, good humor, and infectious charm. People, for the most part, have respected me; but they have loved her.

Mary Ann has been the catalyst for any success I have had. I have never found her basically wrong in her analysis of situations or persons. Her instant readiness to receive my parents into our home when the need came, even though she must have known how great her own sacrifice would be, made it possible for me to continue my ministry. My love and respect for her, never adequately expressed, are still the greatest and most consuming emotions of my life.

Malcolm Muggeridge, the beguilingly articulate British literary critic and editor, who finally became a great Christian, writing in the second volume of his autobiography about his marriage to Kitty Dobbs, expressed well my own feelings about Mary Ann: "So, it was borne in upon me that Kitty and I belonged together; that somehow, to me, the shape and sense and sound of her existence in the universe would always be appreciable in every corner of it, and through all eternity."[2]

Mary Ann and I have one child, a son, Earl Stephen, born November 28, 1948. After earning his baccalaureate degree with honors from Emory & Henry College in 1971, he went on to take a master's from American University and a Ph.D. from the University of Virginia, with additional graduate work in contracts and grants. He was managing editor for two years of the public policy journal *This World* and in partnership with a well-known ethicist edited a major anthology about the nuclear crisis. He now holds a significant position in the Office of Research of the United States Department of Education in Washington. Among his recent publications are the widely distributed report of a committee he organized on drug prevention curricula in public education and the 1990 edition of the Federal Government's standard classification of instructional programs. Stephen is married to the former Edeltraut Gilgan, daughter of a splendid Hamburg, Germany family, who holds a responsible position with the World Bank. She formerly worked for the foreign service of the Federal Republic of Germany and received her B.A. degree from George Washington University and her M.B.A. from Marymount University. They make their home in Bethesda, Maryland. We are very proud of our son and daughter-in-law.

To consider further my cousin's insistence upon the importance of family, I must mention her own father, my Uncle Homer, a member of General John J. Pershing's staff in World War I, a strong and intelligent Christian man who became, in his last years, a heroic sufferer as he battled a series of illnesses. He and his wife, together with a maiden sister, my beloved Aunt Nell, who lived with them, made the old Hunt family home at Sulphur Springs a precious retreat for Mary Ann and me and our young son as long as they lived.

My Uncle Bruce, a public educator for forty years in South Carolina's low country, stimulated my respect for the academic. My father's youngest brother, Uncle Bill, who worked with him at Summers Hardware and Supply Company, with his wife, my Aunt Clara, lived and died in Johnson City. Mr. and Mrs. Bert Kyker, my wife's uncle and aunt, were also there, and all of these kinspeople were dear to Mary Ann and me. The warm memory of Mary Ann's Aunt Nola (Mrs. W. I. Broyles) and her hospitable home and delectable cooking in rural Earl Tennessee near the banks of the Nolichucky River still delights me.

The Evolution of My Faith

I was baptized as an infant by Dr. W. F. Pitts and joined the church at the age of twelve after careful confirmation instruction by Dr. O. R. Tarwater, Sr. But the beautiful moment when I myself accepted Christ as my personal Savior came four years later as, alone in the house one Sunday afternoon, I knelt by my parents' bed and asked God to forgive my sin and take my life into His care. I know that people come into the household of faith by many different routes, but I have always been thankful that God allowed me a vivid personal experience of His saving grace, a shining moment to which I have been able to return again and again during periods of doubt and difficulty.

There were two major influences in my life during my late high school and college years. The first of these was an outreach program at my home church, First Methodist in Johnson City, designed to minister particularly to the children of unemployed families in an economically desolate local community during the grim years of the Great Depression. I have described this program in some detail in the second selection in this book, entitled "The Greatest Among You," beginning on page 43. My first understanding of a servant church emerged from this experience; and the *very* influential friendship of Andrew W. (Andy) Bolinger, an older helper who was a remarkable, although largely untutored, Christian, came to bless my life through this undertaking. The program, called the Junior Mission, fostered for me an early interest in the sociology of poverty and the economic mandates of the Christian Gospel.

The other strong influence during this period of my life was an interdenominational (we did not use the word *ecumenical* as readily in those days) Youth Council composed of young people out of twenty-nine different churches ranging from the Protestant Episcopal to the Salvation Army. This effort began as a series of student-sponsored prayer meetings and broadened into a program of city-wide youth rallies held each month during an academic year and featuring well-known Christian leaders of that period. The local ministerial association counselled with us in selecting speakers; and people like Robert E. Speer, Peter Marshall, M. E. Dodd, Harold Paul Sloan, Dr. Howard Atwood Kelly, Dr. James Park McCallie, Bishop Edwin Holt Hughes, and Dr. E. Schuyler English attracted literally thousands of local citizens of all ages, until the monthly meetings sponsored by the Youth Council became a compelling feature in Johnson City's calendar of events. Lifelong friendships were forged among the students at Science Hill High School and East Tennessee State College. Out of this group more than thirty young people from different denominations went into full-time Christian service around the world.

It was the Youth Council that, in the early years of my Christian life, lifted me out of a narrow sectarianism and gave me appreciation for both the liberal and conservative understandings of the Christian faith. I have always been grateful for this eclectic introduction to the richness of religious belief.

Two individuals, one on each end of the theological spectrum, stand out as heavily influential in my life during adolescence and post-adolescence. The first was the Reverend Dr. Joseph Warren Broyles, pastor of my home church in Johnson City, later professor of Philosophy at Hamline University, and president of Snead Junior College and West Virginia Wesleyan College. Dr. Broyles, under whose ministry I heard the call to preach, died suddenly while serving the last institution. After completing his period at Oxford as a Rhodes Scholar, he took his doctorate under Edwin Lewis at Drew. A man of infectious charm, dynamic demeanor, and incisive intellect, he was an evangelical liberal whose eager commitment to God suffused my youthful soul with a desire to turn the world upside down for Jesus Christ.

The second individual, an unapologetic fundamentalist who was the most exciting Bible teacher I ever knew, was Mrs. Emily Miller Barlow. Widow of a prominent attorney and daughter of a beloved physician, her irresistibly scintillating personality and her warmly intimate personal faith brought the religious community of Johnson City easily under her spell as she unfolded the Scriptures in classes that spanned more than four decades. She loved young people and surrounded them with such understanding and affection that many of us came to a place where we felt we owed our personal spiritual growth to her concern, care and, of course, prayers. During the last years of her life, while my wife and I were serving as the Florida Conference's episcopal family, we saw her occasionally in the company of her daughter, Mrs. Anthony Rossi, of Bradenton.

For me to have been influenced by two people so different theologically constitutes an anomaly which may help to explain the fact that my ministry has been such a mixture of liberalism and conservatism and that I have numbered among my dearest friends committed people from both groups.

Education

Dr. Henry Nelson Snyder, president of Wofford College, who gave the commencement address at my college graduation, titled his autobiography *An Educational Odyssey*.[3] In a sense these words describe my own life. I have always loved the adventure of learning, and the books I acquired across the years were my friends as well as my treasures. I never had an opportunity to pursue a terminal degree, although had I known that my church would call upon me to be a college president for eight years, I would have endeavored to do so. Because I can say the same thing for myself, I understand fully what William Barclay meant when he declared, "I know I have a second-class mind."[4] I have never been a scholar, and perhaps only occasionally a serious student. But I have appreciated the great minds with whom my own experiences have brought me into contact.

My actual schooling, with the exception of one particular venture which I shall describe later, was uneventful. I completed

Science Hill High School in Johnson City as a first honor student and went through four years as a day student at East Tennessee State College (now University), graduating with three majors (history, English, and education) as class valedictorian in 1941. (ETSU gave me a deeply appreciated honor in 1991, when it recognized me as its Distinguished Alumnus for that year.) My college career brought me wide experience and regional and national honors in forensics, culminating in a diamond Pi Kappa Delta pin and exposure to public speaking opportunities which, in an invaluable way, helped prepare me for my life's work.

In the fall of 1941, I entered Candler School of Theology, Emory University to study for the ministry. I remember gratefully a number of my professors there but especially Dr. Wyatt Aiken Smart, Dr. Henry Burton Trimble, and dear old Dr. Franklin Nutting Parker, allegedly retired but still teaching occasional courses. Two young professors, Dr. William Ragsdale Cannon and Dr. Mack B. Stokes, made enduring impressions upon my thought and life and later became close friends.

The particular venture to which I have referred was a thesis written out of residence during my convalescence from a persistent illness and in lieu of final classwork which I had to miss. The subject of my thesis, which had the length of a dissertation, was *The Evangelistic Message and Method of Dwight Lyman Moody*.[5] I was assisted in extensive research by Mr. Moody's surviving son, Dr. Paul D. Moody, minister of First Presbyterian Church in New York City. Dr. Moody placed me in correspondence with a galaxy of distinguished men and women who had been either converted or influenced by his father and were still living: Mrs. W. R. Moody (daughter-in-law of DLM), Mr. A. P. Fitt (son-in-law), Dr. Sherwood Eddy, Dr. Gaius Glenn Atkins, Dr. Mary Emma Woolley, Dr. G. Campbell Morgan, Dr. John R. Mott, Dr. Robert E. Speer, Coach Amos Alonzo Stagg, Dr. Henry Sloane Coffin, Dr. William Lyon Phelps, Mr. George C. Stebbins (the hymn writer), and Dr. Howard Atwood Kelly.

My work with Dr. Paul Moody was especially rewarding, and my examination of rare publications and documents related to the life of his father led me to a number of fresh and different conclusions which I have not yet encountered in the numerous biographies of this greatest of American evangelists. Dr. Moody had urged me to publish my findings in book form, but his unexpected death and the pressures of my busy life in the parish ministry cancelled this possibility. My research and writing on this project was one of the most exciting chapters in my total ministry and a major factor in the shaping of my own mind about the importance of evangelism.

My effort to learn has continued across a lifetime, even until now. My personal library of more than five thousand volumes was largely given away at the time of my retirement from the active episcopacy in 1988, but I have retained fifteen hundred choice titles as a working collection. I have kept my interest in higher education and have served as trustee of fifteen different colleges and universities. Ten institutions, including Duke, Emory, and Belmont Abbey (an important Roman Catholic college), have conferred honorary degrees upon me.

Pastorates

I spent fourteen and three-fourths years as a parish minister, serving the following charges: Sardis Methodist Church, Atlanta, Georgia (as a student), 1942-1944; Broad Street Methodist Church, Kingsport, Tennessee (as associate pastor), 1944-45; Wesley Memorial Methodist Church, Chattanooga, Tennessee, 1945-1950; and First Methodist Church, Morristown, Tennessee, 1950-1956. Friends still survive in each of these congregations. My wife and I owe an incalculable debt to the patient, supportive, affectionate parishioners who surrounded us across those early years, endured my immature preaching, and helped us learn how to minister.

I have always believed that the pastoral ministry should have twin foci: the proclamation of the gospel and the care of God's people. Even when my homiletical knowledge was scant, I used to live literally for that shining moment when I would enter the pulpit to preach the Word. I still do. When I compute from my records the number of sermons preached in more than forty-eight years of assigned work and in more than three hundred preaching missions, I find myself amazed by the total: in excess of twenty thousand messages!

But I have always been equally conscious of the opportunity afforded by purposeful pastoral visitation. In nearly a decade and a half of serving local churches, there was no year when I did not make at least two thousand pastoral calls. It took hard work and firm discipline, and younger ministers sometimes smile in tolerant disbelief when I tell them about this. I may have been too diligent in this aspect of my work, especially because of time spent away from my own family; but I always knew, from a source better than the lectionary, what would be a helpful homiletical menu for my people!

I tried to bring great Christian voices into my pulpits in order that my people might have the inspiration that comes from hearing God's giants tell about their experiences of Jesus Christ. Some of those who spoke for me in spiritual life missions during my pastoral years were Dr. John Stewart French, Bishop Edwin Holt Hughes, Dr. John R. Mott, Dr. James T. Cleland, Bishop Ralph Spaulding Cushman, Dr. Ralph W. Sockman, Dr. Clovis G. Chappell, Dr. Clarence Edward Macartney, Dr. Gordon Cosby, Mrs. Catherine Marshall, Bishops (then Drs.) Cannon and Stokes and Mrs. Arthur J. Moore. Some of these preaching missions are still remembered in the communities where they brought blessing.

Emory & Henry College

My invitation to become the fourteenth president of Emory & Henry College in Emory, Virginia, an old and distinguished liberal arts institution of our church, came unexpectedly in 1956. We accepted with a mixture of apprehension and excitement and entered into what may have been the happiest chapter of our entire ministry. For eight satisfying years we worked with young people, faculty, and alumni. I deeply believed that vital Christian education could be accomplished within a context of academic excellence, integrity, and freedom—and I still believe this! We worked to build a strong faculty, expand the physical plant, develop better library and laboratory facilities, establish two endowed lectureships, and cultivate a mutually meaningful relationship between the college and the church. We did all of this in an academic setting that bristled with rich history and sparkled with such surpassing beauty that the late Ralph W. Sockman once described it as the "loveliest campus scene in academic America."

It would be futile to try to tell the story of our Emory & Henry years in this chapter, but I must mention five people without whose stalwart administrative and spiritual comradeship I could not have endured the struggles of those happy but difficult years: the Reverend Dr. William Clifford Mason, Jr., Mr. G. C. (Connie) Culberson, Dr. Thomas L. ("Pidney") Porterfield, Dr. Victor Stradley Armbrister and Dr. Daniel G. Leidig.

Episcopacy

My election as a bishop in mid-afternoon on Saturday, July 11, 1964, actually startled Mary Ann and me. It was necessary for us to work through a substantial emotional adjustment in order to ready ourselves for a major new task which, if there had been any anticipation of it, we had felt lay much further down the road for us. I have always been glad that I was elected before what I regard as the present dubious process of choosing episcopal leaders became fully developed.

Again quite unexpectedly, we were assigned to the large and somewhat prestigious Charlotte Area, comprised of the Western North Carolina Annual Conference, at that time the fifth largest in our connection. To step from the halls of academe onto the demanding stage of regional and general church administration, I found, was neither an easy nor a simple transition. But the people, clergy and laity, were wonderfully helpful; and we spent twelve almost deliriously happy years in the Queen City, attempting to bring leadership to the more than twelve hundred churches for which we were responsible.

During my tenure I organized my first Lay Advisory Council and, with the invaluable assistance of Dr. Cecil L. Heckard, twice a member of my cabinet before his sudden death in 1974, and Dr. Wilson O. Weldon, sometime world editor of *The Upper Room,* started the Institute for Homiletical Studies. This program, designed to improve the quality of the local church pulpit, was generously funded by the late Mr. and Mrs. George D. Finch, Thomasville, North Carolina, and is still operative at this time.[6] I also appointed the first black district superintendent in the Southeastern

Jurisdiction and a very early one in the entire church, Dr. James C. Peters.

Our journeys abroad for the church began in 1970 and continued until 1990, carrying us to four continents and the islands of the Caribbean and the Aegean seas. During our final quadrennium, we built the handsome new headquarters structure in Charlotte and helping to found two new homes for the retired, Arbor Acres in Winston-Salem and Givens Estates in Asheville.

In 1976 we went to the very important Nashville Area, comprised of the Memphis and the Tennessee Conferences. We enjoyed living in Nashville and especially our association with the three general agencies of the church located there and Scarritt College. I wrote my first book, *I Have Believed,*[7] during that four-year period, and it was published by The Upper Room. We loved the people of both the Memphis and the Tennessee Conferences and especially enjoyed our exposure to a portion of Kentucky United Methodism through responsibility for the more than seventy Kentucky charges which were part of the Memphis Conference.

Contrary to our thoughts about what would occur (particularly as the week of Jurisdictional Conference drew toward its conclusion without a hint that we were to move) since both of our conferences had asked for our return, we found ourselves transferred to the Florida Area in 1980. Our residence was to be in Lakeland, a pleasant mid-sized city in central Florida, the site of Florida Southern College. We spent eight happy and, I trust, profitable years presiding over the far-flung work of Florida United Methodism, one of the largest and most vigorous segments of our church in this country.

Again I tried to put a strong emphasis upon better preaching and was able to help found the Institute of Preaching, an enterprise similar but not identical to the program we had started in Western North Carolina. Mr. and Mrs. Frank Sherman, dear and generous friends who lived in Jacksonville, endowed the Institute. Many important programs occupied our time and energy and we fell deeply in love with the magnificent people who inhabit the Sunshine State and who responded so well to the leadership we tried to offer. A major task, by no means glamorous, was to help Florida United Methodism achieve the kind of fiscal solvency which would equip it for the very demanding future we all knew was coming. It was from this assignment that we retired officially on September 1, 1988.

Every bishop, in addition to serving his or her own area, is a general superintendent of the entire church. As tenure develops, more and more general church assignments are added to a bishop's work load. I served as a member of several general agencies of the church across twenty-four years as an active bishop, including the old General Board of Education, the General Committee on Family Life (I was its chair for five years), the General Board of Higher Education and Ministry (of which I was president from 1980 to 1984). I was a member of the Governing Board of the National Council of the Churches of Christ from 1972 to 1984 and of the Executive Committee of the World Methodist Council from 1976 to 1986. I served as chairperson of the American Section of the World Methodist Council from 1982 to 1986 and received the Council's Chair of Honor in 1988.

The last quadrennium of my active work as a bishop brought the most important assignment of my ministerial career. I was elected to chair the Committee on Our Theological Task, a distinguished international group of leaders charged by the 1984 General Conference with the task of writing a new theological statement for United Methodism. This statement, with slight modification, was passed overwhelmingly by the General Conference of 1988, just as I was concluding a year as president of the Council of Bishops.

During the last thirteen years of my active episcopacy, I sought to carry out a special task given to me by the Council of Bishops, the bringing to publication of a definitive biography of Bishop G. Bromley Oxnam. Professor Robert Moats Miller of the University of North Carolina, distinguished biographer of Ernest Fremont Tittle and Harry Emerson Fosdick, accepted my invitation to undertake this massive work. With the help of colleagues, I raised a substantial amount of money to fund his exhaustive research and otherwise worked with him until the book was published by Abingdon in 1990. My years of association with Dr. Miller, who is incurably but delightfully Scottish and Presbyterian, were deeply rewarding—even though certain friends wondered aloud how a classical evangelical (not the less definable contemporary kind) like myself, albeit a liberal on many social issues, could rejoice in helping create a memorial to one described as "the paladin of liberal Christianity."[8]

Upon our retirement, my wife and I were scheduled to go to Emory University in Atlanta, where I would become visiting professor of Evangelical Christianity at Candler School of Theology, my alma mater. An illness prevented my assuming this task, and soon I found myself confronted with an invitation to lead the Foundation for Evangelism, an affiliate of the General Board of Discipleship of our church. The Foundation was headquartered at Lake Junaluska, where we had purchased a home in late 1988.

What I had assumed would be a part-time, temporary position developed into something much larger and more lasting because of my deep commitment to the importance of the eleven programs for which the Foundation is responsible, and also because of the gracious urging of colleagues in the episcopacy and members of the Foundation's Board of Trustees. As of this writing, my work in this capacity continues. It is interesting to note that, while the basic thrust of my total ministry across more than forty-five years was related to Christian education, the final chapter is being devoted to Christian evangelism. I have always been convinced that, within the church, the two belong together. Perhaps my own life can become, finally, a documentation for their indissolubility.

Hero Worshipping and Autograph Collecting

I know that hero worshipping is no longer fashionable. In fact, hero debunking seems in recent years to have become the order of the day. But not for me. Perhaps my love of history helps to explain why I have always cherished data about the famous and the near-famous and, even more so, exposure to them. My personal experiences in these realms have been sometimes inspirational and sometimes ridiculous.

On my first trip to New York City as a college student, I was staying at Dr. Wilbert Webster White's old Biblical Seminary in Manhattan when one cold winter evening I decided to take the subway to the lower East Side for a visit to the famous Bowery Mission operated by *Christian Herald* magazine. The heavy snow falling at the time was almost blinding. Just as I entered the sidewalk in front of the seminary, I collided with a woman carrying groceries and walking in the opposite direction. We both slipped on the ice, and the groceries went in all directions. After we helped each other up, apologizing, I retrieved her groceries and put them in the sack. The accident unnerved me, and I returned to the seminary building to find its doorman laughing. "Did you know that the woman you knocked down was Katherine Hepburn?" he asked. "She lives next to this building."

Some years later, when I was a senior at seminary, my former roommate and dear friend Gunnar J. Teilmann, Jr., already a World War II chaplain, telephoned the dormitory to let me know that he was passing through Atlanta and would have about four hours between trains. We agreed to meet at the old Henry Grady Hotel on Peachtree Street. Running late, I went charging down the steps leading from the street level into the hotel lobby, vaguely aware that a uniformed Marine officer was coming up those same steps. In my careless haste, I sideswiped him and he lost his balance and tumbled back to the floor level. As I offered profuse apologies and explained why I was hurrying, he dusted himself off and broke into a wide grin. "I accept your apology, young man," he said, "and you may tell your friends that you just did what no one but Jack Dempsey did before. You knocked down Gene Tunney!"

These two improbable but altogether factual episodes from my earlier years were complemented by a third unlikely event during my final pastorate. Catherine Marshall, famous author and widow of the colorful Senate chaplain, Peter Marshall, had dinner in our home prior to an evening speaking engagement in my church. She and I went down to the church early, leaving my wife to follow a bit later. Twilight was fading into darkness as we emerged from my car and glanced up at the sky. We were startled to see a strange cylindrical object with a multitude of flashing lights. It was quite large and apparently stationary, and its surfaces radiated a peculiar metallic sheen. Obviously we were the unexpected witnesses of a vividly spectacular UFO, although both of us later became reluctant to describe our experience, lest skeptics pronounce us gullible.

I stood as a ten-year-old boy, clutching my father's hand, at a curbing in Johnson City, Tennessee, the day Herbert Hoover got out of his open limousine, not five feet from us, and walked into the John Sevier Hotel. My limited and always casual association with White House personalities continued when former President Harry Truman, speaking in nearby Bristol, Virginia, paid a brief unannounced visit to the Emory & Henry campus during my presidency. I was walking home from my office when I spotted the imposing black limousine. One of Mr. Truman's escorts recognized me, and the former president and I had an impromptu visit in front of my campus residence, a visit which resulted in an interesting exchange of correspondence between Independence and Emory across a period of years.

I once shared a program with Mrs. Lyndon Johnson, offering the principal prayer when the James K. Polk birthplace was dedicated in Charlotte. Upon another occasion my wife and I sat with President Gerald Ford at a luncheon at Florida Southern College in Lakeland.

I was closeted by the Secret Service with President Jimmy Carter (whom I greatly admire) for an hour in a room at Glenn Memorial Church on the Emory University campus while officials made sure that the sanctuary was secure enough for Mr. Carter to enter. He was to speak, and I was to offer the prayer. Because of the importance of the occasion, I read a prayer which I had prepared carefully. When I resumed my seat, President Carter leaned over and, with a wide grin, said to me, "We Baptists don't write our prayers. We think God prefers them to be extemporaneous and from the heart."

During his 1987 trip to the United States while I headed the Council of Bishops, I had three separate conversations with His Holiness Pope John Paul II in the home of the president of the University of South Carolina. In one of these, the Pontiff spoke animatedly of his friendship with Bishop William R. Cannon.

I once visited with Bob Hope before a service in Marble Collegiate Church in New York City. Both of us had gone to hear Dr. Norman Vincent Peale, with whom, many years later, I was to hold the Ocean Grove Camp Meeting in New Jersey.

My work as college president and bishop inevitably placed me, upon occasions far more numerous than those mentioned above, with well-known people. But my more extensive exposure to great men and women in this century was through fifty years of autograph collecting (letters, documents, manuscripts, etc.). I acquired, often at no expense except postage, a very large collection, including papers of presidents, kings and queens, authors, scientists, military leaders, humanitarians, clergy and many others. I often corresponded at some length with those whose papers I sought for my collection. Occasionally, when my modest means permitted, I bought in the autograph markets and eventually acquired a complete set of presidents of the United States and an assortment of more than sixteen hundred other important examples.

Serious autograph collecting requires, among other things, a sense of history and a kind of unbridled romantic imagination. It was my boyhood reading of the book *The Americanization of Edward Bok* which launched me into this fascinating and engrossing hobby. Bok, himself as avid collector, once asked Oliver Wendell Holmes to write an introduction to a volume he meant to publish on the subject. The "autocrat of the breakfast table" penned the following perceptive paragraph:

An autograph of a distinguished personage means more to an imaginative person than a prosaic looker-on dreams of. Along these lines ran the consciousness and the guiding will of Napoleon or Washington, of Milton or Goethe. His breath warmed the sheet of paper which you have before you. The microscope will show you the trail of flattened particles left by the tesselated epidermis of his hand as it swept along the manuscript. Nay, if we had but the right developing fluid to flow over it, the surface of the sheet would offer you his photograph as the light pictured it at the instant of writing.[9]

I had planned to give my collection to Emory University, where I have been a trustee for twenty-seven years, but I must confess to great disappointment when the director of the libraries at the time I was prepared to make the gift declined to receive it because, in his words, it had "no research value." For the record, Emory President James T. Laney, my friend of many years, expressed sincere regret in a beautiful letter when he learned what had happened.

My collection, housed in forty-two leatherette volumes with cellulose acetate sleeves, carried portraits and brief biographical sketches which I had composed. From a careful personal evaluation, informed by painstaking study of hundreds of catalogues and price lists from dealers across a number of years, I placed its retail value conservatively at two hundred thousand dollars. When it became advisable to sell it because of changing tax laws, I had no time and little opportunity to seek a favorable market and, as a result, realized only a small fraction of its retail worth.

It was half a century of autograph collecting that led me to love biography and history above other forms of secular literature and that cultivated an appreciation for those women and men who, across long centuries, helped to shape human civilization at its best. Unquestionably, the influence of this beloved hobby in my life and the collateral effect of exposure to the lives of distinguished people were among the formative factors in the development of my own thought and system of values. I treasured particularly my friendship with some of the leading autograph dealers of the world, including Mary F. Benjamin in New York and the late Winifred Myers in London, whose rich acquisitions I was permitted to examine, and whose romantic appreciation of the written relics of history matched my own.

I never cease to thank God that I have been privileged to know personally, some casually and others intimately, leaders in the Christian community across the fifty years of my own ministry. A partial roll of names, all of whom helped to shape my own life, would include John R. Mott, Robert E. Speer, Sherwood Eddy, George Arthur Buttrick, Ralph W. Sockman, Paul Scherer, E. Stanley Jones, George MacLeod, Fulton J. Sheen, Samuel McPheeters Glasgow, Paul B. Kern, Edwin Holt Hughes, James T. Cleland, James S. Stewart, Georgia Harkness, George W. Truett, Gypsy Smith, Sr., Elton Trueblood, Benjamin Mays, Peter and Catherine Marshall, James T. Laney, and Billy Graham. Grace Livingston Hill, the popular American novelist who chuckled over making me the villain in her book *The Seventh Hour,*[10] and Dr. Howard Atwood Kelly, Johns Hopkins founder and surgical immortal, were cherished friends of my boyhood and young adult years and helped direct me toward the Christian ministry. The late

Norman Cousins and Nobel laureate Elie Wiesel, outside the leitmotif of Christian orthodoxy, were nevertheless friends and models who impacted my life.

To name my contemporaries in the Council of Bishops and beyond who have been used of God to influence my life would be an impossible task. Their number is legion.

An Anthem of Gratitude

My indebtedness to the many people who have helped me along the way is immeasurably great. My secretaries, eleven of them, are all still living but one as I write these lines. I have often expressed the hope that God may never let them meet in this world! I could never make adequate record of the faithful, loyal assistance which they have provided, nor could Mary Ann and I express sufficient gratitude for their friendship.

The influence of dear and treasured friends across the years makes the task of acknowledgment a larger one than I know how to address. Perhaps Kent Herrin Esq. (distinguished attorney who was my forensic colleague), Dr. Rex Depew (kinsperson as well as beloved comrade), Dr. Ben B. St. Clair, Dr. Ralph W. Mohney, Sr., the Reverend Harrison Marshall, the late Dr. Gunnar J. Teilmann, Jr., Dr. Robert F. Lundy (sometime Methodist bishop in Southeast Asia), Dr. George G. Young (physician and surgeon in Chattanooga), the late Mr. James F. Underwood (my first board chairman), also in Chattanooga, the late Mr. James D. Senter (and Mrs. Senter), Mr. David A. Black and Pat Rees (Mrs. O'Dell) Smith in Morristown, the late Drs. C. C. Herbert, Jr., and Charles D. White in Charlotte, Dr. Lloyd Ramer in Nashville, and Drs. Durward McDonell and Roland D. Vanzant in Florida (all administrative assistants) belong near the top of the list.

Among Christian leaders, in addition to many mentioned elsewhere in this chapter, I value supremely my association with the late Bishop Arthur James Moore (in whose Atlanta garage apartment Mary Ann and I set up housekeeping in 1943) and Bishop Roy Hunter Short, not to mention memorable friendships with other very special colleagues (like Bishops Monk Bryan and Edward L. Tullis of Lake Junaluska and James K. Mathews of Washington, D.C.) in the Council of Bishops. The most important song of my life would need to be an anthem of gratitude to all of those, ordained and not ordained, who have stood by me devotedly in a pilgrimage of service spanning half a century and featuring God's assignment of the Hunts to "a thousand stations of joy."[11]

As I bring this chapter to a close, I realize how prominent among all my convictions has been the reality of Christian hope. I want to think that this is the point at which every piece of writing in this volume ends. It has been a golden thread running through the entire fabric of my ministry. A noble phrase in Zechariah 9:12 puts it well: I have always been a "prisoner of hope."

The future of God's creation is secure in the victory of the Risen Redeemer. I still like Herbert Butterfield's words about facing tomorrow: "Hold to Christ, and for the rest be totally uncommitted!"

This is my faith. I thank God for the strong assurance it has brought me across a lifetime.

Endnotes

1.   Personal letter from Dr. James S. Stewart to the author, dated Feb. 11, 1987, Edinburgh, Scotland.

2.   Malcolm Muggeridge, *Chronicles of Wasted Time, Chronicle I: The Green Stick* (New York: William Morrow and Company, 1973), 140.

3.   Henry Nelson Synder, *An Educational Odyssey* (New York and Nashville: Abingdon-Cokesbury Press, 1947).

4.   William Barclay, *Testament of Faith* (London and Oxford: Mowbrays, 1975), 24.

5.   Earl G. Hunt, Jr., *The Evangelistic Message and Method of Dwight Lyman Moody.* Unpublished thesis submitted to the faculty of Candler School of Theology, Emory University, August 1945, in partial fulfillment of the requirements for the degree of Bachelor of Divinity (later M.Div.). Available at Emory University Libraries, Atlanta, Georgia.

6.   *Ancient Fires on Modern Altars,* Wilson O. Weldon, ed. (Charlotte: The Institute for Homiletical Studies, 1972). The first chapter, entitled "The Tale of A Dream," is by the author and contains in detail the story of the founding of the Institute and the Finch family's involvement in it, pp. 9-16.

7.   Earl G. Hunt, Jr., *I Have Believed* (Nashville: The Upper Room, 1980).

8.   Robert Moats Miller, *G. Bromley Oxnam: Paladin of Liberal Christianity* (Nashville: Abingdon, 1990).

9.   Edward Bok, *The Americanization of Edward Bok* (New York: Charles Scribner's Sons, 1923), 207-8.

10.   Grace Livingston Hill, *The Seventh Hour* (Philadelphia: J. B. Lippincott, 1938).

11.   *Vital Religion*, T. Otto Nall, ed. (New York: The Methodist Book Concern, 1938). An address by Bishop Edwin Holt Hughes entitled "An Affectionate View of the Church," p. 65.

I

Macte Virtute

May 11, 1957, was a day for us to remember: a beautiful old campus bursting with the foliage of late spring, colorful academic garbs, tradition-laden pomp and ceremony, and an unexpected new ministry for the Hunts.

It was the day when the fourteenth president of Emory & Henry College was to be inaugurated. Two bishops had come to speak, and I had crafted, as carefully as I could, my response.

The paragraphs of my address, as I read them again after thirty-five years, reflect the bold idealism of a young pastor who had suddenly departed the sanctuary for the academy and was naively unaware of the formidable resistance which would confront him as he pursued his dreams.

The stately procession that wound into Wiley Hall that day carried in its heart a lyrical confidence that a brighter dawning would break one day over a tired world. And it has, wherever Emory & Henry lads and lassies have pitched their tents. Macte Virtute, *the college motto in classical Latin, translates into English as "Increase in Excellence"; and this still takes place when true sons and daughters of this splendid old college in the hills of southwest Virginia, and of other schools like it, go forth to bless the earth.*

Macte Virtute

I must first express to each of you my genuine personal appreciation and the gratitude of Emory & Henry College for your presence here on our campus this morning, and for your willingness to honor this institution by making room in your crowded calendars for this program.

I pause also to pay my own humble tribute to the memory of a great man who helped to plan for this very hour. Dr. Floyd B. Shelton, chairman of the United Board of Trustees of our three conference colleges, did for higher education here in Holston Conference incalculably more than words could ever tell, and Emory & Henry received vast blessing from his labors. His place will not be filled, but we can be grateful forever for his granite-like character and his unquenchable zeal for the cause that is our common concern.

I read a few weeks ago, in the unpublished autobiography of the tenth president of this institution, the following arresting statement: "I think the wisest move I ever made was when I decided to leave Emory & Henry." A sober and realistic contemplation of my task might urge upon me too serious a consideration of President Weaver's observation, particularly when I scan more than twelve decades of noble institutional history and sense the burden of emulation which the past imposes upon the present. Governors of states, members of the Congress of the United States, more than a quarter of a hundred jurists, bishops of the Church, nationally known educators, authors, heads of great corporations, more than one thousand ministers and missionaries of the Cross, a great company of professional men, and in recent years presidents of the American Medical Association and the National Education Association—such are they who march in the long processional of alumni trained in this historic college of Methodism. To attempt to take up the task of distinguished predecessors, particularly and most recently Dr. James N. Hillman and Dr. Foye G. Gibson, whose wise labors have produced such far-reaching results, is perhaps at best both a risk and a presumption.

And yet, at the call of my Church, I must make the effort. My friends know that I bring to my task the meager equipment of a layman rather than the specialized training of a professional educator; but they know also that I bring to it an unutterably deep conviction that what is known as Christian higher education is, or ought to be, the most effective antiseptic for the deep and dangerous wounds that plague humankind today. Therefore, with humility and with an acknowledged dependence upon Almighty God for wisdom and understanding, I undertake the task committed to me by The Methodist Church.

Against the backdrop of the stimulating words spoken by Bishop Fred P. Corson and Bishop Roy H. Short, allow me to suggest briefly three areas of emphasis which I desire to be paramount in my administration.

Superior Teaching

A college exists to teach, and the ultimate measure of its contribution to human society is the effectiveness with which it does just that. As essential as are plant, campus, library, endowment, tradition—all of these are really peripheral to the central function of the institution. Arthur Guiterman's famous reference to education as Mark Hopkins sitting on one end of a log and James Garfield on the other is a graphic way of italicizing the importance of superior teaching. From Socrates to William Lyon Phelps, the task of communicating truth with accuracy, understanding and challenge has been the beckoning goal of the conscientious teacher.

There are legends here at Emory & Henry—legends of great men now gone whose teaching was creative, stimulating and memorable: Ephraim E. Wiley, Richard Green Waterhouse, James White Cole, Fred Allison, James Shannon Miller, Howell Meadors Henry, Fred Hayes Barber, and others. The sacred privilege of the present administration and faculty is to strive to add to this anthology of legends by means of indefatigable labor, mutual cooperation, and the compulsion of high and holy purposes. A constant refinement of the skill of communicating truth through the classroom and the laboratory must continue to make books, charts, test tubes and musical scores throb with the excitement and the challenge of life.

Always primarily responsible for this accomplishment will be a loyal corps of dedicated and talented men and women who feel a deep concern for a distinctive quality in education and for the personal development of the individual student—the faculty of Emory & Henry College. Because they are who they are, I am confident we may expect great teaching to become increasingly this college's most widely recognized commodity. Let us press with all vigor toward this goal, remembering that identification with high religious principle is incentive for excellence rather than excuse for mediocrity in matters of academic standards.

Training for Churchmanship

It would seem that the church-related college ought to accept as one of its normal and fortunate responsibilities the training of professional and lay leadership for the Christian Church. Pre-ministerial study at Emory & Henry has always been and will continue to be an essential part of the college's education contribution. The plan is to develop a much broader and more effective program of training for directors of Christian education, pastors' assistants, and church secretaries, so that the serious candidate for graduate work in these fields may secure unexcelled preparatory training on this campus and so that the young person desiring to spend less than a lifetime in such service, and therefore seeking a briefer course, may find balanced and adequate, although limited, terminal training here. This development of our offerings can occur, I am persuaded, without any violation of the liberal arts philosophy to which the college is enthusiastically dedicated.

But let me deal for a moment with a wider area in connection with training leadership for the Church. Through specific courses in the understanding of the Bible, in Christian thought and ethics, in church history and church polity, as well as by means of a positively Christian interpretation of other and so-called secular subject matter, it is surely the church-related college's perennial mission to build responsible, intelligent and consecrated lay leaders for Christendom. Creative churchmanship is rarely accidental but is rather the result of thoughtful planning, careful nurture, and the absorption and assimilation of essential data which have been accurately assembled and forcefully presented. There are many state and private institutions where this type of process is gloriously at work; I am a grateful graduate of one such college. However, the church-related institution, by its very nature, is equipped to make a more natural and a more thorough approach to this task. Indeed, the opportunity of the Christian college is nowhere more enviable than at the point of the making of good churchmen; but the training must be sharp and positive, rich and stimulating—nothing nebulous and apologetic will suffice. The production of lay church leaders must not be a vague and peripheral purpose in the church-related institution's catalogue of objectives; it must be among its definite and central goals. Surely a college like Emory & Henry, owing indescribably much to its parent church, will gladly grasp the opportunity to serve in this strategic sphere.

The Development of Christian Character

A cursory survey of actual conditions on American college and university campuses will reveal, when ample allowance for exaggeration is made, an appalling departure from what may be referred to as conventional Christian moral patterns. To some extent this has been true since the beginnings of higher education in this country and is perhaps the inevitable reflection of youth's sudden liberty and desire to experiment. However, the radical release of inhibitions which accompanied World War II and the Korean conflict, together with the alluring encroachments of a secularized society, has multiplied the problem today. Scholars and interpreters of the times as widely separated in their thinking as Pitirim Sorokin, Will Durant and George Arthur Buttrick bear common and weighty testimony to this fact.

Dare one try to state a frightening truth? There must surely be a point beyond which the culture and training of the mind and the progressive downward revision of ideals do not successfully co-mingle. A sensitive conscience cannot escape shameful scars when an individual indulges in premarital experiences that have been justified by a strange new moral logic. If, as some authorities suggest, the percentage of such participation should run alarmingly high, then a veritable revolution in conduct ideals is in the making.

Again, if certain responsible agents of the beverage alcohol industry are even approximately correct in stating that 75 percent of all college men and women are now engaging in some use of their products, then the question is posed: Can genuine learning thrive as a process and can it be constructively related to the development of positive character in such a climate of conduct?

What roles do purity and sobriety ultimately play in the solidarity of the home and the integrity of the republic? Can a generation of cautious Bohemians provide the requisite moral stamina for the benevolent control of nuclear energy? To go further, what is the permanent effect upon human personality of cheating in an examination? Is there a correlation between this regrettable practice and the eventual collapse of truth and honor in a young person's life? If so, the gradual disappearance of functioning honor systems in American institutions of higher learning has tragic relevance where the future of human freedom is concerned.

Perhaps American higher education, because of the far journeyings of its administrators and the distressing immanence of problems connected with building expansion and operational deficits, has neglected a far more essential matter: the health of the student soul on its campus. Perfunctory religious emphasis programs and required chapels cannot stem the tide of moral irresponsibility whose cynical waters lash dangerously at the lovely houses we have builded on the sands.

There must be an eventual moral renaissance on the college and university campuses of our country—and there will be. All of our institutions will come, early or late, to a sober reassessment of the principles which always govern and guide men and women. Emory & Henry chooses to come to that reassessment early, and to join the noble company of those that have already undertaken to demonstrate for our time that an unfanatical but positive Christian ethic can be the comfortable yokefellow of sound learning in the production of wise and consecrated leadership for a crisis era in human history.

It is neither possible nor desirable, however, to contemplate a thoroughgoing cure of an ill so deeply rooted by a series of radical therapies which are essentially negative in nature. Preventive treatment must be used as well, in the form of constructive effort to build up the total moral, ethical, and spiritual system of the modern college or university student. To accomplish this, the old dichotomy between the culture of the mind and the conversion of the soul must be destroyed. The relevance of God and the redemptive process centering in Jesus Christ and His Person and work to the entire educational experience must be acknowledged with a candor and enthusiasm reminiscent of the great religious awakenings of the eighteenth and nineteenth centuries which gave birth to so many of our distinguished colleges and universities. The stimulating position taken by President Nathan Pusey of Harvard in this connection not only shows that a modern union of knowledge and vital piety is possible and intellectually respectable but indirectly rebukes the timidity of some church-related higher education in this area which is so basically a part of its *raison d'etre*.

The clear call of the Christian Church and particularly its Methodist branch in this hour is to a positive and winsome evangelical emphasis on the campus of the church-related institution of higher learning, an emphasis in which trustees, administration, faculty, and students are all cooperatively and creatively engaged. In a climate devoid of fanatical extremism and capable of reflecting with realism upon the problems of today's society, a sane, reasonable, and authentically spiritual presentation of the claims of Jesus Christ must be offered. Techniques of appeal must give evidence of imagination, originality, and a delicate sensitivity to the mind and personality of modern youth.

All subject matter must be taught with valid Christian insights and from the perspective of deep religious convictions. That this can be done without losing essential objectivity and liberty is amply attested by the truest concepts of religion and education. In brief, the college community, undergirded with not only a philosophy but a theology of Christian education, must strive to become a microcosm of the Kingdom where committed people labor together in quest of knowledge, skill and understanding and— by the radiance of their own lives—seek to win others to their commitment.

To undertake to lead a Christian college today is a high and demanding task, worthy of all that any person will ever be able to give. Confident that others of like mind surround me and will share my labors, I would here dedicate my days at Emory & Henry to the emphases which I have just endeavored to enunciate, with the fervent prayer that the God and Father of our Lord Jesus Christ may visit this historic institution with a fresh manifestation of His power, and so make it a light unto Methodism and to the whole Earth.

II

The Greatest among You

This address, given on January 18, 1968, in Cleveland, Ohio, at the annual meeting of the old General Board of Health and Welfare Ministries, celebrated an important event in the life of the Hunt family. A feature of the Board's annual meeting was the induction of new members into the Hall of Fame in Philanthropy in our denomination. One of the honorees in 1968 was Mr. Ralph M. Stockton, a lay member of Centenary Church in Winston-Salem. It was a highly deserved recognition, for Mr. and Mrs. Stockton had devoted generous amounts of leadership and money to the homes for children and the retired in the Western North Carolina Annual Conference. But the honor paid them had additional meaning to Mary Ann and me.

At a time when the heavy expenses associated with institutional care for my mother threatened my ability to remain in the Christian ministry (I might have earned more in other work), Mr. Stockton very quietly and tactfully made available to me the resources of a small foundation at his church. It was this unexpected benevolence which saved my wife and me from financial disaster and made possible the continuation of the kind of care we coveted for my mother.

Ralph Stockton, a retired businessman whose total life was dedicated to Jesus Christ, was one of the most godly churchmen I ever knew, wholly unostentatious in living out his simple but profound faith. I had nominated him for this honor, and watching him receive it brought me enormous satisfaction.

The Greatest among You

Junior's breath was coming quickly and sharply.[1] His small, pallid, bone-traced countenance was strangely and pathetically like a candle whose flame is about to be snuffed out. His eyes were wide open. In their look of questioning wonder was revealed Junior's soul—that part of him which a lame heart could never kill. In the depths of those eyes was the story of a little lad's longing for health, for playmates, for school, for a chance to live. He did not want to die. About him as he sat there in his rough chair—the pain from his heart would not permit him to lie down—stood a half dozen children with whom he had lived and played during his thirteen short years. Their countenances were a study in sadness and perplexity.

Junior's old grandmother, numbed by the tragedies of eighty heavy years, waved a newspaper over the panting form of the sick boy, keeping swarms of eager flies from their prey. In a corner sat the mother, weeping aloud. Outside a midsummer storm with its deliciously refreshing rainfall playing upon tin roofs in musical echoes told of the vigor of the universe. Inside, the solemn watch of death went on. Throughout the day and part of the night the pleading eyes of the brave little patient clung resolutely to life. Then a dull skim fixed itself over them, and the drama moved suddenly and unexpectedly into its inevitable denouement.

Junior died, and I was there thirty-five years ago when it happened—there as a youthful representative of a church that cared and was finding ways and means of treating, in that community of my adolescent years, not only the symptoms but some of the causes of human poverty.

It was 1933, with the United States still in the agonizing grip of the Great Depression; and our hometown, a small mill and factory community, had been hit devastatingly by shutdowns and unemployment. Our middle-sized Methodist church, about to lose its magnificent new Gothic plant because of a crushing indebtedness, had just been assigned an idealistic young pastor, a

Rhodes Scholar with a Ph.D. from a distinguished American university. To this bold and compassionate man and to a handful of his parishioners, including four or five high school young people, came a vision of applied Christianity, a program of outreach to the penniless families of an adjoining factory area. It was a program designed not only to offer a poverty-stricken neighborhood help and hope but also to probe the reasons for such economic distress—and, perhaps most important of all, to involve a typical parish church in a vital effort to confront human need constructively.

The church plant had a splendid gymnasium and to it the children of the factory community were brought after school twice a week for a vigorous athletic program, dramatically overdue shower baths, a brief Bible class, visits to a circulating library, a medical clinic and a soup kitchen. Regular pastoral visits into the homes from which the children came were instituted, and cottage prayer meetings complete with a Peter Bilhorn folding pump organ were begun. Food, fuel, clothing and medicine were distributed; and a highly effective employment bureau was founded. Church officials undertook conversations with factory and mill owners and city government officials, looking toward the facing of basic problems. Transportation to and from Sunday services was provided, and a carefully groomed, somewhat self-centered middle-class Methodist church suddenly found in its midst a shabbily clothed, not always freshly washed contingent of men and women and children who had only pennies for the offering plates but who could sing the old songs with more gusto than the congregational natives!

There were difficulties, but the therapy worked both ways; and soon the church had members from the new neighborhood. Then, from the tiny, bad-smelling hovels on narrow, crowded streets, from the plain, poor people with their strained, hollow eyes and emaciated faces, there came suddenly and gloriously a sequence of modern miracles. Employers became creatively interested in providing better working conditions and wages as the depression receded. A new school was built; wretched rental property was repaired and painted; streets were cleaned and resurfaced; a recreational park was built; two community churches virtually deserted for years became alive and vital.

Back at our home church the people from the factory area kept coming. Two of their sons heard the call to preach, and our church undertook the cost of their education. Today, thirty-five years later, the good results that began to appear in the thirties persist still, and the stories of lives and homes permanently redeemed by that remarkable ministry are plentiful and thrilling.

I was one of the teenagers enlisted by my pastor and church for this fruitful service, and it was during these months and years that I gave myself to Christ and His ministry. Long ago now, in 1936, I wrote for Dr. Orien W. Fifer's *Christian Advocate* an account of this work under the title "The Tale of a Dream." In this article I told the story of Junior and acknowledged the profound effect upon my own life wrought by my involvement in the effort of a church to do Christ's work among needy people.

I share with this distinguished American Methodist audience in this year of our Lord 1968 my own vivid recollection of those faraway days, if for no other reason than to assure us all that the blessed concept of a *servant church* is not an entirely recent insight! The glory of the Christian gospel has always been its meaningful identification with human need and suffering—the plain but magnificent fact that "the greatest among us" have ever been, in the dear Savior's name, at the service of those who on every hand need us so desperately. And nowhere is this identification clearer or more exciting than in the institutions for which this Association has responsibility.

Let us note in recalling "The Tale of a Dream," to which I have referred, certain simple, basic facts. First, *there was a church that cared.*

There are three Greek words which have seemed to summarize the New Testament idea of the ministries of the Church: *kerygma,* meaning the proclamation of the Good News; *koinonia,* meaning the community of love; and *diakonia,* meaning the Church as a servant people. All of us are aware that recent concern for the renewal of the Church has in large measure centered in a rediscovery of the rich implications of these Greek terms, with perhaps greater emphasis upon *diakonia,* the Church as a servant people, than upon either of the others.

Indeed, this is not a *new* concept. The story of a Church's compassion and concern for humanity is as ancient as the New Testament. Dealing only with modern times, and that fleetingly, its murmur was in the exciting saga of William Wilburforce's toils to free the slaves of Britain, in Elizabeth Barrett Browning's songs protesting child labor, in General William Booth's Salvation Army music, and—far more than some have been willing to acknowledge—in the benevolent afterglow of the Moody-Sankey meetings in Manhattan's old Hippodrome, in Scotland, and elsewhere.

After the turn of the century, the murmur became full voice, and the prophetic statesmanship of men like Walter Rauschenbusch and Herbert Welch began to move the Christian Church out of its cloistered, comfortable corners into the thronged byways of human need. This was the time of the formalization of our church's conscience on great issues in the Methodist Social Creed and also the time of the appearance of some of the immortal hymns of social concern—Frank Mason North's "Where Cross the Crowded Ways of Life," Harry Emerson Fosdick's "God of Grace and God of Glory," John Oxenham's "In Christ There Is No East or West," and William P. Merrill's "Rise Up, O Men of God."

Who is able to trace the causal relationship between these spiritual developments of half a century and more ago and recent achievement in the promotion of civil rights and fundamental freedoms and in the creation of patterns of assistance for the needy and unfortunate around the world? But surely it exists, and we may well be proud that our church is no newcomer to the forum where pleas for earth's underprivileged are heard. Let me quote from a ringing address on this general theme:

With all its faults and failures, with all those inconsistencies of belief and of conduct which might make rivers of water flow mournfully from Christian eyes, the Church must receive large credit for its work of education, of philanthropy and of reform. Every child, every needy and oppressed man, finds safety and deliverance in the Gospel which has been through these centuries proclaimed by the Christian Church. There have been eddies and back-currents which have made the stream look sometimes hesitant or reactionary. But, speaking in the large, the Church has been the friend of education and intellectual progress, the helper in efforts for the weak, the vicious, the enslaved, the struggling, the disheartened.

We must, however, measure our achievements not by history but by ideals. It is not the question whether the Church has done something; has it done everything? Is its work accomplished? Is its mission fulfilled? If the business of the Church is to continue the enterprise which Jesus undertook, we must confront his program: "The Spirit of the Lord is upon me," he read out of the ancient Scriptures, "because he hath anointed me to preach the Gospel to the poor; he hath sent me to heal the broken-hearted, to preach deliverance to the captives, and recovering of sight to the blind, to set at liberty them that are bruised, to preach the acceptable year of the Lord." Has it all come true yet? Are the captives all set free? Are the broken-hearted all healed and the bruised delivered from their distresses? Has the acceptable year of the Lord arrived, the jubilee of freedom and restoration and equity? Is the Kingdom of God fully established, with its righteousness, its peace, its universal joy?[2]

The speaker was Bishop Herbert Welch, then president of Ohio Wesleyan; and the date was 1908. But that address, first composed sixty years ago, would be appropriate for the Uniting Conference in April of this year—an event which its author, by God's amazing providence, expects to attend!

The Church has cared and continues to care. Perhaps the distinguishing hopeful hallmark of our tragic moment in history is a widespread and infectious indignation against tyranny and inequality, prejudice and poverty, racism and inhumanity—product of the slow leaven of the Christian doctrine of man at work in time and culture. Occasionally in our day, the sharp meaning of Christian concern is blunted by attitudes and techniques which represent a radical departure from the Church's mood of other decades and—to some of us at least—from the New Testament climate itself.

One hears and reads of Black or White Power, of urban violence attempting to wrest from spasms of anger and hatred better housing and fairer employment opportunities, of radical efforts to "restructure" the Church through maneuvers which, if employed by the Establishment, would be bitterly condemned. One hears and reads and wonders, wonders that a very ancient Christian term, the term *love,* seems to be so conspicuously and wholly absent.

Vast impatience with a recalcitrant and sometimes ethically unscrupulous society, long decades of futile waiting and suffering— these are offered as acceptable and defensible rationalizations by those who believe that even the Church must participate in the revolutionary *modus operandi* of our time. But, as Norman Cousins so incisively suggested in an editorial in *Saturday Review,* there is a clear limit to what can be justified as a means to even the most desirable ends. Those who have moved beyond the climate of Christian love, as it is again and again delineated in the New Testament, have outdistanced Jesus Christ himself. The doctrine that any means is justified by a good end shatters the whole structure of ethics and makes of Christianity a forlorn wail in the wilderness and of man himself an inhuman tyrant.

The noblest and the most sovereign of all human freedoms is the freedom to do what is right. It is this that emancipates the human being, sets him free in the glorious freedom that belongs to a kinsman of the Almighty. It is this that helps him rise to the full dignity of his humanity and enables him to attain complete stature as a citizen in God's universe. It is this that brings quietness to his soul and a song to his spirit. And this is possible only when his will is utterly controlled by love itself—not some soft, sentimental substitute but the ethically muscular love that fills the pages of the Gospels and the correspondence of St. Paul.

I remember an incident from my old Epworth League days when a group of us were guests in our pastor's living room. In the gathering twilight, there came a knock at the front door of the parsonage. When the minister answered the knock, all of us in the living room could see that the visitor was a notorious town character, a woman hopelessly addicted to narcotics whose life had become a cluster of years that the locusts had eaten.

In a whining, tortured voice, she began her plea for money with which, as everyone knew, she intended to purchase more dope. Our pastor interrupted her sentences with a quiet, tender greeting whose sympathy and gentle courtesy I can still hear across the years: "Will you come in, Mother?" It must have been the word *mother* that did it. The woman at the door stopped her speech, dropped her head, and tears began to flow down her sallow cheeks.

"No," she stammered, "but-but-but, I thank you for speaking to me like that." The glory of the Church is that it has been saying in a thousand different ways across nearly two millennia "mother" to the misunderstood, the forsaken, the tormented in the human family. The Church *has cared,* has been sensitive to human need in its myriad manifestations.

The Church was there when Junior died, and the Church cared, not only about his death but about the sociological conditions which surely contributed to it.

Vast new problems loom on the horizon of the dangerous tomorrows immediately ahead: poverty in the midst of an affluent society, the idea of first-class citizenship for people of all races dimmed by the spectra of inadequate and segregated housing, famine in vast areas of the earth, the brutal horror of war, etc. Involvement in the quest for a solution to these problems is magnificently inevitable for the Christian—*but the involvement must always be compassionate, an expression of concern in the spirit of Christian love.*

Second, in that far-off episode, *there were people who responded.*

There is a story about John Tauler, the fourteenth-century German mystic, meeting a beggar and saying to him, "God give you a good day, my friend!" To which the beggar replied, "I thank God I have never had a bad day." "Well, then, God give you a happy life," said Tauler. But the beggar retorted, "I have never been unhappy." "What do you mean?" asked Tauler. "Well," replied the beggar, "when it is fine, I thank God; and when it rains, I thank God. When I have plenty, I thank God; and when I am hungry, I thank God. And since God's will is my will and since whatever pleases Him pleases me, why should I be unhappy?" Tauler, perplexed, inquired, "Who are you, anyway?" "I am a king," replied the beggar. "You a king! Where is your kingdom?" "In my heart," whispered the man in rags. "In my heart."

This story serves to italicize that emphasis upon the importance of the individual which is at the heart of Christian anthropology. The Bible has no more royal term than the "whosoevers" that sparkle like gems in so many of its passages. They are all gloriously individualistic, magnificently personal!

For God so loved the world, that he gave his only begotten son, that *whosoever* believeth in him should not perish, but have everlasting life. (John 3:16)

And the Spirit and the bride say, Come. And let him that heareth say, Come. And let him that is athirst come. And *whosoever* will, let him take the water of life freely. (Revelation 22:17)

How strikingly out of harmony with much of modern life and Christianity! Depersonalization is everywhere apparent—the almost inevitable result of automation, cybernation, and urbanization. Religion, consciously or unconsciously, has followed this trend. Evangelism is spoken of more in terms of frontal attacks upon social evils, involvement in the human struggle, than in terms of leading individuals into meaningful relationships with God. The social concerns enterprise is moving away rapidly from the more individual problems of alcohol and personal morality and focusing upon the vast *en masse* evils of society like war and poverty.

The missionary undertaking is not as concerned with the conversion of the person in another culture to Jesus Christ as with assistance to the people in overcoming tyranny and enslavement. The local pastor, dedicated wholly to the great principles of applied religion in community life, sometimes has disdain instead of respect for the individual in his church, and may indeed have no helpful word and very little time for the member who is wrestling with some vast problem inside himself.

Now, to be sure, there is in all of this contemporary depersonalization a kind of deeply dedicated concern for people *en masse*—the elimination of racial discrimination, the confrontation of poverty, etc.—but, I sometimes fear very little for people *as individuals.*

I received a Christmas card this year whose illustration depicted a terrible slum with aimless, disheveled, filthy human beings wandering about. Beneath the picture were these lines (and I am still reeling from them): "These are the people of God. This is the city of God." And six years ago when Sir George MacLeod of the celebrated Iona Community in Scotland visited my college campus, he reminded us unforgettably at a luncheon that Jesus Christ was not crucified on an altar between two candlesticks; he was crucified on a garbage dump outside the city with two thieves, with men passing by, women weeping, and soldiers gambling at the foot of the cross for his garment.

All of this spells involvement, inevitable involvement, for each one of us, as it always has. But how can we keep involved with society's struggles without losing our identification with persons and individuals—God's "whosoevers"? For it seems to me that our preoccupation with war, racism, and poverty may cause us to forget or neglect the gentler, brighter but just as valid concerns of Christianity for ministries of healing, loving, encouraging, comforting—the kind of business in which members of this great board are engaged daily.

Dr. Harry Emerson Fosdick, in a memorable sermon preached more than three decades ago, said:

> As a Christian preacher, I am doing my best to be realistic in this pulpit during these difficult days, but I have an understanding with my soul about what realism means.

> For one thing, realism is degraded when it slips down into the idea that only ugly things are real. Some people are so afraid of being sentimental and idealistic that they manage their thinking and their living as some men write their novels, as though sewers were the only real things and mountain streams were not real too...Slums are real but so are humble and beautiful homes like those from which some of us derived. Sewers are real but so is a brook I know

In the leafy month of June,
That to the sleeping woods all night
Singeth a quiet tune.

Judas Iscariot is real but so is Jesus Christ. If man is going
to be a realist, let him go through with it![3]

An indispensable part of the Church's ministry in any age is
that of helping human beings caught in the traps of earthly suffering
to find release, comfort and Christian rehabilitation. Bishop Paul B.
Kern, trying to recover from the heart condition that took his life a
few months later, wrote in his last Christmas message to friends, "I
am thankful for nurses who make the sick comfortable and life
bearable when one's horizons tumble in." I know a preacher reared
in a Methodist children's home who feels such a debt for this
heritage that he cannot talk about it enough. In the midst of our
protest marches over Vietnam and metropolitan ghettos, we may
not mean to lose sight of man's more individual needs, but
sometimes we do.

Too, the mediation of Christianity's historical power to
redeem, rehabilitate, comfort and strengthen the individual is
dependent in a very real way upon the kind of fundamental faith in
a living God and in life's eternal dimension which has gone into
eclipse in many parts of the so-called Christian world in our time. It
is easier for the radical theology in either its bolder or milder
manifestations to organize a protest march than it is for it to offer
biblical peace and the assurance of life everlasting to a lonely and
bereaved senior citizen! Part of the depersonalization of our time is
frightened rationalization!

Robert G. Middleton, distinguished American Baptist
minister, writing in *Christian Century Pulpit* a year ago on "How to
Be an Avant-Garde Theologian," deplored that modern
sophisticated religious thought has no place in it for the great
affirmations, for the Christian doctrine of man, or for the discovery
of life as a joyous experience.[4] One senses the rightness of Dr.
Middleton's perspective—and then one begins to recall in response
to his point a cluster of haunting expressions from the Bible:

"balm in Gilead"
"beauty for ashes"
"showers of blessing"
"more than conquerors"
"walking in the midst of the fire"
"songs in the night"
"exceeding great and precious promises"
"the treasures of darkness"

Keith Miller, that remarkable and candid Texan who wrote *The Taste of New Wine,* has now given us another book, entitled *A Second Touch,*[5] filled with common sense and exhilarating naivete. In it he poses the question, "Can Christ give the Christian Church a second touch, so that we can begin to see the world of the Personal?" This is the idea I am trying to lift up.

As a young man, I saw *individuals* respond to the Church's ministries. This was part of my tale of a dream, part of my experience with Junior and many others. *But I never saw individual response prevent or postpone constructive and redemptive social or corporate progress!* Indeed, in our territory of mission, the two went constantly hand in hand. Why cannot this be so today?

The only real foundation for any defensible anti-institutionalism in this or any day is the charge that the institution no longer meets human need. The Christian Church, the Establishment, the power structure, can silence its critics with startling swiftness by turning its immense momentum dramatically in the direction of a meaningful ministry to persons—not by remote control, not by osmosis, but by actual contact and encounter!

Here are children adrift without a home . . .
Here is a dear elderly person needing care the family cannot
provide . . .
Here is an unmarried expectant mother, grimly aware of her
lonely plight and ready to reconstruct her life . . .
Here is a family with a mentally retarded child, baffled, panic-
stricken . . .
Here are the sick in a day when the poor man can scarcely afford

to lose his health—here they are by the multiplied tens of
thousands . . .
Here are the lonely, the bitter, the frightened, the grief-stricken,
the morally defeated; here are the suffering, the tortured, the
would-be suicides; here are the millions for whom a Savior
died and for whose help a Church was founded . . . .

Now let the Church concentrate its vast wealth and its rich
faith upon simple, timeless ministries to people as persons, all the
while continuing and strengthening its witness against those
practices in society which perpetrate insult and damage to human
life and dignity. Even in our time, the chorus of critics may become
a choir of friends!

Finally, in that event thirty-five years ago, *there was the
essence of real religion.*

If my early exposure to the ministry of my home
congregation as a *servant church* working among needy human
beings taught me any one truth greater than all the others, I suppose
it was a lingering and growing conviction that all of this in which I
was involved as a teenager under the guidance of my pastor was,
after all, the very essence of the deeper meaning of the Christian
religion. In my more sophisticated hours of academic
enlightenment, I have argued with myself repeatedly that such an
understanding of religion is really inexcusable oversimplification,
but in those treasured but rare moments of spiritual insight one
experiences through the years, I have questioned my own critique.

Speaking a number of years ago at a dinner initiating a
Salvation Army fund drive, that highly respected, distinguished,
and candid pundit, Walter Lippmann, whose own odyssey of
growth in appreciation of religion is as dramatic as that of Paul
Elmer More, said, "The final faith by which all human philosophies
must be tested, the epitome of all party creeds, all politics of state,
all relations among men, the inner nucleus of the universal
conscience, is in possession of the Salvation Army."

One remembers what Dr. William Lillie of the University
of Aberdeen refers to as the finest of all the tributes paid to General
Booth. An ex-prostitute, next to whom Queen Mary had sat at
Booth's memorial service, said to the queen, "He cared for the likes

of us." One recalls the ringing sentences of Vachel Lindsey in his poem "General William Booth Enters into Heaven":

Booth led boldly with his big bass drum—
(Are you washed in the blood of the lamb?)
The Saints smiled gravely, and they said: "He's come,"
(Are you washed in the blood of the lamb?)
Walking lepers followed, rank on rank,
Lurching bravos from the ditches dank,
Drunks from the alleyways and drug fiends pale—
Minds still passion-ridden, soul powers frail:
Vermin-eaten saints with moldy breath,
Unwashed legions with the ways of Death!

Real religion—beyond our sophistication and our confusion—is still ministry to human beings across the whole wide spectrum of their needs, still a "cup of cold water" given in His Name.

I remember, from those same early days, Andy. A redeemed alcoholic doomed to an early death because of the physical ravages of his dissipation, a plain ordinary automobile mechanic who found Christ and became the probation officer for our town's juvenile court, he was at the very heart of our local church's mission to people, the pastor's first lieutenant and the superintendent of the whole effort. The people in the factory neighborhood where we labored loved him with an intensity that defied description.

One cold and rainy autumn afternoon Andy took fifty children to the Ringling Brothers and Barnum and Bailey Circus in our town, and exposure to inclement weather brought an onslaught of pneumonia from which his weakened constitution could not recover. One of the vivid memories of my adolescent years is the thronged sanctuary of our church the afternoon of his funeral, with hundreds turned away for whom there were no seats. A former governor of the state, the mayor of the city, judges of local and district courts, all mingled with the people whom Andy loved best, the boys and girls and their parents from the poverty-stricken area where he had struggled to bring rehabilitation and hope. The funeral procession that wound its way toward Happy Valley Cemetery late that afternoon was more than two miles in length. And in our town and among the dear people who ministered to me more than I ministered to them, his memory is still a fragrance.

I submit to you, ladies and gentlemen, that a Church with this kind of ministry, to use Dr. Reinhold Niebuhr's searching word, will never be "trivial" in any age! And these institutions represented in this assembly are the Church at its most Christ-like task, the Church identified with the hurt and the promised glory of the people of God in the cities of God! In the faithful discharge of your responsibilities and the creative confrontation of your opportunities lies a major answer to today's critics of the Christian Church.

Endnotes

1.   The material on pp. 44-46 was used in my book *I Have Believed,* ch. VII, pp. 113ff. It is reprinted here by permission of the publisher, The Upper Room.

2.   Herbert Welch. I have been unable to find this quotation in Bishop Welch's autobiography or his other published material. I seem to recall that he handed me a leaflet with this statement in it during a conversation at a Council of Bishops meeting in Louisville, KY, the last, I think, which he was able to attend.

3.   *The Christian Century Pulpit.*

4.   Robert G. Middleton, "How To Be An Avant-Garde Theologian," *The Christian Century Pulpit* (January, 1967).

5.   Keith Miller, *A Second Touch* (Waco, Texas: Word Books, 1967).

III

On Books and Values

This is an address on liberal arts education, particularly the Christian version which one expects to encounter on the campus of a church-related college or university. Delivered on the occasion of the dedication of the Lucy Cooper Finch Library at Peace College in Raleigh, North Carolina, on October 17, 1969, it was later published in pamphlet form by the college.

My friendship with George and Lucy Finch, members of the founding family of the original Thomasville furniture dynasty, dates back to a February day in 1965 when, with Dr. Frank Jordan, I visited them to request their financial support for the new Homiletical Institute I was trying to establish. Snow was falling heavily and the roads were so icy that I had to travel from Charlotte to Thomasville by public bus. I can still see the Finches, visible through a haze of snowflakes as they stood in their door to welcome Dr. Jordan and me with the fragrant aroma of country ham prepared for our lunch drifting out upon the winter air. Three hours later I boarded a bus for Charlotte with their affirmative response in my possession.

On Books and Values

Someone has defined a private college as a cluster of small buildings, with ivy creeping around on the outside and the faculty creeping around on the inside. You and I who understand the role which the private and church-related institutions of higher education have played in the history of our land and in the conservation of the highest human and divine principles in civilization know better than this. I am deeply and genuinely honored to be present for this important occasion in the life of Peace College and to have this opportunity to express again my abiding conviction that the seriously sincere Christian college is more terribly needed today than it ever has been before. I am glad to have opportunity to pay tribute to my Presbyterian friends and co-laborers for their vision in establishing and maintaining this significant Christian junior college for women.

Furthermore, I am especially privileged to be present at the dedicatory service for the Lucy Cooper Finch Library, when all of us delight to honor a distinguished citizen of the state of North Carolina, who, for many of us present, is also a dear friend. Mrs. Finch, as many here are fortunate enough to know, is a gentle, gracious, kind, and hospitable lady deeply dedicated to her family, her church, and a carefully selected but deliberately small group of other interests. She and her husband regard their stewardship of giving as being a sacred and demanding responsibility to be handled with as much care, discernment, and administrative caution as a personal financial transaction in the world of business which they know so well. To be chosen by them for philanthropic attention is a coveted compliment to any institution.

The Library in Today's Society

The essential nature of an educational institution is probably suggested more accurately by its library than by any other facility associated with it. It is the heart of any campus. A library (the word being derived from the Latin *liber*) is a collection of written, printed, or other graphic material (including films, slides, phonograph records, and tapes) organized for use. Here the vast, accumulated treasures of human knowledge are cataloged and stored, excitingly accessible to those who would furnish their minds and deepen their understanding.

The library is not a recent addition to the paraphernalia of learning as is the language laboratory. It is very old—as old as Ashurbanipal's great collection of cuneiform texts at Nineveh in the 600's B.C., or the famous Athenian holdings associated with the schools of Plato at the Academy and of Epicurus in the fourth century before Christ. But it is also very new, as new as the Lucy Cooper Finch Library at Peace College—having survived the ordeals of two and one-half millennia and having assimilated with curious grace incredible and interminable explosions of knowledge.

There is something hopefully incongruous about a library in today's world with its restless, breathless activism. A library speaks of ordered thought, intellectual concentration, careful reflection and evaluation, silent meditation, the quiet excitement of creative discovery. All of this is set over in juxtaposition against the violence of Vietnam and the city's ghetto, against racism, LSD, hippies, the rebellion against the Establishment, the moral revolution, and the walk on the moon.

In real candor it must be admitted that the influence of books has come upon a questionable moment in the long history of humanity. Mr. Gallup, in a poll taken a few years ago, determined that in spite of constantly enlarging expenditures for education, the percentage of adults who read books is steadily decreasing.

One needs to be even more concerned about the sobering and well-documented fact that modern young people often do not read—not really. Perhaps to them bodies of knowledge are relatively unimportant in contrast to arenas of action. The precise science of the astronauts in Apollo 8 is the fad of "squares," as Anne Morrow Lindbergh once said in a perceptive essay in *Life*. They are the pigs who read their Bibles and get things done—far, far removed from the hippies and the Black Panthers who live where the action is. It is the strange contemporary tension between Cape Kennedy and Greenwich Village!

The Student for Whom Libraries Are Built

At the heart of campus problems and possibilities today stands a certain type of young person almost radically different from the young people of our generations, yet a homegrown product, the result at least partially of the frustrations, illusions, hypocrisies, compromises, and affluence of his parents' world. He (and I employ "he" generically in this lovely citadel of feminism) is a disturbing blend of idealist, iconoclast, rebel, ingrate, dreamer, reformer, seeker, and mixed-up kid. He has been hurt by his elders' gross insensitivity to human suffering and injustice and revolted by their selfish inconsistencies between profession and deed.

He is gullible and doesn't know it—the ready prey of unscrupulous interlopers who use his idealism for their darker purposes. He is often profane and vulgar, and the morality he would die for is a morality that frequently ignores and even shatters conventional sexual mores and concentrates on issues like human rights and war. Although he is ideologically ready to destroy without having planned how to rebuild, glibly affirming that anything—or even nothing—would be better than the status quo, he and the majority of his kind usually avoid violence and practiced destructionism save on occasions when the provocation is severe.

He turns you off, often but not always politely, if you are over thirty. He is more opinionated and prejudiced than those he loudly condemns for being that way—but he won't admit it. He will not read books that deal thoughtfully with another point of view, nor will he hear addresses or sermons which espouse philosophies he has already dismissed. He plays with Marxism and other radical world views as a kid fools with fireworks—not meaning to get hurt but chancing it for the kicks. He has no racial hang-up and pities you because you do. He means to turn this world upside down and is impatient to get on with the job. It often seems that he couldn't care less about *your* sense of values and commitments—but, in a departure from integrity of which he chooses to be unaware, he is willing and eager for you and the decadent system you represent to pick up the tab on his revolutionary antics.

He deifies freedom, but sometimes it isn't the brand of freedom implicit in Western history. He is often against the institutional church, but he isn't against Jesus. He simply can't see very much obvious connection between the two. He is enormously bitter about Vietnam and terribly suspicious of the military and industrial complex which he is pretty sure bears major responsibility for it.

And—curious though it seems—his magnificent obsession and his principled polemics can still be interrupted and even postponed by the kind of gastronomical interlude that provides heaps of hamburgers and french fries and stacks of blueberry pies!

This college student in whom I deeply believe—male or female—is one of those for whom libraries are built. He, or in the case of Peace, she, needs to read, to study, to master content, to revel in the great and important writings of the centuries and of the present moment, to sharpen powers of concentration and comprehension, to assimilate, organize, interpret and interrelate, to dream . . . .

A Personal Appreciation of Libraries and Books

I think of biography as the type of leisure-time reading which has meant the most to me across the years. From a long-ago perusal of *The Americanization of Edward Bok* I gathered interest in autograph collecting and journalism. Then came Mrs. Howard Taylor's *Borden of Yale '09;* Dr. Harvey Cushing's volume on *Sir William Osler;* Lord Charnwood's *Abraham Lincoln;* Eve Curie's life of her mother; *Apologia pro Vita Sua* by John Henry Cardinal Newman; William Allen White's life of Calvin Coolidge, *A Puritan in Babylon;* Herbert Hoover's three-volume *Memoirs* (with the lyrically exquisite chapter on Lou Henry, his wife); C. S. Lewis's spiritual autobiography, *Surprised by Joy; Life and Letters of William Lyon Phelps;* Van Wyck Brooks's *Helen Keller: Sketch for a Portrait;* P. W. Williams's *General Evangeline Booth;* and lately, Turnbull's sparkling volume *Thomas Wolfe.*

There are others and will be more, I hope. Today's youth are not hero worshippers; they *may* be hero-debunkers instead! But I found biography therapeutic, enabling me to see my own warts in humbling contrast to other less-blemished complexions. Was it Ralph Waldo Emerson who said, "There is no history; there is only biography"?

I am a library addict—uninhibited, unfettered, enthusiastic, happy. When I was a college president, I used to spend my Saturday afternoons on campus, with the aid of my master key, browsing in the receiving and preparing rooms of the Emory & Henry College library to keep abreast of new acquisitions and publications.

My good friend, the head librarian, tolerated my clandestine wanderings but never fully approved of them. I had a cluster of adolescent idiosyncrasies: I could not bear to see lovely dust jackets thrown away. I was sometimes critical of a professor's requisitioned purchases because a specific title in his field which I had been wanting to read was not included. I sometimes couldn't bring myself to wait for a fascinating new book to be catalogued and shelved and so quietly purloined it for a week or two—thus throwing the library staff into convulsions of consternation which became tremors of indignation when they discerned my unusual if not illegal practices.

One day Miss Power called me at my office. "Mr. President," she said in Arctic tones, "as nearly as we can tell and in line with our strongest suspicions you have had the new volume of Karsh's *Portraits* for four and one-half weeks, and we think it only fair that the chairman of the Department of Art, who ordered it, should have it for a day or two before it goes into his permanent reserve section. How about letting me send over to your house for it?" One of the heavier sacrifices entailed in becoming a bishop was the abandonment of my leisurely library explorations and the humiliating resumption of the proletarian practice of card-signing for purposes of book borrowing!

The Critical Need for Liberal Education

I am conscious of harboring my own exalted ideas of the consummate importance of books and libraries because of a prior commitment which I have made in my mind and soul to the principle of *liberal education*—a concept which is more than an aphorism to a Christian minister who deposited eight years of his life on the campus of a church-related college. Apart from a fresh and terrible awareness of the judgment and redemption of God, I can think of nothing which our violent, cynical, nearly nihilistic age needs more than it needs a recovery of commitment to those insights and goals which are implemented by liberal studies, those pursued without any instant or visible utilitarian purpose.

John Stuart Mill, in his inaugural address as rector of St. Andrew's University, described the purpose of an educational system as being to make "capable and cultivated human beings. Men are men before they are lawyers or physicians or manufacturers; and if you make them capable and sensible men, they will make themselves capable and sensible lawyers or physicians."[1]

One of the real dangers of contemporary pressures is that we are tempted to bypass liberal education for technical knowledge—an adoption of a basic European theory of training in which young people go directly from secondary studies to a university program focused almost altogether upon the practical, the professional, the utilitarian. This, when finally implemented here, would write "finis" over the whole unique idea of the American college. Justice Felix Frankfurter, one of the best minds in twentieth-century American jurisprudence, replied to a young man inquiring about how he should prepare for a legal career in words that illuminate nearly perfectly the *raison d'etre* of liberal education. I quote Mr. Justice Frankfurter:

The best way to prepare for the law is to come to the study of the law as a well-read person. Thus alone can one acquire the capacity to use the English language on paper and in speech and with the habits of clear thinking which only a true liberal education can give. No less important for a lawyer is the cultivation of the imaginative faculties by reading poetry, seeing great paintings, in the original or in easily available reproductions, and listening to great music. Stock your mind with the deposit of much good reading, and widen and deepen your feelings by experiencing vicariously as much as possible the wonderful mysteries of the universe, and *forget all about your future career*.[2]

Marten Ten Hoor, in his brilliant essay entitled "Education for Privacy," insists that the only way to improve society is to improve one's self. We must, he declares, live well with ourselves before we can live well with others. An earlier and immortal English voice, John Milton, said the same sort of thing in a shining sentence: "I call, therefore, a complete and generous education that which fits a man to perform justly, skillfully, and magnanimously all the offices, both private and public, of peace and war."[3]

These are alien accents in today's activistic vernacular. The strictly personal has vanished in the chorus of the crowds, just as religion's individual pietism has surrendered to the massive involvement neurosis of the moment. But in a world where people are initially individuals and where single votes still determine policy among free men, who shall say that one day the cacophony of noises from huddled humanity *en masse* shall not cease, and the regal significance of the person and his scale of values be sensed once more? This is the precious, timeless meaning of the liberal arts, the glory of the little college, the relevance of books and libraries.

Three goals inhere in the work of institutions like Peace and its senior college comrades. The first is the enlargement of the sphere of human inquiry (embracing matters like basic research, the battle against disease, the complex arena of human relations, and the evolution of international law). The second is the development of an educated taste. Cardinal Newman in his classic work *The Idea of a University* wrote great words on this subject: "It aims at raising the intellectual tone of society, at cultivating the public mind, at purifying the national taste, at supplying true principles to popular enthusiasm and fixed aims to popular aspiration, at giving enlargement and sobriety to the ideas of the age, at facilitating the exercise of political power, and refining the intercourse of private life."[4]

The third objective is to lure and lead students into the discovery of meaning which will lend dignity and cohesiveness to life. Paul, in Romans 8:21, spoke of creation's purpose to emancipate man, that he may be "set free from its bondage to decay and obtain the glorious liberty of the children of God." Colleges like Peace, with their unembarrassed stand for the kind of human and humanitarian values represented in great books across the centuries, have sought these goals and, in the seeking of them, become lighthouses for civilization and free cultures and governments. No one can assess accurately their role in our own land or their exciting potential in helping the United States to solve the perilous problems of the seventies.

Threats to Liberal Education

The Peace Colleges of our century may be seriously threatened this afternoon by a cluster of pending developments on the horizon. One of these is the proposal that church-held property *not operated for profit* shall be taxed. Another is the projected restriction on foundations in the current—and badly needed—effort to revise internal revenue laws. A third could prove to be the Supreme Court's forthcoming consideration of a plea that private or church-related institutions of higher learning may not receive any public monies whatsoever.

Implicit in these converging threats is the possible collapse of private and church-related higher education in America. If this should occur, the considerable percentage of educational responsibility borne now by these institutions would of necessity suddenly devolve upon public colleges and universities and would result in a literally unbearable additional financial burden on the taxpayer. But worse still for our nation, the *historic duality* of the private-public system of higher education would be destroyed, together with its invaluable structure of checks and balances. *All* education would be taken over by the government, and *we could well have tragic occasion to recall that never, in such circumstances, has academic freedom emerged unscathed!*

While pausing to pay grateful tribute to state-supported higher education and its galaxy of distinguished teachers and administrators—nowhere brighter than here in our own North Carolina—we must as thoughtful citizens reaffirm that the church-related college has been historically the quickening conscience of all institutions of higher learning. It may well be, in the midst of today's fresh complexities, that the Christian university, as Sir Walter Moberly suggested, is virtually an impossibility; but it is still gloriously a fact that the Christian college can be a reality. To allow any combination of circumstances, political, sociological or economic, to suffocate it and the liberal learning for which it stands would constitute unmitigated tragedy for our country and for civilization.

Conclusion: Today's Significance

So, the dedication of the Lucy Cooper Finch Library has implications and ramifications far, far beyond this structure, this campus, and this company. If, as A. E. Housman once said, the love of truth is the faintest of human passions, then we dare not allow to be destroyed that which lends saving strength to its frailty.

In *Life's* perceptive essay on the tragic death by heart attack of Swarthmore College's youthful president, Courtney Smith, in the midst of that institution's heated fray with black and white militant students in early 1969, there appeared a magnificent couple of sentences: "The tragedy of Courtney Smith is a peculiarly American tragedy, devoid of villains, full of good intentions, ultimately disastrous. Perhaps it is *the* American tragedy."

So the "pleasant greens" of our nation's church-related and private campuses, dedicated to reason and invisible values, have become narrow capes with angry waters from within beating on one side and terrifying waves from without crashing over the other. It is a crisis whose foreboding dimensions are virtually unsensed in the culture made healthier and more hopeful by these intrepid little schools. Their destruction, as the *Life* essayist would put it, is being contemplated in a setting "devoid of villains, full of good intentions." To allow it to happen would be, indeed, "ultimately disastrous"—"*the* American tragedy."

The importance of little colleges and their inviting new libraries, if one man's understanding of liberal education is valid, is in their calm, reasoned insistence upon a structure of values both relevant and imperishable—even in a day of naked materialism and raucous violence. A famous preacher of our time, when a student, was listening to a radical lecturer in Hyde Park, London. The speaker spotted in the crowd a man wearing a clerical collar and asked him, "Why don't you take one world at a time?" The preacher seemed embarrassed and made no reply, but the student, who was to become a preacher, answered, "He can't, and you can't." The lecturer was about to turn on his respondent when another college man interrupted to ask, "Anybody ever die in your house?" The lecturer stopped and then said bitterly, "That's hitting below the belt."

So life is composed of both the temporal and the more-than-temporal, the visible and the unseen. The little colleges and their collections of knowledge and wisdom, housed in libraries, have precious trusteeship over *both* of life's meanings. In an age where technocracy has outdistanced understanding and wisdom in dangerous fashion, this is surely of surpassing significance. Therefore, within this context of concern and hope, we prepare to dedicate at Peace College this lovely new building, the Lucy Cooper Finch Library.

Endnotes

1.   D. Elton Trueblood, T*he Idea of a College* (New York: Harper & Brothers Publishers, 1959), 99.

2.   Ibid., 99-100.

3.   Ibid., 95.

4.   John Henry Newman, *The Idea of a University* (London: Longmans, Green and Company, 1929), 177-178.

IV

Crisis in Marriage

I gave this address on August 14, 1971, at the program of the second World Family Life Conference held in Estes Park, Colorado, just prior to the Twelfth World Methodist Conference in Denver. At that time, I was serving as chair of the General Committee on Family Life of the United Methodist Church.

I have two distinct recollections of this occasion. The first is that all of my baggage had been lost in Chicago as I was enroute to the Estes Park meeting. I spoke in a borrowed shirt and a wrinkled suit! The second recollection is that there was mixed reaction to my address. An element in the leadership of the old Board of Education strongly favored liberalization of our church's viewpoint on matters of sexual conduct in order to assimilate the permissiveness of situation ethics prominent at that time. My address opposed such liberalization and was criticized by some of my own United Methodist friends (not including Dr. Edward D. Staples, able and beloved head of Family Life in our denomination). I recall how support for my position came from an unexpected source. A well-known Harley Street specialist, a Methodist physician from the United Kingdom, arose and offered vigorous commendation for what I had attempted to say.

Our own General Committee on Family Life, unpopular because of its alleged conservatism, was abolished in our church's restructuring process the following year. Officers were not warned of this, and there was no opportunity for a final meeting.

Crisis in Marriage

Let me begin by quoting a paragraph from the pen of the late Dr. Carl Michalson, Andrew B. Stout Professor of Systematic Theology at Drew University until his tragic passing late in 1965:

> The most dramatic crisis of our day is taking place in the institution of marriage. Gradually the frequency of divorce is transforming the structure of marriage into a polygamous form. To be sure, it is only a "one-at-a-time polygamy" and it rarely adds up to more than deuterogamy. It is a social crisis, nonetheless, in which the character of a major institution is on trial.[1]

Had Professor Michalson lived another six years, in all probability he would have written with greater urgency and even stronger rhetoric. The crisis in marriage in this country, and also in certain other parts of the world, has been compounded by a series of developments in the last few years and the result, for the concerned Christian man or woman, is definitely one of baffled terror. I propose to discuss this crisis wholly from an American perspective and as the point of view of one person only, as practically and dispassionately as is possible this evening. I trust that my presentation may be offered within a context of restraint and flexibility which I deem to be an essential climate for the Church's evaluation of the current situation in this delicate and basic area of human relations.

A Theological Prologue

Christians—actually, more broadly, people of a Judeo-Christian background—believe (some lightly, others profoundly) that marriage is of God. Scriptural authority for this perspective is abundant and ranges from Genesis 2:18, "It is not good that the man should be alone," to Psalm 68:6, "God setteth the solitary in families," to Mark 10:9, "What therefore God hath joined together, let not man put asunder." There is a variegated plethora of additional passages in the Old Testament, the Gospels, St. Paul (particularly 1 Corinthians 7), and St. John the Revelator.

Of course, the boldest and most memorable allusion is the classical reference to the marriage relation as illustrative of the kinship between Christ and His Church to be found, among other places, in Ephesians 5. The latter picture forms one of the bases for the sacramental view of marriage in Catholic theology, attacked so vigorously and, in my opinion, with much confusion by Martin Luther, who regarded the marriage ceremony as a worldly or civil act for which the Church has no constitutive importance, and yet insisted that marriage itself is a divine institution—albeit a *remedium peccati,* a "remedy for sin" and a "hospital for the sick." The Protestant view, evolved from the Lutheran position, holds marriage not to be a sacrament because Jesus Christ did not institute it as he did Baptism and the Lord's Supper, but regards it as "a solemn act in which the grace of God is poured upon (a man and a woman)."[2]

The Christian view of marriage issues from a cluster of basic biblical doctrines. One of these assuredly is the doctrine of God, the Source of all. This is summarized splendidly in the best of all definitions of God: "God is love" (1 John 4:8). Love does not exist in isolation; it shares good things. Therefore, God made us, made us to live in love with Him and to enjoy His blessings.

Another biblical doctrine is the doctrine of man, epitomized in Psalm 8:4-5: "What is man, that thou art mindful of him? and the son of man, that thou visitest him? For thou hast made him a little lower than the angels, and hast crowned him with glory and honor." This is an exalted anthropology, linking Creator and creature, and making a human being something of infinite preciousness whose proper relation to his fellows in life's most intimate experiences can never be tawdry, cheap, or self-aggrandizing.

A third biblical doctrine is the doctrine of the relation of the material and the spiritual: "Know ye not that your body is the temple of the Holy Ghost which is in you?" (1 Corinthians 6:19). Christianity regards the material as the instrument of the spiritual and establishes a sacred gradation of values which gives something as concrete as sex an aura of deeper, invisible meaning. It becomes, in Rudolf Otto's memorable words, *mysterium tremendum et fascinosum*—"a mystery terrible and fascinating."

One could marshal an impressive array of illuminating paragraphs on the subject of Christian marriage by the great minds and spirits of the Church and the household of faith: St. Augustine, Sören Kierkegaard, Francis de Sales, Karl Barth, Emil Brunner, Rudolf Bultmann, Nikolai Berdyaev, Dietrich Bonhoeffer, C. S. Lewis—and the list goes on and on. An objective historian of human civilizations would have difficulty speaking adequately concerning the tremendous impact of the Judeo-Christian message on the solidarity of the home and family, including such collateral concerns as marriage, the sex relationship, monogamy, fidelity, parenthood, and the like. It is a pleasant privilege to read in the literature of autobiography references and tributes to spouses whose roles in shaping the accomplishments of great leaders are so often celebrated with quiet but grateful eloquence. I think especially of the late Bishop Edwin Holt Hughes's chapter on his wife in *I Was Made a Minister,*[3] and of our former U.S. President Herbert Hoover's exquisite writing about his brilliant and charming Lou Henry in his two-volume *Autobiography.* In such instances the theology of marriage becomes a veritable doxology in history!

It is from this deliberately lofty vantage point of consideration, at the conclusion of a theological prologue, that I would invite our attention to the more earthy and even sordid aspects of the crisis in marriage which we are considering.

Diagnosis

Symptoms in the Current Situation. It ought to be stated emphatically that there are positive aspects of the contemporary situation with regard to marriage and the family in this country— and doubtless elsewhere as well. For one thing, the United States is a place where the present popular concept of marriage, having passed through many experimentations and stages in its development, has achieved monogamous stability and a historically and legally meaningful facade of fidelity.

Beyond this, there has been a general abandonment of the intolerable and non-Biblical view of sex as something "dirty"—an overdue emancipation from the crippling and debilitating bonds of

Puritanical prudery. The openness with which sex is accepted, discussed, and taught in present-day America surely contributes to a more wholesome attitude toward an important aspect of life and offers substantial hope for happier marriages in the days ahead. It is of particular significance to record the Church's acceptance of, and occasional leadership in, the evolution of this more normal and healthful attitude toward sex—which, incidentally, may constitute one of the more obvious rediscoveries of biblical truth and teaching in our time!

Other positive signs include, of course, the elevation of the status of women, larger enlightenment in the complex territory of child-rearing, the availability of technical assistance for planned parenthood, dramatic improvements in obstetrics and pediatrics, ways to scrutinize problems like abortion both with idealism and realism, a developing national conscience in the area of minimum income for families, and recognition of creative possibilities in leisure. But the current situation may not be predominantly hopeful. To quote Dr. Michalson once more, "The wilting of the institution of marriage is significantly related to the flowering of secularism."[4] A corollary of the rise of secularism is the sexual revolution, acknowledged by nearly everyone but understood by very few. It had its roots in a number of processes at work in human culture and history during the last century.

One of these processes was that of biblical criticism—the beginnings of a new and freer attitude toward the Holy Scriptures and the consequent release of the Christian conscience from at least a portion of the ancient apprehension which accompanies disobedience to the Bible's teachings and edicts. The relaxation of the traditional influences of orthodox religion, usually Bible-based, certainly helped to usher into existence a new day of human freedom in many areas of life. Without doubt, the lessening of the Bible's authority in the popular mind became a conspicuous factor in the secularizing process and its attendant developments.

Another factor in the inception of the sexual revolution was the widespread development of the scientific method of inquiry and its subsequent focus upon the study of sex. Among the pioneers in this movement were Sigmund Freud, an Austrian Jew and physician; Havelock Ellis, the massively brilliant English psychologist; and a cluster of three American investigators, Alfred Kinsey, William Masters, and Virginia Johnson. Also worthy of mention were people like the Marxist Friedrich Engles, the champion of women's rights Ellen Key, and the English philosopher and mathematician Bertrand Russell—each of whom celebrated the idea of free love and the destruction of the traditional attitude toward sex. A somewhat impressive and greatly varied literature promoting the idea of sexual liberty has been amassed during the last half century and has given the sexual revolution an aura of alleged academic respectability. Much of this literature has been critical of conventional Christian restrictions on the understanding of sex—and, we must confess, justifiably so.

The sexual revolution is promoted by less impressive writings as well, prominent among them *Playboy,* a magazine boasting today a readership greater than the combined subscription lists of all the scholarly journals published in this country. In spite of its pseudo-philosophical editorial position represented at interminable length in the *trialogue* of the editor Hugh Hefner, the basic appeal of this magazine is to a mind dedicated to a philosophy of pleasure akin to ancient Greek hedonism. Hefner constantly indicts the Judeo-Christian tradition for its "antisensual" attitudes and condones temporary relationships between the sexes characterized by complete freedom and predicated upon a low anthropology which really regards man or woman as a *thing* with a brilliantly cultivated brain.

While *Playboy* is perhaps the most sophisticated of the sex publications in this country, there are *many* which undertake to develop the same themes on lower levels and with more blatantly pornographic approaches. And perhaps more insidious and harmful is the shocking array of hard-core pornography in novels and nonfiction, turned out in assembly-line quantities, available on nearly every street corner in a marathon distribution effort propelled by economic motivation and legally protected by the Supreme Court of our country. A visual concomitant is an amazing quantity of X-rated pornographic movies shown now in all the major cities.

Over and above publications and photography there are the nearly incredible facts of contemporary practice in our country. For example, beyond reasonable doubt American youth are now engaging in premarital sex to a much greater extent than ever before, encouraged by the nominal security provided by modern contraceptives—especially the "pill." Along with their sexual encounters go involvement with drugs, soft and hard; excessive use of alcohol; and often the development of bizarre lifestyles and philosophies. Communal living is but one such lifestyle practiced by the youth subculture and is surely a symptom of organized protest and withdrawal where present-day societal practices are concerned. Not unrelated to this type of phenomenon is the steady spread of co-educational dormitory living patterns and open visitation privileges on the campuses of American colleges and universities, including many of the distinguished institutions of the land.

This speaker happened to be engaged some months ago in dialogue with an extremely attractive high school group in one of our very large churches in Western North Carolina, and the subject of attitude toward marriage arose. It was startling, to say the least, to hear at least 80 percent of the youth present for this discussion comment negatively upon marriage as an institution and declare that their own acceptance of marital bondage (as they put it), if it occurred at all, would be because of social expectancy and security and not because of personal conviction that the relationship was either valid or necessary. One does not know how typical such reactions may be, but one suspects that more contemporary young people in the United States than immediately appear to be involved are scrutinizing the entire concept of marriage and raising fundamental questions about its social and/or moral values.

Beyond the whole area of concern just mentioned is the practice of extramarital relations in our contemporary life here in this country. Anthropologist Gilbert Bartell, in an important new book recording a careful scientific study of this development, says that there may now be as many as two million middle-class Americans involved in voluntary group sex, including mate-swapping, voyeurism, homosexual engagements, and the like. He suggests that more than 8,000 married couples in greater Chicago and more than 4,000 in Atlanta engage in such practices.

The promotional enterprise associated with group sex is now said to involve the regular publication of more than fifty magazines, running the gamut from shoddy pornographic tabloids to discreet glossies, devoted to deliberate procuring within this context. With the popular caption "swinging," participation in group sex has produced its own philosophical and practical rationales to the extent that a great many people have been led to believe that such activity is important therapy for sick marriages and as such should be accepted by society at-large. It is interesting to include here a cryptic comment by a New York critic named Molly Haskell, contained in her report about group sex in Greenwich Village: "Like their fellow Americans, swingers have now gone from Puritanism into promiscuity without passing through sensuality."

Even more bizarre practices, like marriage ceremonies for homosexuals, can be recorded as part of the current scene. Beyond the shadow of a doubt, popular acceptance of the institution of marriage and conventional sexual guidelines is at an all-time low in U.S. culture. However, it would be accurate to observe that much of the contemporary obsession with sex so evident in this country is the result of wider and more effective communication and the elimination of much of the earlier fear syndrome because of improved contraceptive techniques. It *may* indeed be true, as some claim, that the actual practice of premarital and extramarital sex is not dramatically greater than in other generations—but just more openly discussed and consequently better known.

One other point ought to be made just here. Perhaps the saddest of all the results of the sex obsession with which our country is afflicted is the imminent peril that our people, having seen and heard and had too much, will revolt against the great and precious reality of sex itself which is one of the loveliest gifts of a good God.

The Contributing Philosophical Cause. Looking beyond the necessarily sordid recital just offered, I will try to identify the background cause of these developments in contemporary thinking and practice. I propose that this cause is related to the revolutionary transition in ethical principles today. The old authoritarian ethic has been scrutinized ruthlessly and all but abandoned, perhaps because of the virtual disappearance of biblical authority alluded to earlier.

In my lay judgment a permanent or near-permanent successor to the authoritarian ethic has not yet been discovered or proposed. We have come to a kind of ethical "halfway house" in the situation, or contextual, ethics suggested by men like Professor Joseph Fletcher of the Episcopal Theological School, Cambridge, Massachusetts, and Professor Paul Lehmann of Union Theological Seminary, New York City.

Situation ethics in a very real sense is as old as Aristotle, and describes a practice entered into by all of us, even those committed to authoritarian ethical principles, at one time or another. Simply stated, its expression in Fletcher's thought is based upon this query: What does love, or *agape,* require of a person in a given situation? Professor Lehmann, using fundamentally the same approach, poses this query: What does belief in Jesus Christ and membership in His Church require?

I think the best critique I have read of Fletcher's thought has been offered by Dr. Robert E. Fitch, dean emeritus of the Pacific School of Religion, in an article which appeared first in *The Christian Century* and later was included in a symposium of articles edited by Dr. Harvey Cox entitled *The Situation Ethics Debate.*[5] Dean Fitch says that Fletcher's situation ethics is more *absolutist* than anything to be found in Immanuel Kant. He says the absolutism of love is the most tyrannical absolutism that one can encounter in life.

Dean Fitch brings three primary indictments against the Fletcher system. The first has to do with the ambiguity of the two terms, *love* and *situation.* The second suggests that there is a lack of realism involved in Fletcher's treatment of social ethics. Professor Fletcher insists, for example, that love and justice are the same, and Dean Fitch points out that historically this has not been so and that the liberties so dearly celebrated in Fletcher's book have usually required either a Constitution or a Bill of Rights or a system of laws to implement them in human society.

Third, the dean accuses Professor Fletcher of what he calls semi-Pelagianism: not sufficient cognizance of the sinfulness or the suffering of the human race or, put another way, a failure to demonstrate ample awareness of the meaning of the Cross. Dean Fitch has an illuminating statement in his critical essay. He says, "If on the pilgrimage of life, I could be sure that I would always encounter a Joseph Fletcher, then perhaps I could entertain his concepts. But suppose that instead I should encounter the Grand Inquisitor. What then?"

I remember well that when I was still at Emory & Henry College, we invited a brilliant teacher of ethics, a well-known member of the faculty at a distinguished American institution of higher learning, to come to our campus and speak both to the students and to the faculty club. When he addressed the faculty, his subject was "Situation Ethics." In the course of his presentation, he used an illustration from a contemporary novel in which an act of adultery was alleged to be a supreme manifestation of the principle of love. Later, in a coffee session, I asked this professor how he would deal with murder. Quick as a flash he replied, "I can think of numerous instances where murder in a community would be the *supreme* act of love." I know, of course, that such an extreme response may not constitute a fair vantage point from which to appraise situation ethics. What troubles me is that a supposedly responsible, knowledgeable mind can come out at such a place and make such a statement. When I interrogated him further, he failed to alter his position at all.

I must say that I have been profoundly disturbed by the fact that philosophical leaders like Fletcher and Lehmann have seemed to accept the reality of moral change in contemporary life uncritically and, as a matter of fact, to welcome it as a cultural development which deserves recognition and assimilation rather than a peril which ought to be deplored and resisted. A viewpoint more acceptable to me is that of the distinguished Jewish philosopher, Dr. Will Herberg, graduate professor of philosophy and culture at Drew University, who in an address made the following statement:

Sexual irregularity among young people has always been common enough. While there is no doubt of marked increase in pre-marital sexual activity among the younger generation today, the real moral problem is provided not by the girl [or boy] who goes along, but by the girl [or boy] who shrugs her shoulders and says, "Well, so what? What's so bad about sleeping around?" To violate moral standards while at the same time acknowledging their authority is one thing; to lose all sense of the moral claim, to repudiate all moral authority and every moral standard as such, is something far more serious. I sharply disagree with those Protestant theologians who hold that society is evolving a new morality based on the application of love for others to each concrete situation rather than upon rules and regulations. This is a dewy-eyed optimism. A realistic look at contemporary values shows that what's actually happening is a rejection of all moral restraint in favor of a way of life governed by a self-indulgent quest for pleasure and fun.

I am convinced that a part of our sexual satiation today is traceable to the widespread popularity of an ethical philosophy which adapts to the culture instead of quarreling with it. And, if this is so, then surely the ethical dilemma in our day is responsible for the moral muddle in which our people and particularly our young folk find themselves. We have paused culturally at an *interim* ethical position, one that offers little promise of permanence; and this perspective is being presented in religious utterances, in the literature of religious education, and in position papers developed by policy-making bodies in the Church.

There are other ethical proposals appearing on the horizon, such as the *"rule Agapism"* of United Methodism's Professor Paul Ramsey of Princeton University and the philosophical, or moral, ethics of Dr. Walter Muelder of Boston University. However, these alternative systems, far more satisfying to some of us, have not acquired the popular image necessary for the arousal of general interest at this time.

I, for one, would affirm that the moral symptoms so apparent in contemporary culture are the result in major measure of the fundamental ethical bewilderment in which civilization finds itself at this moment of its history. This is the parent malignancy in human society which is producing much of the social malaise confronting us.

Prescription

Let me, in conclusion, and with the modesty appropriate to my own lack of professional competence in this field, suggest a cluster of ways in which a Christian, and particularly a Methodist churchman, may become constructively and creatively involved in the confrontation and cure of the existing crisis in marriage. These ideas, to be sure, represent but one man's thought.

One, the Church must accept the *good* things implicit in what we have called the sexual revolution, rather than undertake a massive and blindly Puritanical resistance to *all* new perspectives. There is important background reading which could reinforce our determination at this point, including such excellent books as David R. Mace's *The Christian Response to the Sexual Revolution* (Abingdon Press), Helmut Thielicke's *The Ethics of Sex* (Harper & Row), and even the older C. S. Lewis volume *The Four Loves* (Harcourt & Brace).

Two, the Church must undertake to know and understand the Christian position on the sacred and theological meanings of marriage and its related themes and to disseminate this knowledge effectively among its members and constituents.

Three, the Church, because of the sheer terror of the current crisis, must articulate again its insistence upon basic biblical standards where sexual and marital relations are concerned. *It must not be afraid to take a stand counter to the trends of contemporary culture.*

Four, the Church must define defensible Christian positions and then vocalize them intelligently on such critical issues as birth control, sex education, abortion, artificial insemination, homosexuality, divorce, racially mixed marriages, and genetic engineering.

Five, the Church must sharpen its skills in *teaching* youth and young adults its insights about sex, marriage, and the family. Most of our present problem derives from the Church's abject failure to teach effectively and urgently.

Six, the Church must offer healing love, forgiveness, and hope to *all* of those who have lost their way in modern life—from the hippies to the swingers! The Church is many things, but *it is always and forever a shop where broken lives can be repaired.* Canon T. Guy Rogers, writing in *The Church and People,* suggested significantly, "No one on behalf of the Church ought to be allowed to handle the disagreements of married people who does not believe quite fervently in the power of conversion and the immediate influence of Christ on the lives of people today."

There is a lovely story of a young woman whose life had been broken on the reefs of moral error and who attended a communion service in a little kirk in the Scottish Highlands. When the invitation to join those at the Lord's Table was given, she demurred. The minister, knowing her life, held forth the sacred elements to her and said gently, "Take it, lassie; it's for sinners!" The grace of the Lord Jesus Christ is for sinners, and also for those who are confused and in trouble.

Seven, the Church, in a renaissance of pastoral concern and ministry, must help families confront and solve the *many* problems they face—including childlessness, children with congenital handicaps, retardation, children in rebellion, teenage marriage, forced marriage, infidelity, chronic illness, terminal disease, tragedy, grief, marital discord, the presence of aged in-laws in the home, financial reverse, career collapse, and failing faith.

Eight, the Church must increasingly magnify and interpret the *great occasions* of life such as marriage, birth, baptism, confirmation, and death. In the holiest sense and in the light of the gospel's teachings, these are family festivals, either of joy or sorrow.

Nine, the Church must undertake to arrange for all family members—especially youth—to have the kind of experiential encounter with God which remains at the heart of the Wesleyan interpretation of religion. As the great T. W. Manson said years ago, the teachings of the Christian religion are for *kingdom people:* "The moral demands of Jesus presuppose a changed nature and disposition in man; they imply a previous conversion."[6]

Perhaps the challenge today is for Church liberals to hear once more a call to what is fundamentally an evangelical thrust. The Church's dichotomies have nearly destroyed it across the years, and surely the time for their own destruction is overdue. The activism so vigorously celebrated in the Christian community today depends finally upon a rediscovered pietism. It may not be possible to secure the attention of Church members and constituents in this sophisticated hour of human history unless the Church learns afresh how to present *its basic message of God's love for sinful men.* The distinguished journalist Louis Cassels, senior editor of United Press International, said to an audience of preachers: "If you persist in handing out stones when people ask for bread, they'll finally quit coming to the bakery." Perhaps it is time for this fundamental message about the communication of the gospel to be heard again by ministers, bishops, and lay people. Tolstoy summed it all up long ago: "God is the name of my desire!"

Conclusion

There is a crisis in marriage, and perhaps we have dissected it too thoroughly. But there is also a glory about marriage which, in the mind of the Christian, transcends any crisis. Francis de Sales, in his *Introduction to the Devout Life,* had this paragraph:

> If the glue is good, two pieces of wood glued together will cleave so fast to each other that they can be more easily broken in any other place than where they were joined. God glues the husband to the wife with His own blood. For this cause this union is so strong that the soul must sooner separate from the body than the husband from the wife.[7]

Years ago, as a young pastor in Atlanta, Georgia, I had a fascinating old couple in my little church. Each had passed the biblical allotment for a lifespan; each was in fragile health complicated by mutual overweight. They had been married to each other for more than fifty years, and they had one child who lived only a few short months and was buried in a tiny grave in the country cemetery adjoining the churchyard. They were not technically well educated, but they were Christians deeply and ecstatically in love with each other. They used pet names: he was "Chic" and she was "Trixie." They held hands at church picnics and as they walked from the sanctuary to their car. I watched them and found my own assessment of the institution of Christian marriage thrillingly elevated by their lovely example. I thought then and have thought many times since of Felix Adler's moving words written in 1930, and I trust I shall not be considered overly sentimental if I elect to close this address by quoting them:

Together they have traveled the road of life, and remembrance now holds them close, remembrance of many hours of ineffable felicity, of a sense of union as near to bliss as mortal hearts can realize, of high aspirations, pursued in common, of sorrows shared—sacramental sorrow. And now, nearing the end, hand-in-hand, they look forth upon the wide universe, and the love which they found in themselves and still find there to the last, becomes to them a pledge of the vaster love that moves beyond the stars and suns.[8]

This is the glory of Christian marriage—a glory that overshadows crisis.

Endnotes

1.   Carl Michalson, *Faith for Personal Crises* (New York: Charles Scribner Sons, 1958), 114.

2.   Edwin E. Voigt, *Methodist Worship in the Church Universal* (Nashville: The Graded Press, 1965), 144.

3.   Edwin Holt Hughes, *I Was Made a Minister* (New York: Abingdon Press, 1943).

4.   Carl Michalson, 115.

5.   Harvey Cox, *The Situation Ethics Debate* (Philadelphia: Westminster Press, 1968), 116 *ff*.

6.   T. W. Manson, *The Teaching of Jesus* (Cambridge: Cambridge University Press, 1963), 299.

7.   Francis de Sales, *Introduction to the Devout Life*. Quoted in Michalson, 114.

8.   I have searched diligently for the source of this quotation and have verified its accuracy from other copies in my notes but have been unable to identify the publication from which I procured it.

V

Aspects of Our Methodist Heritage With Particular Focus upon One Of Its Distinguished Transmitters: Bishop Roy Hunter Short

---

I was privileged to preach this sermon on June 16, 1972, at the final session of the Louisville Annual Conference in St. Paul United Methodist Church, Louisville, Kentucky. The occasion was a special tribute to Bishop and Mrs. Short prior to Bishop Short's retirement after twenty-four years as an episcopal leader of The United Methodist Church.

It was a great honor to be invited to speak at this event, primarily because of the relationship which the Hunts have had with the Shorts over a long period of time. Bishop Short was our resident bishop across his twelve years in Holston Conference. They were our neighbors during the four years we served the Nashville Area, having retired in that city. It was during this period that I arranged with the Upper Room for the publication of Bishop Short's biography written by the late Bishop T. Otto Nall, entitled Builder of Bridges.

Aspects of Our Methodist Heritage With Particular Focus upon One of Its Distinguished Transmitters: Bishop Roy Hunter Short

Look unto the rock whence ye are hewn, and to the hole of the pit whence ye are digged. . . .   — Isaiah 51:1

Introduction

The America of history was a rugged land when our forefathers undertook to carve the early colonies out of its wilderness. Something of very great significance happened in those pioneer days and kept on happening for a hundred years. Following the wave of civilization surging westward across unbroken terrain was a sturdy little army of pioneer preachers of the gospel, many of them Methodists. They had no elaborate organization or visible means of support; they rarely knew whence would come a night's lodging or the next meal.

They traveled on horseback or afoot with no roads save an Indian trail, fording streams, exposed to storms, prostrated by fever, wasted by malaria, but indomitable still. Dressed in their deerskins and homespuns, they were in almost constant danger from wild beasts and hostile Native Americans. Their libraries were a Bible and a hymnbook; their sanctuaries the open woods and prairies and perhaps an occasional crude cabin. Their preaching was simple, straight from the heart, not always careful of the King's English but full of the strong doctrines of repentance and grace.

These men founded the churches in which Americans worship, laid the foundations upon which our Christian institutions have since been built, and wrought our Methodism out of the hardy stock of a wilderness era. Their courageous sharing of Jesus Christ is woven like a luminous thread into the very fabric of our nation's history.

Looking down the corridor of the years, we can see a noble procession of those who have bequeathed to us much of what is now our own religious and ecclesiastical legacy: the Wesley brothers, once brief sojourners on the Georgia coast, who loved to ride the narrow turnpikes of Old England in search of men who needed God more than they loved the artistic Anglican ritual; Francis Asbury, who never married a woman because he was wedded to the great task of shepherding the lost sheep of Christ; Peter Cartwright, whose rugged compassion was as rough as his saddlebags but whose heart was like that of a little child in the presence of a man with spiritual need; Matthew Simpson, pouring his frontier gospel eloquence into the structuring of DePauw University and counseling the sixteenth president of the United States during the darkest hours of the Civil War; Francis J. McConnell, crusading against industrial injustice; and John R. Mott, the Ulysses of modern missionaries, at Lausanne, Edinburgh and Jerusalem designing contemporary ecumenism.

Tonight, proudly, we add another name to this company: Roy Hunter Short, who, combining sensitive spirituality with creative churchmanship as circuit preacher, district superintendent, metropolitan pastor, editor, and bishop, has served well the far-flung Methodism he so deeply loves. In a deeply personal sense and with what amounts to inexpressible appreciation, my wife and I regard Bishop and Mrs. Short as our own episcopal family. They occupied this role from 1952 until 1964, and our indebtedness to them was so immeasurable across those years that we have continued to regard them, with many added reasons, in that same relationship since then. My acceptance of this invitation to visit the Louisville Annual Conference is really an acceptance of an opportunity for a pilgrimage to pay tribute to "my own" Bishop and his dear companion.

What, then, is this Methodist Heritage of which we are thinking this evening, the Rock from which we have been hewn, and how has it been exemplified in the life and career of the Bishop of the Louisville Area? I propose that its components are *conviction, perception, message,* and *witness.*

Conviction

One of the most helpful writings, from my own perspective, to come from the pen of Bishop Short is the little *Spiritual Revival for Our Day,* published by Tidings eighteen years ago. It has been a treasure in my own library since it appeared. One of its most searching chapters deals with the great principles of our faith as they are suggested in the Prologue of the Gospel of John. These principles compose the unchanging anatomy of Christianity, the convictions at the very heart of our understanding of the Christian message. Surely, the moment is here to re-emphasize these matters to our people. I mention three of them.

The lostness of humanity. The early Methodists believed profoundly that man, without God, is a lost being. They never presented sin in festive terms; to them it was as basic as life and as common as collard greens in Georgia.

Sin is the denial of God and the arrogant presumption by which we try to play God. Sin is human pride in all its disguises, disobedience against the Supreme Authority, irresponsibility, failure to respond to Him, idolatry, unbelief when God proffers His gift of trust.

Philosophically, one may wonder if the epitome of sin is not humanism—the blatant, blasphemous assumption that God is not, that He is not necessary, and that any introduction of the hypothesis of God only serves to complicate in a hopeless sort of way the human scene and equation.

Oddly enough, in an era when many preachers have ceased to talk of sin, novelists and dramatists are discovering it afresh. Witness Albert Camus' *The Fall* and William Golding's fictional treatment of original sin, *Lord of the Flies.* And witness Eugene O'Neill, Tennessee Williams, even John O'Hara.

For some, sin is more elemental and uncomfortably specific. It can be in a child's attitude toward a parent, in a preacher's reaction to his appointment—and in a congregation's perspective on the preacher, one going or one about to come. It is still in the seven deadly wrongs spoken of by Christians since the fourth century: pride, envy, anger, slough, avarice, gluttony, and lust.

The subtlety of sin's peril is its ever-contemporary disguise—the fact that it is always incognito. Gambling becomes sweepstakes for hospitals, liquor-by-the-drink becomes a necessary overture for prosperity, adultery becomes therapeutic expression of personal freedom, envy—again in the case of the preacher—may become a justifiable indictment of the Establishment for its failure to recognize a person's innate capacities. And so, on and on. When a man begins to see through sin's disguise and to confront his own problem with it, then he is moving toward God: St. Paul came to this point in Romans 7:15-25: "I do not understand my own actions... . I can will what is right, but I cannot do it... . Wretched man that I am! Who will deliver me from this body of death?"

This was early Methodism's starting point—its basic earthy realism.

A Divine Redeemer. The early Methodists had the same concept of Jesus Christ which Charles Lamb suggested in his well-known statement: "If Shakespeare were to come into this room, we should rise to our feet; if Christ were to enter, we should fall upon our knees."[1]

The entirety of our gospel is predicated upon the fact that God sent His own Son to be the Savior of the world. The Church's assessment of Jesus Christ has constantly insisted that He is more than a mere man, a good and great teacher, a splendid example and a noble martyr: Christians have always held him to be Incarnate God, Divine Redeemer. It is this kind of fundamental faith which causes a great preacher to say, "You can afford to have hope in a world where Christmas comes out of a stable, the Son of God out of a smelly little village, and twenty centuries of Christianity out of a tomb."[2] And so, Bishop Short says in his little book *Spiritual Revival for Our Day,* it is the conviction that we possess an all-sufficient Christ which enables us to affirm with deep assurance:

> I know a world that is sunk in sin
> That no man's art can cure;
> But I know a name, a name, a name,
> That can make that world all pure.

An experience of God in saving grace. The early Methodists were indestructible optimists because they insisted upon seeing mankind not as it was but as it might become.

This conviction is rooted, of course, in the surety of God— God living and able and loving. Our departure from emphasis upon the reality of God in our own souls during these latter days is traceable not so much to a new psychology as it is to a diluted theology: we have not been that sure of God Himself! If I could, I would preach a sermon on the great Old Testament text about the nature and existence of God: I AM THAT I AM!" (Exodus 3:13). Shame on us for trying to alter the nature of God to fit our little philosophical presuppositions! Do you recall what John Newton wrote: "If you think you see the Ark of the Lord falling, you can be quite sure that it is due to a swimming in your own head!"?

We try to dodge this encounter between God and our souls to escape its cutting edge. The gospel is so direct and pointed, utterly uncanny in its penetration to the heart of our sin and weakness. We try desperately to detour. It was so with the woman of Samaria in John's Gospel. Suddenly Jesus asked her to go and call her husband, and she told him she had no husband. "Thou hast well said...," he replied, "for thou hast had five husbands; and he whom thou now hast is not thy husband." The poor woman was shaken to the quick and she tried to shift the issue by changing the subject. She saw Mount Gerizim in full view and thought it would do as well as anything: "Our fathers worshipped in this mountain; and ye say, that in Jerusalem is the place where men ought to worship" (John 4:16-20). But it was no good; she couldn't get away from those steady, piercing eyes.

This is conversion; it may be sanctification; it is an epiphany. It is the mystical point where the experiential authenticates the rational. D. T. Niles put it quaintly in his Gatlinburg lectures when he referred to it as the Christian's privilege of living in the *passive voice*—assured by the knowledge that we have been loved by Jesus Christ.[3]

The late Nels Ferré, the brilliant contemporary American theologian, spoke of his experience of Divine grace in almost lyrical language: "The birds sang a new song that night and the trees all wore halos...the very air was softer and utterly mysterious. Never can I forget the strangeness and the wonder of it all."

This deepest of all convictions about an experience of God's saving grace, the coming from heaven of a force able to cleanse and redirect life, is at the heart of Methodism in any century. One simply cannot belong in the Wesleyan succession and not believe it deeply.

Perhaps one of the substantial reasons for a recession in religious interest during recent years is that too many contemporary pulpits have been "trumpets giving uncertain sounds" where the rudimentary convictions of the Christian faith are concerned. Assuredly, the failure to regard with urgency such cardinal truths helps to account for the collapse of evangelism in our day. The consuming obsession to win people to God appears only in the preacher who has unshakable convictions about sin, a Divine Savior, and a transforming experience of redeeming Grace.

Whenever I have read anything from the pen of Bishop Short or been fortunate enough to hear him proclaim the gospel in sermons, I have been certain that the great articles of the Christian creed have always been for him a superstructure to which he fastens the details of his message. He affirms this in his own words in his book *Evangelism through the Local Church,* published in 1956:

A church, to be a truly evangelistic church, must believe something concerning God. It must believe that He is a Father who loves all his children with an unfailing love, who is not willing that any of them should perish, and who, to the end that they might be saved, was willing to give the greatest of all possible gifts, the gift of His only begotten Son.

To be a truly evangelistic church, the church must believe something concerning man. It must believe that men are lost until the salvation of God comes into their lives...

A church, to be a truly evangelistic church, must believe something concerning Christ. It must believe that He lives and is available in our present-day world and is abundantly able to save all that come unto God by Him.[4]

I have felt across the years a blessed kinship with "my Bishop" because of the central certainties about God which I am convinced we share. It was the late Dean Lynn Harold Hough of Drew Seminary who said near the end of his life, "Our civilization is falling apart for want of a sufficient number of great believers." Recovery of the *conviction* at the heart of our Methodist heritage would inform our pulpits with new authority and fresh power.

Perspective

Our Methodist heritage, it seems to me, has always featured an unusual ability to understand the nuances and innuendoes of the particular moment in time when the communication of the Christian gospel was being attempted. From Mr. Wesley's decision to leave the decency and order of Anglican worship and proclaim on the highways and in the fields the glad tidings of salvation, to the almost terrifying efforts of the Dallas, the St. Louis, and the Atlanta General Conferences to meet specific human and social problems with the resources of the Christian religion, the story of our church has been one of correct interpretation of the times and appropriate response to their challenge.

I measure my words with extreme care when I say that I have never known a person more competent in such interpretation and response than Bishop Short. As some of us have observed him discharge with consummate efficiency and wisdom the complex responsibilities of secretary of the Council of Bishops, the highest administrative office in our church, we have often felt that, quite literally, he has taken United Methodism gently but firmly by the hand and led it safely over the rough and dangerous terrain that lies between yesterday and tomorrow.

The years of Bishop Short's episcopacy have been a period filled with critical and turbulent issues: war, race, theological transition, the separation of church and state, ecumenism, the moral revolution, and struggles for power within the Church. Scores of times, his brilliant and insightful analyses of the problems related to such crises, presented to the Council of Bishops in carefully prepared papers, have enabled the chief pastors of the church to understand issues accurately and to deal with them constructively.

I have often said that I have never known a person who could look farther down the road of the future and perceive with more prophetic sureness what might be expected to occur than Bishop Short. To a casual observer, there is frequently an aura of mystery about his crystal ball; but to those who know him best, it is quite clear that massive study and thought, disciplined and organized by an unusually fine mind, explain his startling proficiency as a seer of things to come. Surely, this church of ours has been the beneficiary of magnificently unique ecclesiastical statesmanship in the career of the Bishop of Louisville!

Perspective, then, is that component in our Methodist heritage which keeps us contemporary and relevant. It can cause us to respond to the times by using a combo in worship—or it can insist upon fair representation for an ethnic minority on a strategic board. It keeps telling us that the gospel, in both its vertical and horizontal dimensions, must be marketed in wrappings and ribbons appropriate and fashionable for the hour—or more basically, that religious faith always and everywhere must seek to "serve the present age." This quality of flexibility and adaptability, historically a hallmark of Methodism, may be its finest guarantor of permanence in the family of churches. But we who must share its implementation in days ahead may only pray for those gifts of insight and understanding which have made Bishop Short such an effective architect of perspective during his six quadrennia in the episcopal office.

Message

Message is the *communication* of the great doctrines of religion clearly, vividly, fervently, and effectively to a human audience. It is Beethoven taking the fundamental rules of musical composition and turning them into his "Moonlight Sonata." It is Shakespeare or Browning using the tools of versification and rhyme to make Hamlet's "Soliloquy" or "Rabbi Ben Ezra." Our Methodist heritage, when all is said and done, may actually be more message than anything else. Men like Wesley and Asbury were able to fashion from their theological convictions clarion calls to conversion and discipline, to service and obedience.

The desperate need of modern United Methodism is for the *whole* message of the Christian gospel in its ancient purity and power to be let loose once more among the nations.

What is the gospel? It is the revolutionary and redemptive love of God in a tormented soul and in all of earth's tortured human situations—made real and available by a cross. It is the strange and remarkable assurance, witnessed by an empty tomb, that out of incredible chaos keep coming Divine purpose and order.

Adam Burnet, minister of St. Cuthbert's in Edinburgh, told of an evening during World War I when he stood not far from the tall spire of a village church somewhere in France. Oddly enough, firing on both sides of the line had subsided and in the momentary stillness Burnet watched the sun set in a blaze of glory upon the horizon. Suddenly and without warning a single shell screamed through the twilight and the top half of the church steeple dissolved with a shocking roar. Almost at that very moment a flock of swallows, nesting there, rose slowly above the smoke and flying debris, flew about for a moment, and then settled back quietly and with a certain dignity on top of the wreckage where their nests had been located. Adam Burnet said that this reminded him for some strange reason of the *greatness of God.* After the foundations have been shaken and men of ill will have done their worst, God's greatness remains immutable, illimitable, unimpaired by all that has happened.

No minister has read the eighth chapter of Romans to a dying person and sensed an exquisite, almost audible silence of blessed comprehension enfold the sick room without realizing afresh that this gospel is something infinitely beyond a human being. Let loose in the earth, proclaimed from the pulpit, it will do in any age what John R. Mott used to call its "wonder works."

But the message of the gospel has to be presented differently in our time. We are living in a *changed* day, and the change has been so sweeping that it is not yet fully understood. Unless we do recognize the radically altered world in which we must present the message of the gospel, we simply shall not be effective.

Perhaps I may illustrate in a homely way. A teacher of the Urdu language whose grasp of English was something short of total, wishing to reward an American woman who had done exceptionally well under his instruction in mastering the Urdu language, sent her a bouquet of flowers along with this card: "These, dear lady, will fade and die, but you will smell forever!" Just as the nuances of language have to be understood if communication is to be effective, so the nuances of the times must be comprehended if the message of religion is to be spoken effectively in any given era.

Preaching, as Phillips Brooks said in his Lyman Beecher lectures many years ago, is the bringing of truth through personality. The brightest glory of the Methodist heritage in every age has been the ministry of preachers who literally have lost themselves in the wonder and power of their message. Three years ago some of us heard the telecast of the Bell Telephone Hour in which the featured person was Pablo Casals, the celebrated cellist, conducting a group of summertime musicians here in our country. We watched and listened as the ninety-year-old maestro poured the terrible intensity of his own soul into interpretations of Mozart and Schubert, demanding sheer perfection from those playing under his baton. At the conclusion, while Casals walked away from the cameras, Donald Voorhees said, "He is content. He has made music again—the *one thing for which he lives."* There it is!

> Phillips Brooks in Boston's Trinity Church . . .
> Robert Murray McCheyne in St. Peter's, Dundee . . .
> Frederick W. Robertson at Brighton, England's
>   famous seaside resort on the Chalk Cliffs . . .
> George Whitefield preaching in the fields . . .
> Otto Dibelius in the Marienkirche in Berlin . . .
> Sam Shoemaker in Calvary pulpit, Pittsburgh . . .
> Roy Hunter Short here in St. Paul's, Louisville . . .

All of these and others like them have been men whose own lives reflected the goodness and glory of the Lord and who cared desperately about the gospel. They had prepared themselves to mediate the message by total encounter with the Redeeming Lord. John Henry Jowett spoke of such an experience in a person's life during his Lyman Beecher Lectures: "The Call of the Eternal must ring through the rooms of his soul as clearly as the sound of the morning bell rings through the valleys of Switzerland, calling the peasants to early prayer and praise!"

In a deeply satisfying way, Bishop Short has illustrated for me the haunting power of the Christian message as it is offered through preaching. There is always the danger that administrative responsibility will produce an erosion of pulpit creativity, and surely a certain amount of this is inevitable for all who have been called into connectional obligations for the church. But I have never felt that it affected Bishop Short as much as others. I have never heard him preach poorly, or undertake to bring a message which did not lay strong hold upon my own soul.

Across the years since I have been privileged to know Bishop Short, I have discovered him making new sermons and sharing choice ideas with friends as the result of an experience of writing the night before on some particular text. It may be a reflection of his training in a Presbyterian seminary that his sermons are always strongly biblical in their orientation, but it is certainly a testimony to his own practical, businesslike approach to life that they are ever down-to-earth, filled with illustrative material taken from everyday happenings, and beamed to the actual needs of his listeners. The lyrical quality of his own spirit often breaks through his preaching. Occasionally he closes a message by moving into the melody of some great hymn, and this lovely practice beautifully suggests the fact that in his own heart and life theology long since has become doxology. One has the impression that preaching the Christian message, for him, is a matter of frightening urgency.

I submit to you that this part of our Methodist heritage needs desperately to be rediscovered in our time in all of our annual conferences. No one could possibly estimate the change for the better which would be wrought in our local churches if the full potential of their pulpits could be realized. In his Yale Lectures in 1957, Dr. Niles referred to preaching as being *prolepsis* as well as *proclamation*—having the strange and wonderful power of holding within itself even now a taste of the future's magnificent triumph.[5] Professor Joseph Sittler, in his exciting little book *The Anguish of Preaching* suggests the same basic idea in the following words:

> The preacher in a special posture stands between the "it is finished" and the tremendous word of the apostle "the whole creation waits with eager longing." To be a preacher is not only to know eschatology as a report and an agenda item in systematic theology; he is, in the anguish of his task, the eschatological man.[6]

Paul Scherer in that great book which proved to be his valedictory, *The Word God Sent,* referred again to the idea of *prolepsis:* "Something is right now that was wrong before: something profound in the universe that was worth all the rest."[7]

Over all of this is the sunrise glow of the Holy Spirit's presence in power to communicate, to convict, to convert, to inform with new hope and fresh joy. This, as someone has said, is the Church's hidden secret—the *sixth* reason for the victory of Christianity, to be added to Edward Gibbon's *five* reasons in the *Decline and Fall of the Roman Empire.*

This is why plain men and women, simple men and women, sinful men and women who have been saved by grace, may preach the unsearchable riches of Jesus Christ with quiet confidence!

Witness

All four approaches to our Methodist heritage being used in this address are intimately interrelated, and each overlaps the others in some sense. But I would have us recognize at this point that a particular uniqueness, something over and beyond the other categories, is implicit in the concept of *witness.* If *conviction* suggests the minister in his role as a theologian, if *perspective* calls to mind his function as analyst and statesman, and if *message* envisions him as preacher, then the idea of *witness,* while it involves all of these, speaks primarily of him as a human being, a warmly compassionate person, one for whom the Lord Jesus Christ died.

The impact of the church occurs in the end through people. Programs have to be personalized, and even institutions are but lengthened shadows of individuals. So, the quality of the Methodist heritage, to return to the Introduction of this address, is inseparably associated with people like the Wesleys, Bishop Asbury, Peter Cartwright, Bishop Simpson, Bishop McConnell, John R. Mott, and Bishop Short. They, after Jesus Christ, are also the rocks from whence we have been hewn.

This may be an appropriate time to insist again upon the primacy of New Testament goodness among all of us who bear the gospel's message.

Perhaps no words have been more openly despised in recent theological circles than *pietism* and *moralism*—and to some extent understandably, for honest folk see in them a violent misuse of the preaching event and a verbal microcosm of the age-old Pharisaism and hypocrisy so often grave embarrassments to the Christian community. But the pity is that modern rejection of these terms has sometimes been mistakenly extended to imply a tragic deprecation of the whole idea of ethical quality and personal integrity in an individual's life.

Put another way, *pietism* has been associated with *piety* and *moralism* with *moral sensitivity*—and the latter has been abandoned with the former! Cleanness of thinking, speaking, and living is in many quarters no longer regarded as an unmistakable hallmark of Christian faith. Indeed, filthy speech, unconventional morals, and sometimes loosely rationalized violence have in these latter days been justified by religious argument and sometimes advocated by stellar names in the religious community.

But this is essentially wrong. Religion can never get away from the simple, devastating fact that its experience has to make a *qualitative difference* in a person's life and relationships. To deny this is to surrender to the largest of all illusions. One cannot remember the teachings of Augustine, Anselm, Calvin or Wesley, much less the troublesome New Testament witness to the personal purity and devotional discipline of Jesus, without realizing that the severing of personal piety from theological reflection—indeed, from Christian discipleship—is, put mildly, a peculiar development.

The plain and simple fact is that sermons, through the centuries, have had their greatest power when they have been preached by *good* people, people whose own lives quietly but surely mirrored the gospel they spoke. Not by people who have thought they were good and intimated so, but by those whose ways of living have been mightily influenced by the cleansing Christ. One recalls the words of Professor John Knox: "When I think of men in the ministry who have helped me most, I think not of the gifted but of the good."[8] The man or woman of the cloth who is wholly secular, tarnished a bit by involvement in certain aspects of the new morality, fresh from the freedom of a martini and the glib use of four-letter words in dialogue, had better skip the sixth one when he or she preaches on the Beatitudes: it's just possible that his or her hearers may be unsophisticated enough to question the preacher's understanding of the words, "Blessed are the pure in heart: for they shall see God"! Do you remember Charles Dickens's comment about one of his characters: "He was fuller of virtuous precepts than a copy book, but like a guide post that pointed the way but never went itself"? Even Nietzsche, quoted often in other connections these recent years, took up the cry with these words: "These Christians must show me they are redeemed, before I will believe in their Redeemer!"

But there is more than the ancient quality of being blameless (to use the *Book of Discipline's* word) in one's personal life involved in the "silent sermon" offered by the character and personality of the preacher before any word ever escapes his lips. There is his own deep, moving *personal dedication* to the message of his sermon. The intensity of the preacher's own commitment becomes the really authentic climate of eloquence in which his sermon finds its most forceful articulation. The preacher who "gets it over" gloriously subordinates the fashionable parlor manners of homiletics to the terrible urgency of his message. His words tumble over each other in pleading power as the awful intensity of his own conviction becomes an irresistibly infectious thing speaking to a congregation new and shattering truth.

But *behind this kind of preaching is a life*—a life made lean by the discipline of austerity, a life wrenched away from the soft lap of luxury and set in its pilgrim way with a ruthless solitariness of purpose, a life that has been crucified with Christ and now knows Him in the full and blazing power of His resurrection. How hopelessly the affluent society has softened and spoiled the modern preacher! His or her ancient and formidable dedication to a Strange Man on a Cross has too often been replaced by an impotent addiction to intricate intellectual gymnastics in theology and philosophy—and by worldly ambition. We are men and women without a passion, ordained but no longer burdened with the gospel. And our own pious unconcern communicates itself unfailingly to congregations who "couldn't care less."

In quite another vein, the pleasantly innocuous minor evidences of a person's *humanness* have always had some appeal to the public and often have helped men and women to identify with him in spite of the fact that there is "a great gulf fixed" between them and him on other counts. I remember my delight when I first learned that Immanuel Kant couldn't pass a cookie jar without reaching for its contents and that Charles Spurgeon, the immortal London Baptist, smoked big black cigars. Even the affinity of President Richard Nixon for meatloaf and chocolate pudding may have helped to destroy barriers between the White House and ordinary citizens!

I must confess that I speak of Bishop Short at this point with certain trepidation, for I remain acutely aware of the fact that he, more than anyone else in our church, is still "my own" bishop! The expressions which I have normally used in his company have reflected the polite restraint appropriate to this relationship—and to contemplate departure from such verbal decorum is startling, if not frightening, to me. But here goes!

I think of a cluster of perhaps little-known data related to the Bishop of Louisville, some of them documented by my own experience:

For the most part, his clothing has always been severely and even painfully clerical—although, it should be noted, he has revealed recent latent tendencies to sartorial wildness in the acquisition of an off-white shirt, a brown suit and what at least faintly resembled a paisley tie!

He is a connoisseur of good foods, with what must surely be an exquisitely sensitive palate, but his culinary preferences sometimes plunge to plebeian depths, and include white bacon and grits. I recall one time when he spent a delightful period recounting the number of delicious dishes which could be contrived from a grits base. I remember another and memorable occasion when both of us were at the Bellevue-Stratford Hotel in Philadelphia for a church meeting and he squired me away at noon to a picturesque nearby haunt known as "Oyster Alley," where we sat together in a crowded little restaurant enjoying, the finest of oyster stew served family style!

His native neatness has surely been one of the easier explanations for his remarkable administrative efficiency. His library is carefully pruned and contains only the books he cherishes, particularly his unusual and valuable collection of biographies of the bishops. His desk is clean, and a letter received one day is usually responded to before the next. The unusual amount of traveling involved in his responsibility as secretary of the Council of Bishops has caused him to keep a bag available at all times, already packed and prepared for a journey. His experience in tripping about over the world has taught him what he may never have been able successfully to communicate to his wife— the advantage of traveling light!

His demeanor upon all public ecclesiastical occasions has always been the soul of propriety and even somber sobriety. But to see him emceeing a game and contest period at a cabinet meeting or a staff retreat, some sort of foolish headgear established jauntily above his white locks, would cause any Methodist preacher to do a startled double take!

I have already alluded to the artistic manner in which the Bishop has been known to modulate from the final paragraph of a stirring sermon into the first stanza of some familiar hymn, pitching the tune unerringly without aid of instrument, and leading the congregation in the singing of all the stanzas. I believe I have not mentioned that ordinarily the hymn chosen will be a very old gospel song, perhaps not included in the average modern hymnal, but beloved by many members of the congregation who, quite frankly, have not thought of it, much less attempted to sing it, in many a moon. One of his favorites, frequently invoked in our mutual Holston days, was "Footprints of Jesus," and I doubt if the Bishop ever learned that there was one loyal but irreverent member of his Cabinet in those days who insisted upon humming softly the chorus of this song whenever his episcopal leader hove into sight or stood up to speak!

What great personality has ever been without endearing eccentricities? They are the accouterments of his humanness. But over and beyond the foregoing recollections where Bishop Short is concerned, I must affirm and applaud for all of us the gentle warmth, the unfailing sympathy, the quiet kindliness, the patient courtesy, and the genuine humility of a man who, as far as this one preacher knows, has never taken even the shortest step outside the circumference of Christian gentlemanliness. More significantly, there has been the constancy of impeccable integrity every step of his way. It has been easier to believe in God and Jesus because he has been their faithful witness! One remembers Kierkegaard's shining statement, "Purity of heart is to will one thing," when one thinks of Bishop and Mrs. Short.

Conclusion

"Look unto the rock whence ye were hewn, and to the hole of the pit whence ye are digged ...." Oftentimes the thrust of history proves to be the safest and surest propulsion into tomorrow. Dean Robert Cushman of Duke used to say to me, "When you read, Earl, read the old books, the standards, and not the 'fluff' of today. You will find far more help for solving modern problems in them than you will in contemporary writing." I am persuaded that we need to rediscover our Methodist heritage as a church and to gather from that rediscovery the strength of timeless principles which have been ours in the past and are now required to give our modern mission meaning and productivity.

As we have examined four aspects of that heritage this evening, it has been easy to recognize once more that institutions, even the Christian Church, are usually the lengthened shadows of individuals. So our speaking of all these matters in terms of the distinguished ministry of Bishop Short has been highly appropriate.

I, for one, confront the future of United Methodism and the entire Christian enterprise with unfaltering confidence. I know the storms that break upon the shores, the confusions that plague and threaten the household of faith. Some years ago, the actress Deborah Kerr granted an interview on her experiences in making the film *Quo Vadis*. At one place in the picture, lions rushed at her while she was fastened to a stake in the Roman Colosseum. A reporter asked, "Weren't you afraid when the lions made a rush at you?" She replied, "No, I had read all the script of the movie, and I knew that Robert Taylor would come and rescue me!"

A good sentence with which to approach any Christian task is that one: "I had read *all* the script." So I believe—and I record my belief in your presence—that there is immortal hope for the mission of the Christian Church in this apocalyptic age. "Unto Him be glory in the Church by Christ Jesus throughout all ages, world without end. Amen" (Ephesians 3:21).

Endnotes

1.   Charles Haynes Holmes in an article in *Current Religious Thought.* 1951; and this is quoted by Gerald Kennedy in *A Reader's Notebook* (New York: Harper and Brothers, 1953), 150.

2.   Paul Scherer, *The Word God Sent* (New York: Harper & Row, 1965), 189-190.

3.   D. T. Niles, *The Message and Its Messengers* (New York and Nashville: Abingdon Press, 1966), 44.

4.   Roy H. Short, *Evangelism through the Local Church* (New York and Nashville: Abingdon Press, 1956), 20-21.

5,   D. T. Niles, *The Preacher's Task and the Stone of Stumbling* (New York: Harper & Brothers, 1958), 112.

6.   Joseph Sittler, *The Anguish of Preaching* (Philadelphia: Fortress Press, 1966), 32.

7.   Paul Scherer, 65.

8.   John Knox, *The Integrity of Preaching* (New York and Nashville: Abingdon Press, 1957), 62-63.

VI

United Methodists and Roman Catholics:
A Contemplation of Christian Unity

A cherished delight of my years on the Charlotte Area was the joy of knowing and loving Mike Begley. Bishop Michael J. Begley of the Roman Catholic Diocese of Charlotte, a jovial, warmhearted Irishman who was the embodiment of the spirit of Vatican II, was my dear friend and frequent luncheon companion. We spent six Christmas Eves together in the Mecklenburg County Jail visiting and praying with the prisoners and making telephone calls for them, while our lay people sang carols and distributed treats. Together we sponsored a week of lectures by Archbishop Fulton J. Sheen for the ministers of our two churches. Every year Mike preached in our great First United Methodist Church, and I preached in St. Patrick's Cathedral.

This address was presented to a distinguished group of United Methodist and Roman Catholic lay people and clergy at Myers Park United Methodist Church, Charlotte, North Carolina, on November 21, 1973. The occasion was a luncheon co-sponsored by Bishop Begley and myself for the purpose of developing a better understanding between our two communions.

A rewarding part of my entire ministry has been working alongside my Roman Catholic friends. I prize my Doctor of Humane Letters degree from Belmont Abbey College and the autographed photographs I have received from Pope Paul VI and Pope John Paul II.

United Methodists and Roman Catholics: A Contemplation of Christian Unity

I suppose there ought to be very little that is newsworthy about this particular gathering. Seen in its truest sense, it is simply an occasion when friends of Jesus Christ are sitting down to luncheon together in Christian fellowship. I heartily hope that this may be the prevailing memory which all of us are able to carry away from today's experience.

But for other reasons today's meeting has important additional implications. It is part of a widening movement to bring our two churches into better understanding and closer fellowship, and as such it has significant ecumenical dimensions. Serious dialogue between the Roman Catholic Church and the World Methodist Council was inaugurated by a joint commission from the two communions as early as 1967, and important sessions devoted to these conversations have been held in Italy, England, Malta, and at our own Lake Junaluska. Participants in these discussions have included some of the stellar names of Roman Catholicism and World Methodism, and it is to be noted that a very important and interesting report of this enterprise is being made available for all of us attending this luncheon.

Who can define the origins of modern ecumenism? Perhaps they are as old as our Lord's high priestly prayer recorded in John 17. To be sure, in every age, God has had His dedicated servants from different communions whose breadth of spirit and compassion of heart have quickly recognized the grounds for unity provided by a common confession of faith in Jesus Christ. Dr. Albert C. Outler, one of the prime movers in United Methodism's share of contemporary ecumenism, had the following words at the close of one of the chapters in his little book entitled *That the World May Believe:*

Mott and Temple planted; Oxnam and John XXIII have watered—and others with them. But it is God who has given the increase and who will bring us into the *fullness* of that community, the promise of which we are already beginning to know.[1]

If Methodism, through giants like John R. Mott, inaugurated any part of the current ecumenical emphasis, then it surely must be acknowledged with profound gratitude that Roman Catholics, through that remarkable Christian man John XXIII, began a number of years ago to take commendable initiative in the same endeavor. I pause to pay one United Methodist minister's humble tribute to Angelo Giuseppe Cardinal Roncalli, who became Pope John XXIII, a man both utterly divine and utterly human, who dared to open windows upon the entire Christian community until fresh air and new light came flooding in to bless us all. He convened the Second Vatican Council, founded a Secretariat for Christian Unity, and authored the encyclical *Pacem in Terris,* which introduced an unprecedented appeal for cooperation among all people, even including unbelievers. The remarkable spirit of this transparently good Christian leader sought out many of the ancient prejudices of the Church's clerical statesmen and replaced them with a fragrance and a sense of love. I suppose all of us have been bold enough to insist that he belonged to the *entire* Christian world. I shall never forget what I heard Dr. Outler, ordinarily a profound and sometimes didactic scholar, say about Pope John: "He was so human that he could have written the script for 'Bonanza!'"

There were surely more folk responsible for the present fortunate turn of events than Pope John XXIII. Enlightened Methodists whose ancestors had been taught that the Roman Catholic Church was a kind of "synagogue of Satan" and that the Roman Catholics were out to take over, by fair or foul means, began to realize, because of the breadth and brotherhood of Vatican II, and also because of a new climate here in our own country, that they should be ashamed of this libel. Roman Catholic scholars began a serious study of contemporary Protestant theologians; and Protestants, interested in corporate worship, explored the liturgical revival among Roman Catholics—discovering to their surprise that the great Catholic liturgists were striving for a simplicity of Christian worship at its center and not for its ritual elaboration.

Great Roman statesmen like Augustin Cardinal Bea and Bishop Jan Willebrants began to steer the largest of Christian communions into ecumenical waters. Fortunately, we had, as official observers to Vatican II, a cluster of Methodist leaders of the caliber of Albert Outler, William Ragsdale Cannon, and Robert Nelson, whose broad knowledge and catholic spirit enabled them to respond gladly and intelligently to the invitation to join in the voyage.

It ought also to be noted that Methodism's founder, John Wesley, more than once introduced thinking which was compatible with the idea of an ecumenical fellowship between Roman Catholic and Methodist peoples. His well-known sermon entitled "A Catholic Spirit" and his *Letter to a Roman Catholic* are important documents at this point. It must be remembered that Mr. Wesley was aiming to found not a church but a Religious Society, and that the absence of any creedal test as a condition of Methodist Society membership is not to be interpreted as Wesleyan indifference to purity of doctrine. I quote below a very important paragraph from his *Letter,* written in Dublin on July 18, 1749, and lately edited by Michael Hurley, S.J., and published in the United States by our Abingdon Press:

> My dear friend, consider: I am not persuading you to leave or change your religion, but to follow after the fear and love of God without which all religion is vain. I say not a word to you about your opinions or outward manner of worship. But I say, all worship is an abomination to the Lord, unless you worship him in spirit and truth, with your heart as well as your lips, with your spirit and with your understanding also. Be your form of worship what it will, but in everything give him thanks, else it is all but lost labor. Use whatever outward observances you please; but put your whole trust in him, but honor his holy name and his word, and serve him truly all the days of your life.[2]

To be sure, there are problems, deep and vexing, sometimes all but insurmountable for the honest thinker. One of these has to do with the principle of *authority in the Church.* Both of our traditions have very strong episcopacies, and both, in this regard, run counter to the mood of the times. The Pope, as a matter of fact, is himself Bishop of Rome. There is far more authority attached to the episcopacy in our two churches than there is, for example, to the episcopacy in the Protestant Episcopal or Anglican Church and those branches of the Lutheran Church where the office of bishop exists. As a happily irreverent soul among my circle of friends likes to put it, Catholic and Methodist bishops "bish"!!

I once heard Bishop F. Gerald Ensley of our United Methodist Church refer to a passage in one of Thomas Carlyle's essays where he contrasts *the force of lightning with the pale and spasmodic glow of a lightning bug,* using this startling juxtaposition to illustrate the substantive difference between a Catholic or Methodist bishop and bishops in the Episcopal or Lutheran churches. I am sure there would be many, and perhaps they are even represented here today, who feel that the Church might be better off to deal with lightning bugs than with lightning itself! But at the moment this does not alter the fact of the case.

To pursue the question of authority in the Church a bit further, it should be noted that all Christians deny any ultimate authority to human reason or feeling and that all do appeal to God's self-revelation as the ground of our knowledge of Divine grace and will. We differ *somewhat* as to how we come about this divine revelation—here is where the roads fork. Protestants generally insist upon the Holy Scriptures as the pathway to the understanding of the divine disclosure, while Roman Catholics, at least since the Council of Trent, have held a two-source theory of revelation: the Bible as the constitutive deposit of Christian truth, and *tradition* as the interpretative action of the Church in determining what Scriptures mean. When the Holy Scriptures seem obscure, Protestants normally appeal to the whole of the biblical message or to denominational confession for assistance. Roman Catholics, on the other hand, turn to the *magisterium,* or the teaching authority, of the Church, and with that the court of last resort has been the Bishop of Rome, or the Pope.

It is interesting to note that Roman Catholicism in recent years has seemed to become more aware of the role of the Bible in the determination of authority in the Church, while Methodists have seemed to become more aware of the importance of tradition in this process. Hopefully there is movement toward a more common perspective on this matter, but it must be admitted that much additional dialogue is needed if this very obstinate problem is to find resolution in the minds of the people from the Methodist tradition. Quite frankly, along with some of the Mariological dogmas and the doctrine of the infallibility of indefectibility of the Church, it is the office and authority of the papacy which frighten people of our particular communion; and, quite as frankly, the appearance upon the horizon of a man like Pope John XXIII serves to confuse, if not to convert, our critics of Rome!

Another area of serious disagreement, as well as an area of fascinating agreement, has to do with the *ministry*. Who may rightly administer the Church's sacraments? What about the problem of order and ordination? How many orders should there be, two or three? How may the representative character of the ministry be conferred so that the historic continuity of the Church is properly safeguarded? How can we hope to reunite the ministries of our divided churches without engaging in some sort of ritual which seems to deny the authenticity of earlier ordination and, therefore, amounts to repudiation of someone's ministerial credentials received and exercised, imperfectly to be sure but in good faith and not without the blessings of God?

However, it is important for us to note that the Joint Commission Report on Roman Catholic and World Methodist Council dialogue enumerates some very significant areas of agreement with regard to the whole concept of the Christian ministry. Among these are the following:.

1.   Primary authority and finality of Jesus Christ as the One through whom the ministry is ultimately authorized
2.   The importance of the work of the Holy Spirit in calling people into ministry
3.   The understanding of the ministry primarily in terms of a *full-time* function embracing a cluster of specifically religious or ecclesiological duties
4.   The understanding of the ministry as, in some mysterious way, an extension of incarnational and sacramental principles

5.   The shared recognition of prophetic and special ministries with their distinctive moral and charismatic qualities
6.   The "connectional" character of the ministry
7.   The need for high standards of education and spiritual training for ministry

There is, perhaps, but a bare beginning of that ultimate understanding between our two communions which can result in a blessed Christian reunion. But let us rejoice that the beginning has come, and let us permit ourselves in glad amazement to note the rapidity with which changes in attitude and feeling have developed in little more than a decade of time. Vatican II in 1964, in the section called "Decree of Ecumenism," chapter 3, part 2, promulgated November 21, 1964, spoke thusly of believers outside the Catholic Church:

The Christian way of life of these brethren is nourished by faith in Christ. It is strengthened by the grace of baptism and the hearing of the Word of God. This way of life expresses itself in private prayer, in meditation of the Scriptures, in the life of a Christian family, and in the worship of the community gathered together to praise God. Furthermore, their worship sometimes displays notable features of a liturgy once shared in common.

The faith by which they believe in Christ bears fruit in praise and thanksgiving for the benefits received from the hand of God. Joined to it is a lively sense of justice and a true charity toward others. This active faith has been responsible for many organizations for the relief of spiritual and material distress, the furtherance of education of youth, the improvement of social conditions of life, and the promotion of peace throughout the world.

And if in moral matters there are many Christians who do not always understand the Gospel in the same way as Catholics, and do not admit the same solutions for the more difficult problems of modern society, they nevertheless want to cling to Christ's Word as the source of Christian virtue and to obey the command of the Apostle: "whatever you do in word or in work, do all in the name of the Lord Jesus, giving thanks to God the Father through Him" (Colossians 3:17). Hence the ecumenical dialogue can start with the moral application of the Gospel.

This is an enheartening word, as enheartening as the companion fact that United Methodists have seen fit to remove from their foundational documents adverse reference to the Roman Catholic Church! Progress is being made, guided by the spirit of the Christ who long ago prayed "that they may all be one; even as thou, Father, art in me, and I in Thee, that they also may be in us, so that the world may believe that Thou has sent me. The glory which thou hast given me I have given them, that they may be one even as we are one" (John 17:21-23, RSV).

Perhaps much of this ecumenism is being accomplished because of the depth of human need and despair at this moment in history. Years ago I heard the celebrated Anglican missionary, the late Sir Wilfred T. Grenfell, tell an amusing but haunting story. He said he had returned from his medical work in Labrador to make a speaking tour through Canadian and American cities for the purpose of raising funds to carry on his labors. In a certain church in Seattle, Washington, Dr. Grenfell chanced to tell the story of a native woman in Labrador whose leg had had to be amputated and who desperately needed an artificial limb. At the close of the message, a woman came forward and told Dr. Grenfell that she would bring to his hotel the next morning an artificial limb which had belonged to her deceased husband, with the hope that he would accept it as her gift for his Labrador patient. In relating this occurrence, the famous missionary concluded with this telling sentence: "When I, an Episcopalian, took from this Presbyterian woman an artificial limb which had belonged to her Methodist husband and which she had promised to me as the result of a sermon delivered in a Baptist church, my Roman Catholic friend in Labrador could walk again!" This is the spirit of Christ at work in an ecumenical setting to bring healing to the hurt of the world. And this, surely, is the exalted mood of today's luncheon fellowship and the high and holy resolve of all of us as we set our faces toward the future.

Endnotes

1.   Albert Outler, *That the World May Believe* (New York: Women's Society of Christian Service, 1966).

2.   John Wesley, *Letter to a Roman Catholic,* Michael Hurley, S.J., ed. (New York and Nashville: Abingdon Press, 1968), 53.

VII

Common Glory

This is a sermon given at St. Patrick's Cathedral in Charlotte on January 13, 1974. It seeks to identify some of the common ground on which Roman Catholic and United Methodist Christians stand.

It has been my experience throughout my entire ministry, and especially during the episcopacy years, that ecumenical relations with our Roman Catholic friends depend in large measure upon the views of the particular United Methodist and Roman Catholic bishops involved in each instance. I have already paid tribute to Bishop Michael Begley of the Diocese of Charlotte. I also must mention Bishop James Niedergeses, who served the Diocese of Nashville at the time I presided over the Nashville Area of The United Methodist Church. He exemplified superb brotherliness and the highest level of ecumenical understanding and vision. The shared sorrow resulting from the deaths of our two mothers during my Nashville tenure provided an added bond which united us in Christian fellowship.

Common Glory

Neither pray I for these alone, but for them also which shall believe on me through their word; That they all may be one; as thou, Father, art in me, and I in Thee, that they also may be one in us: that the world may believe that Thou has sent me.

—John 17:20-21

Here, perhaps, is the Magna Charta of ecumenism. Our Lord, in His great high priestly prayer, is pleading for the unity of His Body and remembering that such unity is an indispensable ally of all our efforts to communicate the Christian faith. Thoughtful, intelligent Christians of all communions must deplore the scandal of division within the household of faith. The way back together is not a simple path, and the journey may be long and wearisome. But, thank God, the desire to travel in this blessed direction has been planted deep in the hearts of multitudes, high and low, brilliant and unlettered, who live in these chaotic times.

This Sunday night and next are historic occasions in the life of our city and in the annals of the Christian community. As the United Methodist people and I receive with humble joy the hospitality of my dear brother Michael, his colleagues, and the good members of St. Patrick's, I pray that these two evenings may make it easier and more desirable for us to live, love, worship, and serve together not simply as Catholics and Methodists but as sons and daughters of the King of Kings who share a common glorious faith in God the Father, God the Son, and God the Holy Spirit. May these happy hours, in a small way and in our hearts at least, help to heal the brokenness of Christ's body.

We speak too often of the things that separate us. May I, as one Christian man, refer briefly this evening to three compelling ideas which, as I see them, help to unite us? To be sure, our interpretations of them may differ at a variety of points, but I suggest that tonight we celebrate central rather than peripheral matters.

Certainty about Great Religious Elementals

To believe is difficult—especially for the honest man who is a careful thinker. Life seems to be filled with monstrous inconsistencies, and the tragedy of evil defies rational explanation. Somewhere in John Henry Cardinal Newman's immortal autobiography of his thought, *Apologia pro Vita Sua,* is this sentence: "Thank God that He has shielded me from what intellectually might easily come on me—general skepticism."[1] The miracle of faith, if it is real, does not come easily. Alfred Lord Tennyson, laureate of England, was right when he said:

> There lives more faith in honest doubt,
> Believe me, than in half the creeds.

One cannot assess fully the incredible inroads of the secularization process. We live not simply in an age of cool and assured indifference but of brutal hostility to spiritual values. The voice of our Lord seems an odd and curious and unpleasant impertinence, "the distant music of the horns of elfland, lovely perhaps, but actually unreal and unworthy of serious consideration in this vivid and passionate and hard and masterful world."[2] Modern man, through the prevenient intercession of the Holy Spirit, occasionally struggles in resistance to this agnostic climate—as in the cases of Augustine, John Henry Newman, Lecomte du Nouey, Pierre Teilhard de Chardin and Paul Elmer More. But it *is* a struggle, and the valiant souls who win in the enterprise deserve homage from us all.

We cannot make the agony of belief less stringent and demanding; but through a rebirth of affirmative emphasis upon the great doctrinal legacies of our churches, we can make initial steps more accessible and vast and important resources for the effort more readily available. The Roman Catholic Church has long known this and, to my best knowledge, has consistently practiced it. The United Methodist Church is moving now, praise God, in the direction of a similar stance. We seem to be engaged deliberately in the gradual recovery of the great cardinal beliefs which compose our faith in the Christian gospel. The days of creedal draught are surely in their twilight. This is an obvious return to our Wesleyan position, for the little Oxford don, to whose insights we owe our sectarian origin, was never in doubt about what he believed where God, Christ, sin, forgiveness, prayer, and the holy life were concerned! His theology was doxology, and his trumpet never gave an uncertain sound.

It has been my observation that significant and lasting social action by the Christian community always and forever rests back upon deep and authentic conviction about the great doctrines of the gospel. There is a historic sequence of idea and deed, conviction and mission, faith and action. Before the imperative of the Great Commission came the indicative of God at work through Jesus Christ in his incarnation, his death on the cross and his resurrection. But this has been, in recent decades, the lost movement of the symphony. A great Presbyterian, commenting upon the absence of intelligent and zealous commitment to the important articles of the Christian creed among church people of this generation, declared that "the Christian religion is often today identified with pious ethical behavior and vague theistic belief, suffused with aesthetic emotionalism and a mild glow of humanitarian benevolence."[3]

All of us know that the Holy Spirit uses for the conversion of men and women a proper exposition of the great truths about God and Christ and man which are in the message of our Lord. We can never really explain how the fires of faith are kindled in the human breast, any more than we know why a tulip has a heat of four-and-one-half degrees above the atmosphere, why the song of a lark is always in the same key, or why bees make their combs hexagonal. But we do know that the central certainties of our holy religion, through a Power quite beyond us, produce in human beings the sort of experience and knowledge to which Alfred Lord Tennyson referred in the first stanza of *In Memoriam:*

> Strong son of God, immortal love,
> Whom we that have not seen Thy Face,
> By faith and faith along embrace,
> Believing where we cannot prove.

LEFT: **When the Hunts were young and their ministry just beginning:** on the steps of old Broad Street Church, Kingsport, Tennessee, August, 1945.

BELOW: **The inauguration of the author as four-teenth president of Emory & Henry College, May 11, 1957.** Bishop Roy H. Short is reading the charge as Bishop Fred Pierce Corson, who spoke, listens.

The inaugural party, on May 11, 1957. With President Hunt, from the left, are Senator W.N. Neff, Dr. Thomas F. Chilcote, Jr. (later to become the seventeenth president of Emory & Henry), Dr. W.C. Mason, Jr., Bishop Corson and Bishop Short.

The author's consecration as a bishop, Lake Junaluska, North Carolina, July 12, 1964. Participating, from the left, are Bishop Short, Bishop Walter Gum, Bishop Arthur J. Moore, Dr. William R. Cannon, Dr. E.H. Ogle and Bishop John Owen Smith.

A special tribute to Dr. Harry Denman in the summer of 1967. From the left are Bishop Paul Hardin, Jr., Dr. Denman, the author, Dr. Billy Graham and Dr. Lee F. Tuttle.

The author as an autograph collector, circa, 1971. This composite photograph, with examples from the author's collection, went out over the wires of the Associated Press from Charlotte, North Carolina.

With Dr. Peter Marshall (second from the left), 1940. Others in the picture, from the left, are Dr. William R. Rigell, the Rev. Harrison Marshall and Mr. Harry Smith.

With Dr. and Mrs. James S. Stewart, third and fifth from the left, 1966. Others are Dr. Wilson O. Weldon and Mr. and Mrs. George D. Finch.

ABOVE: **With Archbishop Fulton J. Sheen, 1974.** Others, from the left, are Dr. H. Claude Young, Jr., and Mr. George D. Finch.

BELOW: **The author and Mrs. Hunt** with Dr. and Mrs. Albert C. Outler, Bradenton, Florida, 1988.

ABOVE: **Three presidents of Emory & Henry College, 1966.** From the left, Dr. Foye G. Gibson, the author and Dr. William C. Finch.

Below: **At Emory & Henry again, circa, 1972.** From the left, President Chilcote, the author and Bishop H. Ellis Finger, Jr.

The author addressing the World Methodist Conference in Dublin, Ireland, on August 25, 1976.

TOP: **An event at Bethune-Cookman College in Florida, 1986.** The author and his wife are with President and Mrs. Oswald P. Bronson, Jr. The author was Board chairman at Bethune-Cookman 1980-1988.

LEFT: **The author signing copies of his book** *I Have Believed* at the Cokesbury bookstore, Nashville, 1980.

LEFT: **The author speaking** to a university audience in 1978.

GENERAL CONFERENCES

LEFT: **Presiding at General Conference,** Portland, Oregon, 1976.

RIGHT: **Presiding at General Conference,** first session, St. Louis, Missouri, 1988.

LEFT: **Presiding at General Conference,** second session, St. Louis, Missouri, 1988.

RIGHT: **The author preaching** the opening sermon, General Conference, 1988.

BELOW: **Three presidents of the Council of Bishops:** Bishop James M. Ault, retiring president; the author, who had just assumed office; and Bishop Ernest T. Dixon, Jr., president designate.

RIGHT: **The author and Mrs. Hunt,** General Conference, St. Louis, 1988.

The author with Pope John Paul II in Columbia, South Carolina, September 1987.

ABOVE: **The author at his desk in Lakeland, Florida, February 1988.** He is holding the completed report of the Committee on Our Theological Task.

BELOW: **The author's last conference** had just adjourned, Lakeland, Florida, 1988.

A new task! The author as president of the Foundation for Evangelism, at the installation of Dr. James C. Logan, Wesley Theological Seminary, Washington, D.C., October 17, 1990. Others, from the left, are Dean M. Douglas Meeks, President G. Douglass Lewis, Dr. Logan, Bishop Thomas B. Stockton and Bishop Joseph H. Yeakel.

Long ago when Phillips Brooks held consultation hours at Harvard University, it is said that a student arrived at his office with anxious air. "Dr. Brooks," the student said, "I would like to talk over some of my doubts, but I don't want to disturb your faith." Understandably, Brooks is said to have broken out into uncontrollable laughter. How, indeed, could someone disturb his faith, when he knew with such certainty the deep experiences of the soul which only the Christian gospel can adequately interpret for a human being?

I should like to think, and indeed do deeply believe, that our two great churches in this new and demanding day are drawn together by renewed resolution to affirm before an unbelieving world the central certainties of the gospel of our Lord Jesus Christ. In such an affirmation contemporary men and women who are battling honestly for viable philosophies of life and religion will surely discover anchors for their souls and beacons for their minds!

Prayer

There should be no doubt at all that Roman Catholics and United Methodists ought to feel spiritual kinship in their efforts to help the Christian community recover in our day the meaning and power of prayer. Admittedly, there is difference in approaches, but surely none in ultimate purpose. Dependence upon prayer presupposes fresh acknowledgment of the supernatural in religion— something wonderfully therapeutic in the aftermath of Bultmann and the radical theology.

A friend of mine not long ago listened to an address delivered by one of the world's distinguished brain surgeons. The men of a famous breakfast club hung on his words as he described in simple language the physical mechanism of the mind. It was said that day, by an authority in the field, that in any list of five great scientists and brain surgeons, this man's name would appear. He concluded his remarks by describing an operation so involved and confronted by so many unforeseen complications that the patient was under the knife for nearly nine hours. "When at last the tumor was removed," the surgeon continued, "I knew that we had done everything that science could do. There was nothing left in the book. Also I knew that my patient had less than an even chance to recover. Gradually respiration rose until it stood at fifty-six. Her temperature went to one hundred and five. The fatal end was clearly indicated. I did not leave the hospital but went downstairs to rest. Then I did what nearly every other man does in such a crisis. I prayed. I asked nothing for myself but prayed that if it was God's will the mother might be restored to her children and the wife to her husband. Strangely relieved, I fell asleep."

An hour later the surgeon was called to his patient's room. The startled nurse said, "Respiration and temperature are normal, Doctor. I can't understand it." Concluding his remarks, the speaker addressed himself to the clergymen who were present and said, "Sirs, teach us to pray. You are specialists in the field. We are humble, untrained, unknowing laymen. Someone has neglected us. Teach us to pray!"

Many years ago now I preached my first sermon, as a boy of fourteen, on the text John 15:7, "If ye abide in me, and my words abide in you, ye shall ask what ye will, and it shall be done unto you." It was a gloriously simple promise resting upon an incredibly demanding condition. Forty years later, I must say that I have never failed to see the promise of John 15:7 kept by the Almighty, provided the condition has been met. We have tragically underestimated the power of prayer and its revolutionary role in the work of our Lord's kingdom. Oswald Chambers was magnificently correct, even though we may not understand the mystery of it, when he said, "The very powers of darkness are paralyzed by prayer."[4] That intrepid Burmese missionary, Adoniram Judson, as he lay dying, heard of the remarkable answer to his prayer for the Jews when he was a missionary and uttered this testimony: "I never prayed sincerely and earnestly for anything but it came; sometime—no matter how distant the day—somehow, in some shape, probably the last I should have devised, it came."

Tonight in this historic setting, I plead for our two churches to lead our people in a recovery of the power of prayer.

The Pursuit of Holiness

One of the most pleasant privileges I have had since coming to live in Charlotte was that of collaborating with Bishop Begley in the release of a "Joint Pastoral Letter" for Advent 1973. I must now confess publicly that it was Bishop Begley who composed most of the text of this letter. He very graciously offered me editorial opportunity, but when I noticed that the third paragraph of his draft contained a quotation from John Wesley on scriptural holiness, discovered and carefully copied out by a bishop of the Roman Catholic Church, I decided that I had better accept his version without a change and quit while I was ahead! I have read in chapter 5 of the Constitution on the Church in the *Sixteen Documents of Vatican II* sustained and exciting references to the holy life, a theme still familiar and significant to those of us who endeavor to follow in Mr. Wesley's spiritual succession.

I strongly fear that some leaders within the Christian Church have been unwitting accomplices to contemporary moral disintegration in the Western world. One individual indicted in the Watergate tragedy was honest enough to state that his blurred vision of the difference between right and wrong came as the result of instruction in situation ethics under a well-known Protestant clergyman. I remember attending an educational meeting in the days when I was a college president and hearing a well-known professor and minister tell two thousand people that he could think of a number of instances within his own pastoral and professorial experience when the practice of adultery would have been the most Christian of all the options available. At the risk of sounding hopelessly out-of-date, I propose that the present crisis in character plaguing our nation is traceable to a cluster of causes, including that philosophical and theological effort to dismiss the fact of moral absolutes which some leaders in mainline Christian communions have embraced almost uncritically. The Roman Catholic Church's guilt at the point of this heresy has been minimal; indeed, it has properly rebuked many of the rest of us!

In this historic setting I should like to plead that both of our churches urge upon the Christian community the fundamental importance of recovering moral and ethical norms if civilized life is to survive on this planet. There can be no meaningful exploration of the Christian faith which deliberately eliminates the necessity for a *peculiar moral or ethical quality* in the believer's life and performance. It is as simple as that, and no high-sounding rationalizations in favor of pornography and new lifestyles in human sexuality can change for the tiniest second those great imperatives of character which are part of the teachings of Scripture and the tradition of the Church, and as such remain central in the requirements of Christian discipleship!

No one can be good without help from beyond himself. Years ago, after one of her public addresses, a person approached Muriel Lester and said to her, "Miss Lester, God Almighty never made a better woman than I, but I just can't live up to it!" The Christian believes that the life *in Christ* provides an individual with resources and power to "live up to it." For the man or woman willing to pay the price in spiritual disciplines, the actuality of a holy life is one of the precious realities of our religion. It is this reality, lived out quietly in a world of unbelievers, which becomes the most convincing argument for Christianity and the most effective agent of evangelization.

The pursuit of holiness is not our human idea; rather it is a clear prescription of the gospel, as these passages suggest: "...this is the will of God, even your sanctification..." (1 Thessalonians 4:3). "According as He hath chosen us in Him before the foundation of the world, that we should be holy and without blame before Him in love..." (Ephesians 1:4). "...as the elect of God, holy and beloved..." (Colossians 3:12*a*). "God is love; and he that dwelleth in love dwelleth in God, and God in him." (1 John 4:16*b*).

Again I plead. In spite of philosophical and theological detours of recent years, Archbishop Soderblom did not exaggerate greatly when he said, "Holiness is the great word of religion; it is even more essential than the notion of God."[5] I wish that we might lift the grand New Testament term "saint" out of the disrepute into which it has fallen in some quarters of the Christian community. Churches do not canonize in the same manner, but they all have their saints. It is a major misfortune that the different branches of the universal Church know so little of each other's saints. Those who embrace the disciplines which enable God to impart His holiness, in whatever nation or church, are constantly presenting to the world Christianity's most convincing credential: the transformed life. Nothing could possibly cleanse the Church and inform its witness with new vigor and influence like a sweeping resurgence of *New Testament quality* in the lives of believers.

I knew a Methodist "saint" once, the great William E. Sangster, sometime minister of Westminster Central Hall in London. He concluded one of his best books with these thrilling words: "Holiness is not a monopoly of the cloisters, or of one branch of Christendom. The energies of the Holy Spirit are available to everyone who will seek Him . . . . Far above us, we see the saints moving on the snowy whiteness...and we follow after. *Any* man may climb."[6]

Conclusion

Our Lord prayed "that they may be one." Oneness, we need to remember, is far more a spirit than it is a structure—and always a spirit before a structure! The gracious history being made tonight and on January 20 may prove to be, God willing, prologue to many appropriate and exciting events and experiences for Catholics and United Methodists, including fellowship, dialogue, and a variety of forms of Christian service in our city. We need to understand each other, to learn from each other, and to support each other in the great task of witnessing for Jesus Christ today. Together, if we know our own hearts, we would be used of God to share with all men and women His love and truth—used as never before.

Many years ago, so the story goes, Fritz Kreisler, the famous violinist, kept pleading with a certain Englishman who owned a rare and treasured violin to sell this instrument to him, but to no avail. One day the Englishman permitted Kreisler to take the violin out of the case and play it. "I played that violin," said Kreisler, "as one condemned to death would have played to obtain his ransom." When he finished playing, the Englishman was so moved that he said, "I have no right to keep it; it belongs to you. Go out in the world and let it be heard." So it was that Fritz Kreisler used his precious violin, which he called "Heart Guarnerius," as a medium for his wonderful music to bless and inspire the world.

As believers, as practitioners of prayer, as seekers after the holy life, as Catholics and United Methodists, children of the Living God all, shall we not yield ourselves to Him as instruments through which He can pour His blessings into the lives of others? Thus may we help to answer our Savior's prayer in John 17, "that the world may believe that thou hast sent me." Amen and amen.

Prayer

Allow me to close with one of the great prayers of the centuries, the ancient prayer for unity which appears in our new United Methodist Book of Worship and which has a history reaching back into the fourth century and the Liturgy of Saint James. Let us pray.

O God, the Father of our Lord Jesus Christ, our only Savior, the Prince of Peace, give us grace seriously to lay to heart the great dangers we are in by our unhappy divisions. Take away all hatred and prejudice and whatsoever else may hinder us from godly union and concourse. There is but one Body and one Spirit and one hope of our calling, one Lord, one faith, one baptism, one God and Father of us all, so we may be all of one heart and of one soul, united in one holy bond of truth and peace, of faith and charity, and may with one mind and one mouth glorify Thee, Jesus Christ our Lord. Amen."[7]

Endnotes

1.   John Henry Newman, *Apologia pro Vita Sua* (Boston: Houghton Mifflin, 1956).

2.   Lynn Harold Hough, *The Great Evangel* (Nashville: Cokesbury Press, 1936), 13.

3.   James S. Stewart. I heard Dr. Stewart make this statement in a sermon preached at the University of Edinburgh. I have searched his written works but have been unable to find it in print.

4.   Oswald Chambers, *Disciples Indeed!* (London and Edinburgh: Marshall, Morgan, and Scott, Ltd., 1955), 40.

5.   Archbishop Soderblom, quoted in *Encyclopedia of Religion and Ethics, Vol. VI* (Boston: Houghton Mifflin, 1956), 731.

6.   W. E. Sangster, *The Pure in Heart* (New York and Nashville: Abingdon Press, 1954), 250.

7.   *The Book of Worship for Church and Home* (Nashville: The Methodist Publishing House, 1964), 87.

VIII

The Day of the Lord

I had been anxious about this assignment. The Hunts had moved from Charlotte to Nashville only two days before we had to fly to Dublin, Ireland, for the thirteenth World Methodist Conference. I had prepared my manuscript for the keynote address with great care but was not sure that its content could be compressed into the twenty-nine minutes which my good friend Bishop Dwight Loder, program chairman, had declared emphatically would be the maximum time allotted me.

The memory of the evening of August 25, 1976, in the Main Hall of the cavernous Royal Dublin Society is still vivid in my mind. Dressed in my clericals, I stood between the beloved Dr. John Havea from Tonga, whose great mind and heart matched the hugeness of his body, and the handsome, dignified representative of the Lord Mayor of Dublin (who left before I spoke). Mrs. Betty Lou Stroud of Lake Junaluska, now the wife of my administrative assistant, led the vast assembly of Methodist people from more than ninety nations as they sang the stirring hymns of Charles Wesley.

The privilege of delivering this address, with the great audience giving me a standing ovation at its close, was an unforgettable, though humbling experience in my ministry.

The Day of the Lord

Hold thy peace at the presence of the Lord God: for the day of the Lord is at hand: for the Lord hath prepared a sacrifice, he hath bid his guests.

—Zephaniah 1:7

Dr. Havea and other distinguished members of the presidium, my fellow Methodist Christians and friends:

Mr. Wesley wrote in 1746 about the first of his twenty-one visits to Ireland: "For natural sweetness of temper, for courtesy and hospitality, I have never seen any people like the Irish." Certainly those of us who have descended upon historic Dublin, a center rich in history and learning, for the thirteenth World Methodist Conference are already experiencing the warm and gracious welcome about which our founding father wrote so gratefully. I belong to the Methodist family in the United States, and accordingly have a special sense of indebtedness to those eighteenth-century Palatine emigrants, Barbara Heck and Philip Embury, who helped establish Methodism in North America. We come to this lyrically picturesque, though deeply troubled, Emerald Isle with feelings of genuine affection and prayers for Divine blessing and healing upon all the noble Irish people.

I am gratefully conscious of the high privilege afforded me in keynoting this World Methodist Conference. It is expected that twenty-five hundred Methodists from ninety different nations, with delegates and official observers representing sixty different denominations within the Methodist movement, are to be in attendance here. I greet all of you in the name of the Lord Jesus Christ.

I have chosen to speak upon the theme of this conference, "The Day of the Lord." My text is the seventh verse form the first chapter of Zephaniah: "Hold thy peace at the presence of the Lord God: for the day of the Lord is at hand: for the Lord hath prepared a sacrifice, he hath bid his guests."

This grim, startling, darkly hopeful sentence was wrung from the heart and mind of a young prophet, probably of royal descent, who lived and labored in Jerusalem in the 600s B.C. His name was Zephaniah, and his writing is difficult to understand. It constitutes the beginning of apocalypse in the Scriptures. But "the day of the Lord" is a time "when the true meaning of life, of event, of history, of creation itself will be made clear," as Howard Thurman has pointed out. No age or individual can escape this: "(God) will search Jerusalem with the lamps" (vs. 12, RSV). The divine accounting is all-inclusive and embraces those in authority as well as the more humble.

The Day of the Lord! The old order changes: nations rise and fall; sophisticated philosophies smother the flames of Christian adoration; wild license sweeps society like the restless waves of storm-tossed oceans; ancient principles of moral integrity, honesty, social responsibleness, and purity totter and collapse; crass insensitivity to the facts of God and human sin becomes the cloak a modern world wears. Suddenly the faraway message of the little Oxford don seems incongruous, out of place, a religious relic of a bygone age. But it still *is* the day of the Lord—and God is moving over His earth with gentle but relentless persistence. He means to wrest victory from His adversary and to bring the glory of the new Heaven and the new earth, seen of John from Patmos, into and beyond history.

If we are His, and if John Wesley's insights into Christianity have meaning, then I dare to propose that this "day of the Lord" is a clarion call to the people known as Methodists to recover their passion for God and humankind, their magnificent obsession to bring the fullness of the Gospel to a lost and sinful world. The fires that once burned with such intensity but now flicker and fail must be brought to brightness and warmth again. Without abandoning scholarly pursuits and commitment to the high level of rational religion which characterized our founder's splendid mind, we must move beyond preoccupation with little things, theological bickering, and capitulation before pressure groups whose causes are good but whose focus is often distorted. We must move ahead to a rediscovery of our own *first principles* and a rekindling of that original ardor which caused the brilliant son of Epworth to leap on the back of his horse and ride out to save England and the world.

If the ingredients of our message are good and right, then that message *must* be communicated to our day! A church languishing on the shoals of diminishing membership and deteriorating influence must be shocked into vigor again. The intimidation of a secularized civilization must be conquered. The coldness of an institution must become once more the blazing warmth of an experience, the romantic excitement of a movement. We must care that people are living and dying without Jesus. We must believe again that there is no other name given among men whereby we must be saved except the name of our glorious Lord!

> Come, sinners, to the gospel feast
> Let *every* soul be Jesus' guest;
> Ye need not *one* be left behind,
> For God hath bidden *all* mankind.
> —Charles Wesley

Let Dublin be the forum where these cries for spiritual renaissance are heard again in tones so unmistakable that their message shall go 'round the world! Let lovely Eire, land of charm and emerald green, known throughout its history for Christian learning, be a place this week where the Wesleyan world is stirred again to its very depth and led to send forth a fresh word for humankind in the 1970s!

The Day of the Lord: Understanding

I no longer fear the Church will disappear from the human community. I believe Professor James Moffatt was right when years ago he said, "The church is in far wiser hands than our hands, as indeed it always has been." I believe that the Christian Church will survive to the end of time. But I do not read in my Bible scriptural commitment to the survival of The Methodist Church. I am persuaded increasingly that the endurance of our particular expression of the Christian faith will depend upon the honesty, the fidelity, the commitment and the skill with which we apply Wesleyan perspectives to the human situation in our time.

It is difficult for us to face the fact of newness. I read not long ago, I think it was in *The New Yorker,* a description of a certain political figure in our country. The writer said that he was "dragged screaming" into the twentieth century! They—and sometimes we—have accepted with vast reluctance the fact that our world is different from any world with which the Church has had to deal before.

It is a crowded world. The population of this planet increases every week to the extent of the size of a city like Cleveland, Ohio. It increases every year to the extent of the size of Great Britain. Seven people perish each minute from starvation in our world. One-third of those living upon our planet today will carry to their graves physiological and psychological effects of starvation.

It is a polluted world. The cake that we wanted both to have and to eat has turned into a loaf of poison.

It is an imperiled world. Explosives exist this evening the equivalent of 35,000 tons of TNT for every man, woman, and child alive on this planet.

It is a confused world. We live in a period of positive and negative eugenics when for the first time we have the capability of tailoring human beings. We can order 500 Beethovens, a couple of dozen Mozarts. We can make a Hitler or a Mussolini or a Stalin, a Nietzsche or a Bertrand Russell at will. But the tragedy is that our particular generation, high on drugs and low on personal discipline, is not equipped to make decisions like that. Ninety-eight percent of the knowledge we have in the world this evening is knowledge that has come to us in the last decade. We do not have wisdom commensurate with that knowledge.

It is a hopeful world. For the first time, cancer, war, poverty *can* be destroyed—perhaps even before the end of this century.

Martin Marty of *The Christian Century* and the University of Chicago in a recent essay predicted that a comfortable apathy will descend over the Church in the years just ahead. If this malady should visit Wesleyan Christianity, I submit that our portion of the Church would hardly be worthy of survival. Understanding the hours and the moments of the day of the Lord requires of us not only accuracy of insight but also *urgent* application of those spiritual and ethical truths of which we are custodians. Pierre Teilhard de Chardin said years ago, "I am a pilgrim of the future."

So must we be pilgrims of the future, rightly assessing the revolutionary changes which have come in our world and seeking to bring each of them under the bright light of Jesus Christ.

The Day of the Lord: Affirmations

I speak at this point of John Wesley. Someone has said that he was "a pipe for omnipotence to flow through." It is a beautiful description. He was also the effective artificer of certain unique affirmations within the Christian faith. First, there was *assurance of sins forgiven.* The followers of John Wesley at their best have known and claimed the agony and ecstasy of pardon. The importance of God's forgiveness in a moral creation rests back upon the dual realities of Divine holiness and human sin. The climate of compromise which characterizes an age of materialism and happy hedonism shatters the kind of value-consciousness which sensitizes a human being to sin. But the terrible malady remains and cries out for healing.

One thing wrong with the Church today is that it has too many good and respectable people in its pews and pulpits who have never known the unmitigated horror of sin's conviction or the inexpressible wonder of forgiveness and deliverance. The song of Aldersgate is strangely absent from our repertoire. But hear Charles Wesley as he sets in verse the timeless experience of Christians—especially Methodist Christians:

> O Love divine, what hast thou done!
> The immortal God hath died for me!
> The Father's co-eternal Son
> Bore all my sins upon the tree!
> The Son of God for me hath died:
> My Lord, my Love, is crucified!

John Wesley was certain that the fact of sin is the root of all real ills, and he knew from his own experience that human beings can be saved from sin. The experience of redemption can be known in the life of the person to whom it happens by direct perception through the witness of the Holy Spirit as clearly as light is distinguished from darkness. There is an old revival lyric which we used to sing in my country, with these lines a part of it:

> Rolled away, rolled away,
> All the burdens of my heart rolled away!

A church which still proclaims a gospel of deliverance from sin is a church that can command a hearing in a world like ours at any time.

A second unique Wesleyan emphasis is a *contemporary realization of sanctification.* John Wesley used to speak of the Christian life as a house. Repentance was the path, justification was the porch, and sanctification was the parlor—the best room in a house in those days. At his best, John Wesley always viewed sanctification or holiness as *wholeness.* It involved the salvation of impulses, desires, feelings. Wesley would have agreed with General William Booth, who said a religious meeting is like a cup of tea— no good unless it's hot! The bad and good emotions of life—fear, anger, rest, love, ambition, sex—must be transformed by the power of Christian regeneration.

Sanctification meant also the salvation of the mind and manners. In one of his letters, Mr. Wesley wrote to a preacher: "You say you don't read anything but the Bible. You have got beyond St. Paul." He had absolutely no faith in the kind of religion that was not informed and was strongly opposed to the enthusiasm of his day. He believed a person ought to read and offered to give any of his preachers who could not afford to buy literature up to five pounds worth of books.

Wesley also believed in correct decorum and conduct—a sensitivity which may have derived from Susanna's practice of inviting a dancing master to come into Epworth Rectory to teach her children how to act properly in public! He believed that gentlemanliness and ladylikeness are characteristics of sanctification, a conviction not always implemented in these latter days!

Sanctification was also the salvation of the body. Wesley never hesitated to prescribe for physical ills, and long years before psychosomatic illness was described scientifically, he saw the causal relation between mental health and physical healing. In one of his letters he talked about a woman's sorrow causing a pain in her stomach.

All of these salvations—the emotions, the mind, the body—were brought together under the mighty canopy of Love. The characteristic of a saved person in Wesleyan thought was *love*—overarching, overwhelming, penetrating, probing, permeating love. This was the test, not whether a person speaks in tongues, not whether he performs miracles or engages in a healing ministry. The test was love, as the Charles Wesley hymn attests:

> Love divine, all loves excelling,
> Joy of heaven, to earth come down,
> Fix in us Thy humble dwelling;
> All Thy faithful mercies crown!

Any contemporary realization of sanctification must have to do with quality of life, particularly religious quality. In a day of sweeping ethical apostasy, its rediscovery could heal a broken Church and restore a shattered witness.

A third Wesleyan uniqueness is *vigorous focus on social redemption.* John Wesley said upon one occasion: "The Christian religion is a social religion and if you try to make it a solitary one, you will destroy it . . . . Holiness is only social holiness." He didn't have the sophisticated insights into the application of the teachings of Jesus that have come to us in these latter years, but Wesley had a simple formula for it all. A man or a woman who had been saved and sanctified must go out and live forth in human society the implications of that divine Love that had washed away sin and brought dedication to life. John Wesley, interestingly enough, linked sanctification with social action at every point of the way in his theology.

It is unthinkable that Methodist Christians would ignore the human tragedies of our world and avoid redemptive involvement in their solutions. Hunger; racism; the Bomb; the disintegration of family life; drugs and drink; poverty; housing; the tortured struggles of people seeking freedom, identity, and dignity; the incredible excesses of affluence—these are problems that no child of God dare attempt to escape. Hear Barbara Ward, that articulate British economist whose sensitivity to the plight of the oppressed is so sharp, as she probed the consciences of all of us in an address:

> Look, Lord, we are having a conference, we are crowded in, we are all over the place, we are very earnest, and we listen to incredibly long speeches. Lord, don't you think we are doing rather well? But the Lord will say, "How about the widows and the orphans? How about the hungry? Go away," that's what He'll say, because that's what He said then: "Go away, go away, until you have done something about the starvation of the world, until you have done something about this incredible gift of creation that I have given you, until you have caught up with my ideas. Keep away, because you are an abomination before me."[1]

Dr. Hedley Plunkett, past president of the Methodist Church in Ireland, said it for all of us: "Professing Christians must come off their cozy fences of private piety and noninvolvement."

These are our own uniquenesses. They don't belong to anyone else. They belong to *our* tradition. They compose a gospel so total, so richly adequate that even our world with its terrible plethora of problems can be saved by its proclamation and implementation.

The Day of the Lord: Disciplined Living

Even a casual perusal of John Wesley's life reveals to us that he practiced a personal discipline which shames the most structured individual among us. He got up at four o'clock every morning. He said too much sleep was bad for the liver and the eyes. He often began his preaching with a feeling of sickness and concluded his sermon in the full bloom of health, literally preaching away his own illnesses. He husbanded his time in a remarkable way. Old Doctor Johnson, talking to Boswell, said, "John Wesley's conversation is good, but he always has to be on his way somewhere."

There is a lovely fragment in the Wesley biography about a time when his carriage was late coming. He had already put away his papers and gone outside the door to wait for it. Someone standing nearby heard him murmur to himself: "I have lost ten minutes forever!"[2] Measured by that yardstick, we are *not* his followers. We bring to our gigantic task the inept skills of poor and undedicated crafts-people.

God's work across the centuries has been done by singleminded men and women--those who have literally dedicated their all to the Christ--and few of us belong in that rare and elect company. We are more often power-conscious, mercenary, self-centered, addicted to comfort and safety, fundamentally unwilling to sacrifice anything of value for the Kingdom of God. We speak with eloquence and frequency about laying our lives on the altar of total consecration, but our way of living denies our words. And so the Church languishes, diminishing in membership, impotent to address the evils of our time with redemptive power, its flames of faith flickering and uncertain.

There may be no more important thing which could happen to our worldwide Church than a rediscovery of disciplined living. When you become a disciplined Christian, and when you live in an alien, pagan society that no longer is sensitive to the voice of God, there is danger. There ought to be danger in the Church today, my fellow Christians, and there would be if the Church did what it ought to do. The Church needs to move beyond its tomes of talk and give to women and ethnics their full human and ecclesiastical rights. It is a shame that the body of Christ must yet engage in debate over principles as elemental as that. The Church needs to begin to practice what it preaches. The Church has played too long with such issues, as children play with toys. It needs now to address them forthrightly and to get on with other Kingdom tasks.

The Church needs to develop an unmanageable compulsion to win human beings to God. The Church needs to discover a new beauty and power in the institution of Christian marriage. This may well be the most important frontier upon which the church can move in this day of collapsing moral values. The Church needs to make Christian worship so irresistible that when people participate in it they will be changed, reoriented. All of this can come only if we engage in heroically disciplined Christian living. You may remember what George Bernard Shaw said when Mahatma Gandhi was assassinated. "You see how dangerous it is to be really good in this kind of world."

The terrible truth is that many of us are literally unwilling to live the kind of disciplined Christian life which is commensurate with the immense demands of these moments. When I think of the motivation required to change our perspective at this point, I recall what happened to Saint Teresa when she was over forty and had been in a convent for years. One day she went into her private oratory and noticed a picture of the Lord being scourged. She had seen this same picture hundreds of times before, but in that particular moment of revelation she saw it as she had *never* seen it before. She saw God suffering—suffering for love of her. She fell to her knees, sobbing in pain and wonder, and when she arose, she arose a new soul. This was the great divide in her life, the experience which changed everything. She said that she arose with "a sense of unpayable debt."[3] Only such an epiphany in your life and mine can produce the will to disciplined living, only a sense of "unpayable debt" to the God whose we are. May He help it to begin to happen even in us here in Dublin.

The Day of the Lord:
Recovering Our Rapture over Jesus Christ

In one of his sermons, Arthur John Gossip, the great Scottish preacher, said, "Our souls do not sing with sheer gladness as they ought." I do not deprecate institutions, particularly the institutions of religion about which Gustave Weigel said, "They are always dying but they never do." But neither do I glorify them. They are means to an end, never the end itself. Churches and boards and commissions and bishops are all expendable for the glory of God and the furtherance of his gospel. The institutions of our faith are only serviceable when the elixir of Christian experience bursts their sides and pours its fiery liquid of new life and energy over tired timbers as a summer rain revives a field of parched corn. Our souls—even ours here—must sing again with sheer gladness!

A New York newspaper reporter was hurrying out of his apartment on his way to take a subway train. As he went down the stairs he saw a lilac blossom lying on one of the steps. He stopped and picked it up, noticing that it still had a lingering fragrance about it. As he stood there and studied that lilac blossom, this Manhattan reporter suddenly remembered that beyond New York City it was spring in the country. The green things were growing and blooming in the fields. There was a blue mist on the mountains, and there were flowers everywhere. Holding that lilac blossom, he remembered a world which he had forgotten since childhood. I suggest to you and to myself that there is a spiritual world beyond the world we know.

A little girl was asked in class one day to write down the things she thought most beautiful. This was her list: a thrush singing, snow falling, the reflection of street lights on the water, red velvet, the moon in the clouds. Our relationship with the Savior ought to have beauty beyond the beauty of such things. It ought to have joy and ecstasy, the incredible kind of ecstasy that grips the soul of a person who has been saved from his sin and knows that he is a child of the King. E. Stanley Jones put it in his wonderful way: "I felt as though I had swallowed sunshine."

In a day of religious sophistication, in a church which has properly emphasized the intellectual and the rational, in a setting of international culture, I dare to lift one person's voice in a plea that we shall seek to recover a Christian's simple original rapture over Jesus Christ. I pray that the spell of the Savior may fall again upon each of us and upon all our churches, that we may be open to receive His incredible, incomprehensible blessing. William Barclay was right when he said, "Jesus Christ will be in no man's debt."

This is not where our religion stops but where it has to begin—again and yet again. This is the *interior preparation* which we must have in order to go forth and do the work of our Lord at the dusty, dirty crossroads of life. This is the resource that enables us to take Christian positions on knotty social issues and to witness for God wherever there is human injustice and inequity.

Conclusion

The day of the Lord, indeed, is here. We stand under His judgment that we may repent and move into a new appropriation of His redeeming Love. I am very sure the Church of God will survive, but I am still not certain that its Methodist expression can be expected to do the same. This will depend, in part, upon what happens to us here in Dublin. In John 20:19, there is this language: "Then came Jesus and stood in the midst." If this happens in this World Methodist Conference, then the flames of a new Pentecost with both individual and social dimensions will light the life of Methodism around the world. The Day of the Lord, with all of its agony of judgment, will turn into an experience of the Living Word of God. The wonder of the original Wesleyan experience will be reproduced in our time. The Lord Jesus, I believe, does stand in our midst in regal glory, saying to us what He said centuries ago to the woman of Samaria: "If you knew, if you knew the gift of God..." (John 4:10).

Amen and amen.

Endnotes

1.　　Barbara Ward. I have searched diligently but unsuccessfully for some written record of this statement by Dr. Ward. I may have read it in a report of this particular address published years ago.

2.　　Francis Gerald Ensley, *John Wesley Evangelist* (Nashville: Methodist Evangelistic Materials, 1958), 57.

3.　　Thomas S. Kepler, *Leaves from a Spiritual Notebook* (New York: Abingdon Press, 1960), 57.

IX

Preaching Theology

This address was delivered first at the conclusion of Ministers'
Week at Emory University in Atlanta on January 25, 1978. It
followed, and in a sense was a response to, a series of lectures
given by Dr. Jürgen Möltmann of the faculty of the University
of Tübingen in Germany. The following day, in the midst of a
heavy snowstorm which had closed the Atlanta airport, my
wife and I were sequestered with Professor Möltmann in the
terminal for four hours, during which she helped him shop for
souvenirs to take home to his family in Tübingen. We found
him to be a delightful human being.

The same address, with slight modification, was
delivered on October 18, 1982, in Richmond, Virginia, as the
inaugural lecture on the Goodson Foundation, a program
sponsored by the Virginia Annual Conference and designed to
exalt better preaching. This foundation honors the late Bishop
W. Kenneth Goodson, my colleague and friend, a master of
any platform or audience.

The magnificent obsession of my life and ministry has
been the proclamation of the gospel. I have sought to hear and
read the great preachers of our time and to inform my own
pulpit work from their practice of the homiletical craft and
art. I have written and spoken in a limited way about this
critically important theme, but never to an extent
commensurate with my interest and concern.

Preaching Theology

I have elected to use a more general and, to an extent, a more popular approach in this address than would be involved simply in reacting to the theology of hope and liberation at the point of preaching. I shall refer to the challenging subject matter of this particular week, to be sure, but along with many other references. Too, I must confess to a conviction of my own that preaching in this country is still probably more central and significant than Dr. Möltmann may feel it to be in his Germany. However, I surely do not interpret his elevation of the Lord's Supper and congregational praying and speaking as being opposition to the sermon itself but rather a change of focus in the pattern of worship. I speak, as he would wish me to do, about my own observations here in this land and in that part of the Church which I know best.

Preaching is experiencing resurrection! This exciting current development in the Christian community, fully documentable, suggests a more somber prior fact: contemporary preaching had stumbled, faltered, and all but expired as a potent influence—with, of course, some notable individual exceptions. Professor Helmut Thielicke of the University of Hamburg and the famed Saint Michael's Church in that city had a sobering sentence in an incisive little book devoted to this subject: "Anybody who keeps in mind the goals which the Reformation once set for itself can only be appalled at what has happened in the church of Luther and Calvin to the very thing which its fathers regarded as the source and spring of Christian faith and life, namely, preaching."[1] As a matter of fact, the distinguished German theologian and pulpiteer declared forthrightly that the trouble with the Church in our time is the failure of preaching!

One is compelled to ask if there is any causal relationship between some of the more obvious tragedies of our time and the collapse of Christian preaching during recent years. Watergate, whatever else, was a gloomy, nearly incredible commentary on the dreadful evil which can engulf ordinarily respectable and even good people who avoid important questions and pursue wrong goals. The energy crisis, surely more deadly than we are eager to believe, among other things is a sickness in our society produced by the malignant demands of an affluence no longer tempered by austerity and thrift and shorn of a sense of proper priorities. This has sharp relevance to important aspects of Professor Möltmann's thought.

Racism within the household of faith, the dismaying malady which has kept the people of God from leading significantly in the struggle for human rights, is partly the result of inaccurate instruction in the principles of New Testament Christianity, or no instruction at all. Again, there is the realism of this week's insights! Could wise, vigorous, and prophetic preaching have helped to reverse these terrible tides in human events? My query is based upon the recollection that certain historians have noted a grim parallel between the absence of significant preaching from 500 A.D. to 1000 A.D. and the concurrent descent of the Dark Ages over the human scene during the same period.

But our affirmations about preaching come at a moment when there are also legitimate misgivings and concerns. To be sure, preaching, by its very nature, is an act basically out of harmony with the antiauthoritarian mood of our time. Even the contemporary change from a hortatory to a dialogical pulpit approach cannot alter this fact wholly, and the problem remains a very serious one to overcome. Beyond this, when one cares to speak of *thoughtful* preaching (and preaching with theological content would have to be that), he or she is confronted immediately with the almost cultivated shallowness of the contemporary mind, one aspect of the current rebellion against matters intellectual.

I had dinner recently with the president and publisher of the United Methodist Publishing House and was shocked to hear him observe that people simply are not buying serious, difficult books in the modern market. There seems to be a collapse of that muscular intellectual inquisitiveness which once jubilantly mastered involved and difficult propositions and subject matter. Perhaps this is what a thoughtful essayist, writing in *Forbes* magazine two years ago, meant when he suggested that America's love affair with higher education is nearly over. If this dismal development constitutes a major part of the problem of colleges and universities in our land today, as it undoubtedly does, it also has very significant relevance where the problem of preaching is concerned—particularly preaching with content.

There is another kind of preaching, of course, the kind which is more fluff than substance, which is capable upon occasion of drawing large crowds and sending them away under the illusion that they have received something important. Years ago I heard the late Dr. Joseph R. Sizoo, in a lectureship at this university, describe this brand of preaching as being like Postum: it makes you think you're getting what you're not! We have too many "Postum pulpits" today!

The issue may be even more complex. Preaching itself is quite unlike any other form of public address, both in its nature and its objectives. In his Lyman Beecher Lectures delivered some years ago, Dr. David H. C. Read reminded us that preaching is not "the attempt to sow religious ideas," or "a moral prod to the conscience," or yet "an effort to provide mild therapy for the victims of tensions and strain." He goes on to say, "It is certainly not an occasion for a clergyman to air his opinions on everything from the price of meat to thermonuclear war."[2] One might hasten to add that the sermon is not a classroom lecture, although good preaching is always what James T. Cleland years ago called it, *teaching* preaching.

Preaching is, according to the late Harold Cooke Phillips, that distinguished and ecumenically precocious Baptist, "bearing witness to the truth."[3] My colleague Bishop James Armstrong calls it "telling truth."[4] All of us who have ever done it, no matter our favorite definitions of the act, are aware that preaching involves intelligent and responsible dealing with God's Word in the biblical message under a power quite beyond our human skill and understanding. This means competence in exegesis and exposition, areas of homiletical education sorely neglected for my generation— even here at good old Emory! An irresistible compulsion lies upon the preacher to communicate the message, as Jeremiah understood well when he said: "...his word was in mine heart as a burning fire shut up in my bones, and I was weary with forbearing, and I could not stay" (Jeremiah 20:9). True preaching, even when the most careful preparation has been made, is still an event which at some point and in some manner is taken beyond the control of the preacher. Matthew 10:19-20 suggests this: "When they deliver you up, do not be anxious how you are to speak or what you are to say, for what you are to say will be given to you in that hour; for it is not you who speak, but the spirit of your Father speaking through you" (RSV). But a man or a woman must *earn* the right to believe this by gruelling study and toil, and by prevailing prayer. To try to use the Holy Spirit as a labor-saving device is a horrifying prostitution of our calling.

The bottom line of all that I have been saying is the urgent need to convey God's truth effectively through sermon, and this has to presuppose not boring didacticism but substantial theological or doctrinal content packaged as attractively and delivered as persuasively as possible. In this connection, and with the special stimulus of this week as a backdrop, let us notice four ideas.

1. Making Theology Clear and Comprehensible

If you think it cannot be done, you ought to read the stirring sermons and prayers given by Karl Barth over a period of years to the inmates of the prison at Basel, Switzerland.[5] There are times when he sounds like an old-fashioned Methodist circuit rider, and his illustrations range from an allusion to the artist Holbein to an almost nostalgic recollection of his experience of taking cod-liver oil as a child! Or you should buy and read Reinhold Niebuhr's sermons, edited and published posthumously by his wife. These sermons are a study in the prophetic and clear use of difficult passages of Scripture to communicate exciting insights into Christian truth.[6]

Never can my wife and I forget an experience in the fall of 1943 when, with Dr. and Mrs. Mack Stokes, we went over to Agnes Scott College in Decatur to hear Dr. Niebuhr lecture. For us it was a memorable evening, and we saw then what much reading since has only served to document, namely, that his vast and far-reaching social concern was set permanently in a deeply religious context. His words were clear, often eloquent and moving, but most of his gesturing and many of his inflections were accomplished by those piercing, probing, incredible eyes! I remember one sentence in his lecture across all these years: "When Paul speaks of the peace that surpasses understanding, he means it is such because it is a peace that has pain in it." "I am a preacher and I like to preach," he said in 1959.[7]

The sermons of Barth and Niebuhr bristle with deep doctrinal truth, far more thrillingly stated in their preaching than the average person would find to be so in the former's *Dogmatics* or the latter's *Gifford Lectures*. Preaching is dramatically different from scholarly writing or lecturing! The same point can be documented further by a study of the posthumously published sermons of Nels Ferré[8] and the several sermon volumes by Scotland's James S. Stewart. In an illustration used in a sermon at Boston University years ago, Professor George Croft Cell had a startling passage which makes its theological point clearly and vividly:

Out here is Boston Bay and beyond it the Atlantic Ocean. You simply can't tell where one ends and the other begins. Both have the same water, but the ocean has more of it. So it is with Jesus Christ and God the Father. You are safer in your frail boat to try to negotiate the Bay waters than you would be to venture out into the deeper and broader ocean. So Jesus Christ helps you to know God.[9]

Dr. Moltmann, in his newest book published here, declares "What cannot be said simply does not need to be written at all. Simplicity is the highest challenge to Christian theology."[10] His illustration of human community in terms of his own POW experience of sharing bread rations is clear and telling.

The theory which all of these distinguished thinkers seem to have used is a simple one. It is God's truth as expressed in historic evangelical religion which nourishes the human spirit and life; and this truth, albeit complex and complicated in its scholarly or academic statements, *can* be communicated simply enough so that "wayfaring men, though fools, shall not err therein" (Isaiah 35:8).

This philosophy has to presuppose that a preacher will not be afraid to deal with the great theological ideas in the Christian message. One of my fondest recollections of the late Dr. Henry Burton Trimble, sometime dean of Candler School of Theology and the beloved mentor of many of us here tonight, is a series of sermons he preached in a church I was serving during my early ministry in Holston Conference. One sermon was on the subject "God"; another was on "Redemption"; still another was on "Eternity." To a fledgling homiletician this was pure, unmitigated audacity! But he was at his glorious best in those three sermons. They were like Matterhorns bathed in the crystal clear light of beautiful mornings! It takes a lot of study, a lot of living, and a lot of praying to marshal the courage necessary to confront your congregation with the massive theological propositions of our Holy Faith, and to do it in a way that illuminates instead of darkens their glory.

2. Making Theology Practical

Modern theology is in a formative period. Perhaps its principal motif is *liberation*—political, economic, racial, and cultural—and derives from the universal plight of the oppressed and the poor. Its exciting scenarios, sometimes products of thinkers scarcely known to us, are now appearing in Central and South America as well as in Europe. Dr. Moltmann's brilliant writings insist without equivocation that resurrection faith must be expressed in meaningful social revolution and sacrificial living. They imply a call for radical revision in the personal perspectives of the ordinary preacher and for preaching that demands a sterner brand of discipleship than the typical congregation in our land has yet been able to assimilate.

Preaching theology today requires relating the great biblical doctrines to the ugly issues of modern society and thus guiding the people of our parishes into difficult Christian responses to social and national sin. Even when we do it with compassion, the process must necessarily involve an element of pain and a message of discipline. But do it we must, or betray the very gospel we are dedicated to proclaim. The clear presence of pastoral love in the pulpit and out of it will help immeasurably to assure a more effective communication of Christian truth through such sermons.

Let me say two other things about making theology practical. Ours is a day plagued by a plethora of critical and sometimes new issues. These include world peace and the self-development of people, a steadily burgeoning population and inadequate supplies of necessities as basic as food and fuel, genetic engineering and test-tube babies, the failure of character in high places, racism, poverty, the widespread questioning of institutions as fundamental as marriage and principles as old as integrity, the charismatic movement with its perplexing concomitant glossolalia, and the rejuvenation of the church—all of these in addition to sin, sorrow, fear, and suffering!

Even a superficial observer is aware of the fact that there are present in many places of the earth almost inexplicably helpful movements in the direction of solving some of these problems, movements quite totally disassociated from the Christian church. Some of their leaders are not even professing believers, but the end results of their labors seem oddly but comfortably close to the realization of patently Christian objectives. The discerning student of Christian theology should be able to see in these occurrences new insights into the meaning of the doctrine of the Holy Spirit, and perhaps a fresh and more socially oriented appreciation of the significance of the ancient Wesleyan insistence upon the idea of *prevenient grace.*

Isaiah 45:5 helps to make the point in words ascribed to the Lord: "I girded thee, though thou hast not known me." What an amazing comfort it would be if we could but realize that, through the unfettered operation of the Spirit of God, we have unknown and unacknowledged allies everywhere in the human situation struggling along with us for the same goals!

Again, the idea of the resurrection, so indescribably fundamental in Christian theology and surely in the thought of Jürgen Moltmann, perhaps can be illustrated in more down-to-earth ways than we ordinarily employ. In one of my pastorates there was a lovely and radiant young woman upon whose life heavy suffering converged. Her husband was an alcoholic whose tragic condition defied the corrective efforts of successive ministers and a regiment of friends and made him insensitive to the claims of responsibility, honor, and love. Debts rocketed, community derision for the man she loved cut her to the quick, financial duress kept her working though physically ill and decreed that she must not use her earnings for herself. But there was something memorably buoyant about her. She never lost hope. Others did for her, but not she. The commonest kindness, the tiniest scrap of good news became a harbinger of better things ahead in her perennially confident heart. Each new morning was a magic scroll, a parchment of reverent optimism. Life was new, and something marvelous might happen before nightfall! One day I preached on "The Christian Hope" and her eyes danced in excitement as she thanked me for letting her hear a fresh utterance of the message God had given to her long before! She died—all too soon, we thought—but with the banners of ecstatic expectancy flying yet over a debris of terrible heartaches. She was our lady of the resurrection hope. She used to make me think of Wordsworth's lines:

> My heart leaps up when I behold
> A rainbow in the sky . . .[11]

She was living evidence of the reality of the resurrection, and this great Christian truth became the only sensible and practical way to explain her life.

3. Making Theology Sing

Isn't it a tragedy that often the best books go out of print before people of a newer generation are able to receive their messages? I think of two that left an indelible impression on me. The first is a British woman's story of her own personal religious odyssey,[12] told in language so unutterably beautiful that the tale of a painful journey from agnosticism to triumphant faith becomes a symphony of magnificent music about the great certainties of Christian doctrine. It impressed me so much at the time that I told Mrs. Arthur J. Moore and Dr. Harry Denman about my discovery of it, and each of them, after having read it, ordered a hundred copies to give to friends. The title of this slender volume is *The Loneliest Journey* by Frances Jackson.

The other book is *Jerusalem the Golden* by Vermont's unforgettable country preacher, Arthur Wentworth Hewitt, who may have been at once the ugliest and the most scintillatingly brilliant pastor I ever encountered. As someone wrote when it was first published, this little treatment of the idea of Life Eternal "has the bright, burning quality of poetry; yet it remains a cogent and faithfully reasoned discourse."[13] Every believer who has lost a loved one or who stands himself or herself in the vestibule of death ought to have this tiny volume at hand to read for its stirring comfort.

The total impact of these two books and others in their rare category upon my life through the years has been to set the great truths of God to the music of unforgettable beauty and glory. They have made theology into doxology and so have gripped my soul as mere facts and logic never could do. I have known some preachers—alas, too few—with this startling gift. Peter Marshall, whom I heard half a hundred times, was one such, although I could have wished that his own formal training in theological thought had been more adequate. Arthur John Gossip of the University of Glasgow was another.

There isn't anything deadlier or more boring than the presentation of theology which doesn't sing. It *may* instruct, but it rarely inspires. Do you remember James Russell Lowell's comment after he heard Ralph Waldo Emerson's Phi Beta Kappa address at Harvard in 1867? He wrote, "Emerson's oration began nowhere and ended everywhere, and yet as always with that divine man, it left you feeling that something beautiful had passed that way—something more beautiful than anything else, like the rising and setting of the stars." This, dear friends, is what every Christian preacher ought to pray and struggle for gifts to do, even and especially when the Christian truth to be conveyed is stern and unpopular!

4. The Miracle

Dr. Read declares, "When we think of preaching as *mystery,* we are restoring it to its proper place in the enduring life of the church."[14] The Apostle Paul in 1 Corinthians 1:21 says, "For after that in the wisdom of God the world by wisdom knew not God, it pleased God by the foolishness of preaching to save them that believe." A bit earlier (vs. 18) he had reminded us, "For the preaching of the cross is to them that perish foolishness; but unto us which are saved it is the power of God." There is something about preaching which will always defy human understanding, and which can never be captured in the class notes from a course on homiletics.

Perhaps the late Dr. D.T. Niles, the great Ceylonese Christian, came nearest to an explanation when he told the story of Pierre Maury leaping to his feet during a meeting of the Central Committee of the World Council of Churches in Paris and crying out in the midst of a discussion, "This is a *saved* world!"[15] Victory is implicit in the gospel. The idea of *prolepsis* is an appropriate companion for the idea of *proclamation.* When you and I have done our humble best, after a thoroughgoing discipline of prayer and study, a miracle will occur. This, too, is near to the heart of some of the things which Dr. Moltmann has written and said.

Dr. Thielicke summed it all up in a splendid statement near the end of his provocative little book:

God will acknowledge you and He will not let His Word return to Him void. When it returns to you it will be freighted with the answers and the decisions of those who have heard it. And because God Himself is on the battlefield, there is no need for the presumptuous assumption that the right thoughts will occur to you at the right moment. God's own Spirit will enter into you and He Himself will confront men through your poor words. While you contend, Another will contend for you.[16]

I once heard Dr. Stewart say, "No man knows how to preach!" God help each of us to try to learn, and *God help us to learn to preach theology,* if we want our work to last and God Himself to be able to own it.

Endnotes

1.   Helmut Thielicke, *The Trouble with the Church*. John W. Doberstein, trans and ed. (New York: Harper & Row, 1965), 1.

2.   David H. C. Read, *Sent from God* (New York: Abingdon Press, 1974), 30.

3.   Harold Cooke Phillips, *Bearing Witness to the Truth* (New York: Abingdon-Cokesbury, 1949).

4.   A. James Armstrong, *Telling Truth: The Foolishness of Preaching in a Real World*. (Waco, Texas: Word Books, 1977).

5.   Karl Barth, *Deliverance to the Captives* (New York: Harper and Brothers, 1961).

6.   Reinhold Niebuhr, *Justice and Mercy*. Ursula M. Niebuhr, ed. (New York: Harper & Row, 1974).

7.   Ibid, 1.

8.   Nels Ferré, *The Extreme Center* (Waco, Texas: Word Books, 1973).

9.   From the notebook of one of Dr. Cell's students who is a friend of the author.

10.   Jürgen Moltmann, *The Passion for Life* (Philadelphia: Fortress Press, 1978), 9.

11.   From "The Rainbow."

12.   Frances I. Jackson, *The Loneliest Journey* (Philadelphia: Westminster Press, 1949).

13.   Arthur Wentworth Hewitt, *Jerusalem the Golden* (New York and Nashville: Abingdon-Cokesbury Press, 1944). The quotation about the book is from its dustjacket.

14.   David H. C. Read, 30.

15.   From a personal conversation between Dr. Niles and the author.

16.   Helmut Thielicke, 109.

X

Toward a Recovery of the Sacred

This address was prepared for initial delivery on November 9, 1979, as part of a colloquy at Notre Dame University sponsored by A Foundation for Theological Education. It was the concluding address in a program which, excepting myself, had featured presentations by distinguished participants, including Martin E. Marty, Carl F. H. Henry, and Albert Outler. President Theodore Hesburgh of Notre Dame was also in attendance during the colloquy.

The address later became the opening essay in a Festschrift _entitled_ A Celebration of Ministry: Essays in Honor of Frank Bateman Stanger, _edited by Kenneth Cain Kinghorn in 1982 and published by Francis Asbury Publishing Company. It is used here with the permission of the publisher. The same address, somewhat shortened, appeared in_ Christianity Today _for February 8, 1980._

Toward a Recovery of the Sacred

Scripture Passage: Isaiah 64:1-5
For since the beginning of the world men have not heard, nor perceived by the ear, neither hath the eye seen, O God, beside thee, what He hath prepared for him that waiteth for Him.

⊢—Isaiah 64:4; quoted by St. Paul in 1 Corinthians 2:9

The passage of Scripture which I have just read from Isaiah 64 is a prayer on the part of the faithful for a universal theophany, or manifestation of the presence of God. James Muilenburg, writing in *The Interpreter's Bible* (vol. 5, page 739), says that "Out of the *de profundis* of the lament the prayer breaks into its most impassioned and earnest petition." The apparent absence of God (where have we heard that idea expressed before in these latter days?), His indifference, and His silence have to end; and the prophet urges the necessity for a revelation of the divine presence even greater than Sinai (Exodus 19) and the waters of Megiddo (Judges 5). The prophet implores God to reveal Himself in a cataclysmic invasion of the natural order, which was the characteristic expectation implicit in the classical theophanies. The Divine is asked to "rend the Heavens," so that "the mountains might flow down" and "the melting fire...[cause] the waters to boil." At that point the prophet refers to the time "when thou didst terrible things"—reaching back in memory to the momentous events in the period of the Exodus and the wilderness wanderings.

Then comes our text. It is a poetic outburst of praise to the God who performs incalculable wonders for those who wait for Him. Thus the final lines of the passage, reflecting a mighty fervor of prayer and faith, affirm on the part of the prophet (or his disciples) unshakable courage and illimitable hope. "For since the beginning of the world men have not heard, nor perceived by the ear, neither hath the eye seen, O God...what he hath prepared for him that waiteth for him!" It was this great verse which St. Paul, writing in 1 Corinthians 2:9, remembered and, with some simplification, repeated.

This almost vehement supplication for an advent of God, as Dr. Henry Sloane Coffin pointed out years ago, states quite clearly the Bible's faith that it is God who assumes the initiative and Himself works in ways almost beyond the comprehension of human imagination. Here, it seems to me, is one of the most splendid affirmations of the sacred to be found anywhere in Holy Scripture. When I was beginning my ministry and completing my formal education for it, this was an almost incongruous concept. It embodied the idea that the Christian religion is based upon a revelation from God which virtually defies the categories of modern thought. To be sure, the attitude of studied unfaith which some in my student generation encountered reflected what certain religious leaders in those days felt to be a highly appropriate capitulation to the dominance of science and the scientific method. The process of discovery was substituted almost gleefully for the idea of Divine self-disclosure. And thus it was that so many preachers, trained in that tradition, became very little more than *humanists in vestments.*

But pendulums swing. The old-time liberalism, so fashionable in the days of my own theological matriculation, is now long since bankrupt. The pity is that so many people trained under its banners are not really aware of its demise and in their positions of responsibility and leadership are continuing to project programs predicated upon its now outdated presuppositions. One is reminded of Norman Cousins's comment about a former U.S. secretary of state a few years ago: "The Achesons are gone, but unfortunately the ideas and policies which they prompted linger on during an era when their authors would no longer be tolerated!"

The purpose of this provocative colloquy on "The Loss and Recovery of the Sacred" has been to focus the attention of the contemporary church community upon the timeliness and, indeed, the urgency of a new outcry on the part of the faithful for Divine self-disclosure in our moment of history. Our thesis has been serious but simple: acknowledgment of the desacralization of Western culture begets in spiritually sensitive human beings a companion insistence that only a genuine renaissance of the kind of belief in God and His gospel which will make real to us once more both His demanding disciplines and His precious promises can possibly transform the faltering Church we know today into a redemptive force. To employ the moving phraseology of the Song of Songs, such a redemptive force would be "fair as the moon, clear as the sun, and terrible as an army with banners!" (6:10). It is a frightening task to try to encapsulate in these final moments of our fellowship the kind of thinking that can send us forth to become agents of this miracle. Let me explore *four* obvious pathways.

The Glory of the Lighted Mind

Perhaps I may be pardoned by alluding first to a deep concern which issues both from my own love of learning (frustrated, I must acknowledge, by a steadily enlarging plethora of administrative duties) and my years of involvement as an educational administrator—and which has particular relevance in a colloquy composed of so many princes in academe. We seem to be moving posthaste into a largely unrecognized and unacknowledged era of anti-intellectualism in our own country and perhaps in Western civilization. The educational revolution is both sweeping and devastating. In much of our public school system today the element of substantive content in classroom teaching and the factor of disciplined demands upon the student have vanished in a manner so total as to release upon colleges and universities generations of young men and women who not only can neither read nor write with acceptable accuracy but have never been introduced at all to the skills of study and thought. The necessity for hard-pressed institutions to admit such young people, complicated by a fear of economically disastrous attrition and apprehension over costly litigation initiated by disgruntled students and parents, has caused in many instances the virtual collapse of even reasonable standards of quality and, to use a term which still had currency when I was a college president, excellence.

Dean Rosovsky of the Harvard faculty said in a 1974 letter to his teachers, "The B.S. degree is becoming little more than a certificate of attendance." The president of a distinguished church-related university in our own denominational family charged recently that the church has "accepted the pleasure principle of society without firing a shot against it. It behaves like a political aspirant looking for a public image. It forgets and sometimes seems ashamed of the gospel."

These are heavy indictments, and if they are true where the Church is concerned, it is quite easy to understand how they could be basically true where education, always intimately related to religion, is involved. What we have traditionally referred to as liberal education, or the liberal arts, may be in a state of terminal illness in our time. It has always insisted upon exposure to the great books and concepts of the centuries, including the Bible and the ideas of Christianity. It glories in grappling with the hard questions of human existence and experience, the stubborn but intriguing "why" issues. It deliberately seeks to train the student to *think,* and it struggles purposefully to develop an ability to make value judgments. Most significantly, it offers the option of God and informed faith, an understanding of the place of the spiritual in wholeness of life.

There is serious question in my mind, and I come here to the articulation of my second concern, whether or not this nation or Western civilization itself can hope to survive in the years just ahead unless education recovers, on all levels, its sense of the Sacred, its ancient obligation to offer content that builds moral sensitivity and value response and provides exposure to the rich religious legacy of human culture and history. Actually more important is the question, Can leadership for an *awakened Church and its constituent community* be supplied from the ranks of young men and women who are victims of this sweeping desacralization of the learning process?

With the exception of a few of us who are journeymen preachers, much of this distinguished company consists of deeply dedicated Christian educators whose personal involvement in the academic process and whose institutions represent *dramatic exceptions* to the pageant of catastrophe which I have been describing. I have two simple pleas, and I wish that I might write them across our skies in letters of fire. The first is for every one of you, with the rest of us helping as we can, to rededicate himself or herself to the strengthening of *Christian liberal education,* with all that this means, in our time.

I do not believe that the merely church-related college or university has much hope or reason for survival between now and the year 2000. But I believe with all my heart and soul that the *deliberately Christian institution of higher learning,* honest enough not to be ashamed of the gospel and bold enough to demand quality performance in the classroom, will have a ready-made constituency of support among thoughtful people in the Christian community in spite of spiraling inflation and diminishing student enrollment. My second plea is that the Christian community speak urgently and courageously to the college and the university, religious and secular, concerning their duty to build an awareness of the holy or the sacred back into their perspectives and, indeed, their curricula.

One other word at this point: as much as we welcome the resurgence of historic evangelicalism throughout the Christian community in our time, we must face the fact that this very evangelicalism, if it is to have permanent meaning and value, is required to be more than casually conversant with the best in human culture and knowledge. Much of it is not so conversant at the present moment, as witness many presentations on television and radio, and even more utterances in local churches and the printed word. I know that the general decline in the public mind's willingness to study and reflect for itself has to be taken into consideration and the gospel served up even to this kind of intellectually limited constituency. But I know also that unless the Church can continue to discover and train an intelligent and informed nucleus of believers able to relate the Christian gospel excitingly to the wisdom of the centuries, the Church will lack that quality of viable leadership required to accomplish God's will in our time and in the dangerous tomorrows. I plead, in the spirit of the text, for our prayers in behalf of a new divine self-disclosure which can restore, in this moment of history, the *glory of the lighted mind!*

Impervious to the Very Gates of Hell

I speak now of the Church itself. It is in deep human trouble, its fabric tattered and torn by many current agonies and frustrations. It is being blitzed by the community of homophiles and sexual aberrationists. Even a multitude of good and worthy human causes, seeking a significant forum for their pleas, are *badgering* the Church into a compromise of its fundamental roles and functions as the Scriptures define them. A strangely sanctified worldliness, the product of economic affluence and its concomitant problems, has invaded and polluted Christian motivation, disciplines, and commitment. And in the midst of it all, happily engaging in the oldest dodge there is, the Church in too many instances is avoiding addressing its real problems by tinkering awkwardly with its structure and machinery!

The institutional church, God be praised, still occupies a unique position in the life of our society; and, oddly enough, its very presence awakens certain expectations on the part of a population which is not always or even often religiously sensitive. But there is a curious subterranean idea about what the Church ought to be and what it ought to be doing which runs just beneath the surface of public consciousness—perhaps put there by the Holy Spirit Himself, working under the guise of prevenient grace to keep Christians alert to the dangers which confront them. I have an idea that *the general patience of human society toward the institutional church may be running out!* I also have a conviction that those of us who, for better or for worse, have positions of leadership in that church need to recognize this sobering fact honestly and immediately.

To use a sentence which was the title of a good book from the pen of Elmer George Homrighausen nearly four decades ago, I plead that we may learn again how to "let the Church be the Church"! This will call for Christian courage on the part of all of us, and such courage may prove professionally quite costly. For example, I think we must begin to apply again and without compromise the principles of biblical teaching to *all of the problems of human sexuality* so prominent in public thinking today. To be sure, we must have compassion for the deviationist, whether in the homosexual or heterosexual category, and must endeavor with Christian love and gentle but informed evangelistic skill to offer healing and redemptive help to such an individual. But we must declare, always without judgmental malice but always with unmistakable clarity, that *the practice of homosexuality is incompatible with Christian teaching;* and that *the celebration of the joys of sex itself, a nearly sacramental act ordained of God in His love for human beings, is always to be reserved for the marital relationship.* This is the unequivocal teaching of biblical religion, and to compromise it is to injure the witness of the Church mortally in our time.

Moreover, while continuing to cultivate an acute awareness of all social and human problems, we must never allow the Church to slacken its preeminent emphasis upon bringing men and women into newness of life through faith in the saving grace of our Lord Jesus Christ. Historically and biblically this is our primary role and function, but it is a function involving both the *whole* person and the *whole* gospel—which is to say that conversion must include not only a person's right relationship with his or her Heavenly Father but also with his or her fellow human beings! Confession of the Savior and bold implementation of social justice are indissolubly interrelated in the economy of grace.

Again, I am persuaded that the Church, in order to recover its essential servant role in the human family, must deliberately *throw off the unfortunate accouterments of affluence* which have caused its critics to accuse it of mercenary objectives and luxurious self-aggrandizement. Its leadership and membership, to a large extent, must be willing to change their lifestyles and to impose upon themselves once more those time-honored and sacred disciplines of austerity, prayer, study and meditation, and utter self-giving which through the centuries have been the most precious hallmarks of Christian dedication and commitment. What I am saying is simply this: the Church—beginning with people like you and me—must be willing to pay the price involved in the *recovery of its authentic character in our contemporary world,* if men and women are to hear again *with open minds* its ancient evangel and to make their response to it.

The Church, indeed, is in trouble today. No amount of altering its structure or its machinery will eliminate that trouble. The malaise is spiritual. Even when this problem is addressed adequately by the fellowship of believers, the Church cannot expect to experience widespread popular acclaim for the simple reason that it must exist and serve now in a day of enveloping secularism. The times themselves are anti-Christ, and this is the foreboding context within which Christians must accept the fact that their witness and work are to occur. But we may be encouraged by those words spoken centuries ago by the brilliant French scientist-saint Blaise

Pascal: "What a wonderful state the Church is in when it is supported only by God!"

However, there is something additional and of great significance which needs to be said here. A principal part of the Church's function has not yet been referred to in my plea for new evangelical commitment. I have in mind the central drama of worship itself, the miracle of worship, if you please. It is the gathered congregation, come into one place to glorify God and receive His message, which becomes, through the operation of His Holy Spirit, the *energizing event* for all the church's activities. Perhaps there are two ways to look at it.

First, there is *the meaning which the act of worship has for God Himself.* Sören Kierkegaard years ago used an illustration taken from the theatre. He pointed out that ordinarily a congregation regards itself as an audience before which the minister and the choir give their presentation or performance—with God identified in the process as a kind of unseen playwright or producer. However, the great Danish theologian reminds us, the true picture is quite different. The congregation actually is the cast of actors with the minister and the choir serving as directors and prompters offering cues from the wings. The audience is God, and *the entire presentation is offered for His good pleasure and everlasting glory.* We need this corrective thought *to make us bring God back into the center of things* and to help us realize, in the old catechetical language, that our chief end is "to glorify Him and to enjoy Him forever!" In some way we cannot comprehend altogether our recovered effort to delight the Almighty's heart may prove of substantive importance in the fresh release of His saving power in the world for which His son died.

The other way to think of this has to do with the *redemptive transaction* which, again by God's Holy Spirit, occurs in the very act of worship. Mr. Wesley often said that there is in the Word and in the Sacraments as they are proclaimed and celebrated in the Church an objective holiness which produces in the people a subjective holiness, or else the Church is not actually the Church at all. He also taught that *faith itself is a gift of the Holy Spirit* which enables a man or a woman to comprehend spiritual realities, the things that belong to God. It seems to me that the entire theory of corporate worship is here, for it is the fact that the Holy Spirit informs the message of the minister and instructs the minds and hearts of the worshippers which produces a *redemptive interaction* between pulpit and pew and so enables God to do again and yet again His wonder works in the lives of the people.

When you put together the first and the second ways of looking at worship to which I have made reference or, if you please, the objective and the subjective, you have at least a faint suggestion of the power which ought to inhere in this event. Many years ago I heard the first preacher on the Lutheran Hour, Dr. Walter Maier, use as a text Joshua 6:20: "And it came to pass, when the people heard the sound of the trumpet, and the people shouted with a great shout, that the wall fell down flat." Then he gave a telling illustration. When the armies of Napoleon swept over Europe, one of his generals made a surprise attack on the little town of Feldkirch on the Austrian border. A council of the town's citizen leaders was summoned hastily to decide whether to surrender or to attempt defense. In the meeting the venerable dean of the church arose to speak these words: "This is Easter Day. We have been counting on our own strength and that will fail. This is the day of our Lord's Resurrection. Let us ring the bells and have services as usual, and leave the matter in God's hands. We know only our weakness and not the power of God." The council accepted the dean's plan, and in a few minutes the church belfry chimed the joyous bells of Easter. The enemy, hearing the sudden peal, concluded that the Austrian army had arrived during the night, broke up camp, and before the Easter bells had ceased, the danger to the town had been lifted.

My point in all of this is quite simple. The Lord Jesus Christ spoke of building His Church in such a way that the very gates of hell should not prevail against it. As one Christian preacher, I only plead that in this moment of the recovery of the Sacred in our thinking, we undertake to bring to that Church the gift of human courage and integrity and the kind of simple, childlike faith in the power of Almighty God which will enable the Church, cleansed and renewed, to become again in our time the true Bride of Christ and a place where human lives once more are redeemed and transformed through the marvelous grace of our wonderful Lord.

It Doth Not Yet Appear What We Shall Be

The fellowship of Christian believers is earth's ultimate democracy: we are all sinners saved by grace and in this sense all equal before Heaven. We have been deeply concerned during these exciting days with a fresh laying hold upon those ingredients of our holy religion which lie beyond our finiteness; and it may be assumed safely that each of us, in his or her own way, is committed to the fact that this enterprise is basically important for the Christian faith in our time. May I dare to suggest and even to urge that an *essential corollary to the recovery of the Sacred* in the experience of the Church must be of necessity the renewal of that certain elusive quality described as *holiness* in our own individual lives.

I know, of course, that any real goodness which a Christian possesses in himself or herself has to be *an imputed goodness* from God and made possible by the kind of total surrender of life which satisfies Scriptural stipulations. I think I know also that God has arranged His creation in such fashion that He can only work effectively through those believers who strive earnestly for such holiness. One does not meet too many fellow pilgrims who qualify for this category. I myself think immediately of two who greatly influenced my own Christian life.

Professor Leroy Loemker was the greatest teacher I ever had—and the hardest. One of the world's finest authorities on the German philosopher and mathematician Gottfried Wilhelm Leibniz, he was the longtime dean of graduate studies at Emory University and a local elder (in the old days) in The Methodist Church. To a young graduate student struggling to master the formidable vocabulary of philosophy, his brilliance was mesmerizing and the profundity of his thought revealed so articulately in his classroom lectures almost shattering. I shall never forget what he wrote on a book report which I submitted to him in the early days of our relationship: "You can do better than this, Earl; at least I *hope* so!" But he was constantly probing into the minds and lives of the young theologues sitting in his classroom to determine the extent of their motivation, the depth of their commitment, and the quality of their spiritual integrity. With gentle but penetrating courtesy he made us realize what an awesome thing it is to be called to preach the gospel and sent us back to our desks and our knees to search our souls about the authenticity of our Christian experience. I never really told him of my vast indebtedness to him, an omission for which there are excuses but no reasons.

The second such individual who comes to my mind is Dr. Howard Atwood Kelly, one of the four founders of the Johns Hopkins Hospital and School of Medicine, surgical and gynecological immortal, the scientist who worked with Madame Curie to perfect the radium treatment for skin cancer and then tried it out on his own face, one of the quartet in John Sargent's famous painting *The Four Doctors*—and a humble, deeply dedicated Episcopal layman. His avocation in his later years was to find young preachers in the different denominations and to help them think through their calls to the ministry while encouraging them with gifts of books, steady correspondence, and invitations to visit his fascinating library at 1406 Eutaw Place in Old Baltimore. Dr. Kelly, whose startling friendship with his atheistic fellow townsman H. L. Mencken was quite as remarkable as his penchant for writing introductions to his classical tomes on medical and surgical subjects in the Latin language, was an unforgettable Christian, humble, fundamental, Spirit-filled, who left an indelible impression upon me as a young follower of Jesus Christ.

The pursuit of holiness, or the New Testament ideal of personal excellence, is not just a human enterprise; rather it is a clear prescription of the gospel, as these passages suggest: ". . . this is the will of God, even your *sanctification* . . ." (1 Thessalonians 4:3). "According as he hath chosen us in him before the foundation of the world, that we should be holy and without blame before him in love . . ." (Ephesians 1:4). ". . . as the elect of God, *holy and beloved* . . ." (Colossians 3:12a). "God is love and *he that dwelleth in love* dwelleth in God, and God in him." (1 John 4:16b).

Again I plead. In spite of certain curious aberrations in religious thought across recent decades, some being largely responsible for the Church's plight today, the concept of holiness remains the throbbing heart of basic religion. Those who embrace the blessed disciplines which enable God to impart His holiness, in whatever country or church, are constantly presenting to the world Christianity's most convincing credential: *the transformed life.* Very few happenings could possibly cleanse the Church and inform its witness with new vigor and influence like a sweeping resurgence of *New Testament quality* in the lives of believers. The Loemkers and the Kellys helped bring an inescapable rendezvous with God into my own life and started a Divine tremor in my soul which not all the desacralization of three decades has stilled. I pray that we may not leave this colloquy without each of us giving the Holy Spirit fresh regnancy in his or her mind and soul in order that we ourselves may experience the quality of spiritual victory that alone can make us channels through which the message and power of Almighty God may reach and captivate other lives.

A Treasure in Earthen Vessels

My final point must deal with the manner in which we ought to think of the gospel itself in days ahead. It was Dr. George Arthur Buttrick who, responding to an overly elaborate introduction, retorted rather shortly, "There are no great preachers; there is only a great gospel!" And that gospel, purely and simply, is of God Himself. I believe in all the historic doctrines central to the Protestant Christian tradition. It has not been easy for me to come to this point in my own conviction, for I have known my personal ordeal of doubt and bewilderment.

I believe that God is able to save to the uttermost all those who come to Him in penitence and childlike trust. I believe that Jesus Christ died for my sin and rose again from the dead to become the firstfruits of them that sleep. I believe in the power of prayer and the gift of the Holy Spirit. I believe in life everlasting. I believe that the kingdoms of this world shall become the kingdoms of our Lord and of His Christ. I am still supremely confident that the Church belongs to God, not to any of us, and that He will guide those of us who are in it. In my life and ministry I have failed Him many, many times, but He has yet to fail me.

Dare I suggest, as we part company, that our individual personal commitment to our Lord and Savior Jesus Christ and to the entirety of His gospel is what finally will give these days of colloquy permanent meaning in our own experiences and, beyond us, in the life of the larger Christian community?

We have wrestled here with ideas wholly beyond ourselves, ideas that have to do with the forces of Almighty God. They have been essentially concepts related to His spiritual energies and activities—and, therefore, mightier even than His powers in the natural world like the rays of the sun, the tides of the ocean, the wild furies of the storm, the inexorable procession of the seasons, and the slow germination of seeds in the warming earth.

We have been handling—albeit with the heavily padded gloves of careful scholarship—what an unpolished but Spirit-filled preacher in my denomination insists upon calling "the forked lightning of the gospel." We know the Church is in mortal trouble today because much of it has lost touch with the explosive dynamic of that gospel. We are convinced, from our varied backgrounds and viewpoints, that the Church's recovery of this Divine and elemental energy in our nearly apocalyptic moment of history literally *could* set in motion a series of forces, social and political as well as religious, potent enough to bring new life to the Body of Christ—and to the nations of earth.

It is not enough to consider the details of our Christian responsibility in realms such as education, the Church, our own individual lives, and the interpretation of the gospel itself. All this we must do—and then, with absolute and bold abandon, proceed to implement our findings. But one thing more is needful. I put it in a brief paragraph from that remarkable Scottish preacher of this century in whose life the idea of the recovery of the sacred has been lived out gloriously, Professor James S. Stewart of Edinburgh: "Bring everything you have and are to your ministry—bring it without reserve. But when you have brought it, something else remains. Stand back, and see the salvation of God!"

Beyond all of our awareness, praise God Almighty, we who have shared this fellowship believe in the salvation of God. We believe also in the possibility and probability of an immanent new epiphany, a fresh Divine self-disclosure such as that for which the prophet long ago prayed in Isaiah 64. And since we do so believe, I invite you to affirm with me in confident faith:

> Whatever clouds may veil the sky
> *Never* is night again!

Amen and hallelujah!

XI

A Devotional Odyssey

This was an address delivered at the semiannual meeting of the Council of Bishops in Birmingham, Alabama, on November 18, 1982. The president of the Council at that time, Bishop Finis Crutchfield, had invited me to prepare and present this paper.

I reveled in the discipline of preparation necessary to get the address ready, for it required me to review the books I love best in my library, those that have brought me closer to God. When I had finished giving the message before the Council, my dear friend Bishop Monk Bryan, now my neighbor at Lake Junaluska, handed me a note which I shall always keep. On it were these words: "Who else among us could have offered such a paper? Thank you."

A Devotional Odyssey

Some years after I was elected a bishop, I was attending a Council of Bishops meeting in Chicago and saw the late Dr. Georgia Harkness at one of the open sessions.[1] For years I had read her books, listened to her speak at General Conferences, and admired her vigorous intellectual and spiritual leadership in our church; but I had never met her. At the close of the session, I made my way to the place where she was greeting friends and waited in line to introduce myself and shake hands with her. When I began to speak, she interrupted me smilingly and said, "Oh, you are Bishop Hunt!" Then she reached into her purse and pulled out a well-used little book which she opened to a list of names, many of them bishops. "I have prayed for you every day since you were elected to this office," she said. "I knew you because I made it a point to become familiar with your likeness from photographs in order that I might pray more intelligently and warmly."

I was stunned with a sense of humility and deep, glad surprise. I think I realized in that moment, as upon few occasions in my life, the sheer power of the Christian's devotional life and its penetrating, personalized adventures in intercession. I thought then and have thought many times since about Georgia Harkness's spiritual autobiography entitled *Grace Abounding*[2] (her title borrowed, as she confesses in the introduction, from John Bunyan's three-hundred-year-old book *Grace Abounding to the Chief of Sinners*). This is an unusual collection of her lovely and perceptive poems interspersed with beautiful prose describing a distinguished theologian's pilgrimage of developing faith and religious understanding across the years. It is a book my wife and I still treasure very highly.

Every one of us in this Council of Bishops has experienced the subtle but terrifying erosion wrought by administrative tasks upon her or his devotional life. Too often this is manifested in the grim difficulty we encounter as we try to prepare sermons reflecting spiritual depth and fresh theological insight. The effective implementation of our tasks as chief pastors and teachers for the

Church sometimes is plunged into mortal jeopardy by the problem of our own seeming estrangement from God, induced by official frenzy. A determined intentionality is required on the part of each of us if this danger is to be overcome, and in my case at least this must include a ruthless budgeting of sufficient time to *study devotionally*.

In one of the most provocative writings which I have read recently in this field, entitled *Celebration of Discipline,*[3] Professor Richard J. Foster of Friends University in Wichita, Kansas, discussed the four steps of meaningful study: repetition, concentration, comprehension, and reflection. He goes on to emphasize Mortimer J. Adler's idea that the study of books properly involves three separate readings which in time can be done concurrently. The first reading is for the *understanding* of the book, the second for the *interpreting* of the book, and the third for the *evaluating* of the book. Foster also mentions Adler's extrinsic aids to the study of a book, namely *experience, other books,* and *live discussion.* In the midst of a literal smörgasbord of valuable ideas and helps to be found in Foster's book, these practical suggestions impressed me as being highly usable in my own fresh dedication to the task of furnishing my mind and spirit with new devotional content. I commend them to all of us.

The Bible Itself

We are not a Bible-reading and studying people, this in spite of the fact that we are committed philosophically to being such. Unquestionably, the reason saints (in the New Testament sense of this word) are in such tragically short supply in our day is traceable to this fact. I have been impressed by the realization that many of our contemporary problems in The United Methodist Church would find an easier solution if we as leaders and members were commonly committed to a *high doctrine of the Bible.* I do not refer to an indefensible concept of biblical inerrancy or to any other extreme idea of inspiration which is not informed by the best and most reliable of contemporary scholarship. Bibliolaters in their various garments have done grave damage to the Body of Christ through the centuries.

I believe that the Bible is both a human and a divine book, and I accept with humble gratitude all that reverent critics have

discovered and undertaken to communicate to me through the years
of my Christian life and ministry. I remember the delightful story
about Dwight Lyman Moody's inviting George Adam Smith to
speak one summer at Roundtop. Smith is said to have observed,
"You don't want me, Mr. Moody. I believe there are three Isaiahs."
To which Mr. Moody quickly replied, "That's all right! We need all
the good men we can get!" This breadth of viewpoint, plus the
distinguished galaxy of Moody converts who were later to lead in
the development of responsible liberal Christianity, surely is the
kind of thing that made Henry Sloane Coffin, surprisingly, call the
nineteenth-century evangelist from Northfield "the father of modern
liberalism."

I am sure that the study of the Bible must be the beginning
of any significant devotional odyssey for a Christian. This has to
mean the study of entire books, in order to get the spacious sweep
of Scripture. It also has to mean the use of a variety of translations.
My favorites for study and understanding are the Revised Standard
Version, the New English Bible, the New American Bible (prepared
by the Catholic Biblical Association of America), the Phillips
translations, and the now fairly obsolete Moffatt and Goodspeed
versions. Because of my unapologetic affinity for the beauty of
near-Elizabethan English, I still adore the stately prose and poetry
of the old King James Version and often use it in the pulpit even
though young ministers occasionally challenge my practice with
rude insensitivity to rhetorical glory! I am glad there is a newly
revised King James Version and that it attempts the removal of
basic inaccuracies and intolerably out-of-date expressions. I have
not examined it fully.

To be sure, there must be good aids in the study of the
Bible. I have found two which I use most consistently: the old but
still classic *Expositors' Bible* and the newer *Interpreter's Bible*—
both unavoidably uneven in the quality of their essays but still on
the whole satisfactory. Often an individual treatment of a particular
book or theme by a specialist in that area of thought is superior to
commentaries on the entire Bible. In grasping the geography of St.
Paul's travels, I have never found anything more helpful or readable
(not even the works of Conybeare and Howson and the remarkable
book by Sir William Ramsay) than Bishop William R. Cannon's

utterly delightful *Journeys after St. Paul*.[4] This book, published nearly twenty years ago, is in my judgment one of the finest products of the magnificent temperament and gifted pen of our colleague—an encomium which his meticulously scholarly mind probably will not appreciate because, alas, there isn't a footnote in the entire volume!

Other Literature

I doubt if any work has had a larger influence upon my own life than the venerable *Confessions of St. Augustine*.[5] A Latin student in college, I read this work in its original language biennially during my earlier ministry as a discipline designed to keep my knowledge of Latin fresh. Living with the future Bishop of Hippo through his days of unbridled libertinism, his experimentation with Manichaeism and neo-Platonism, and his eventual triumphant growth in Christ is an experience I would covet for every Christian leader.

Moving down the centuries, let me list a few treasures from my own library, each of which has left its lasting impression upon my life. I must warn you that collectively these examples represent a wide span of theological positions, but my devotional appetite has always been happily eclectic.

Let me mention *My Daily Meditation*[6] by John Henry Jowett, sometime pastor of Westminster Chapel and New York's Fifth Avenue Presbyterian Church. His titles make highly suggestive sermonic themes. Then there is a classic from the heart and pen of Oswald Chambers, *My Utmost for His Highest*,[7] the great Britisher's YMCA meditations published posthumously by his wife. Again there is *Streams in the Desert*,[8] the original volume, by Mrs. Charles E. Cowman. This perennial favorite from the heart and mind of a woman with strong Methodist influence in her background is still beloved. Two sequels are not of equal quality.

I never heard the quaint S. D. Gordon, who gave us twenty-two *Quiet Talks* volumes and who carried his devotional gentleness into a pulpit era characterized for the most part by powerful forensics. Gordon was a layman with no academic degrees, and his theology is poles apart from my own; but I can still be deeply moved by reading again his incomparable *Quiet Talks on Prayer*[9] or *Quiet Talks on Power*.[10]

No one has completed a review of the significant devotional literature of our century who has missed Evelyn Underhill's *The Spiritual Life*,[11] first published in 1937. This brief little piece is composed of four broadcast talks couched in the simplest of language. Nor has anyone thoroughly covered this intriguing field of writing who is not familiar with the works of our own E. Stanley Jones, several of which have been reissued in the last few years by Abingdon in its Festival series. I still prefer *Abundant Living*,[12] but there are others perhaps equally helpful—and nearly all of them have the gifted touch of his distinguished daughter, Eunice Mathews, whom all of us love and honor and to whom her father often looked for editorial assistance.

A little book which has meant much to Mary Ann and me is the product of the pen of Robert Elliot Speer, the great lay Presbyterian missionary statesman who with John R. Mott and Sherwood Eddy founded the Student Volunteer Movement, entitled *Five Minutes a Day*[13] and published first in 1943. We picked up fresh copies of a new edition last summer for gifts.

The poetry and devotional writing of Bishop Ralph Spaulding Cushman is well known throughout the Christian world. I myself still like *Spiritual Hilltops*[14] and *Practicing the Presence*,[15] but *Meditations and Verse on Living in Two Worlds*[16] is also worthy of attention. One of the meaningful lessons of Bishop Cushman's life ought to be that a wayfaring person, though a bishop, can still keep a song in her or his soul!

Do you know *Daily Readings from William Temple*,[17] compiled by Hugh Warner and published now by our own press? There is a theological sturdiness and breadth of social consciousness in Archbishop Temple's writing which one does not always find in ordinary devotional literature. Of the same intellectual quality, perhaps even greater, is John Baillie's *A Diary of Private Prayer*[18] and also his *A Diary of Readings*[19]—the latter being a choice collection made by Professor Baillie of brief pieces by great spiritual personalities of the centuries.

Rare in its contribution to my own life is Thomas R. Kelly's *A Testament of Devotion*[20] with its interesting biographical memoir written by Douglas Steere. This is Quaker consecration at its illuminated best.

I went to see Jane Merchant one time, shortly before she died. They took me into a cramped little house, and there she lay on a tiny bed with bars around it—twisted and misshapen, unable to speak, having to communicate by writing painfully upon a slate, a tragic shell of a person whose love of God and life had blessed a generation. I have read her poems for years, and so have many of you. They are like a sudden rainbow after a summer thunderstorm, like a beautiful light in a room that had been dark and foreboding. They are filled with joy and hope as an American Beauty rose is filled with perfume and softness and brilliant color. They have the cross in them, but they never stop until they reach the Resurrection. She was a member of our church, and we published her books. I think especially of the one entitled *In Green Pastures,*[21] poems and prayers related to the general theme of the Shepherd Psalm.

Some of us remember Bishop Costen J. Harrell for his mastery of church law, his unrelenting insistence upon episcopal proprieties, and his unflagging moral energies. Another side of this man who was our colleague is found in his devotional writing such as *Walking with God*[22] and *The Wonders of His Grace.*[23] A member of Nashville's great West End Church, where Bishop Harrell was pastor, told me that each of the brief writings in these two books represents a précis of the West End pulpit during the Harrell era at its very best. They are still good reading!

The best little book of devotional writing I have read in more than a quarter of a century is *The Loneliest Journey*[24] by Frances I. Jackson, an English housewife. It is the tale of a painful journey from doubt to faith told in unutterably beautiful language, a literal symphony of the soul. Published by Westminster just after World War II, it has long been out of print.

There are *new* writings as well, and some of them move me deeply. I have already referred to Richard Foster's *Celebration of Discipline,* one of the most rewarding books to come to my attention in years. And there are the unforgettable writings of Henri Nouwen, the Dutch Catholic who migrated to our country and has moved relentlessly toward the center of Christian truth for our time in a whole series of thought-provoking and soul-stirring books.[25]

He is my wife's favorite writer. Father Morton T. Kelsey, an Episcopal clergyman with an affinity for the teachings of Jüng, has three titles of great significance to me: *Caring*,[26] *The Other Side of Silence*,[27] and *Afterlife: The Other Side of Dying*.[28] Then there is *A Gift for God*,[29] from the soul of Mother Teresa of Calcutta—a book of prayers and meditations. I mention also *A Twentieth-Century Testimony*[30] by Malcolm Muggeridge, the puckish former editor of *Punch,* an unreconstructed institutional iconoclast who nonetheless has one of the most vibrant testimonies to the power of the living Savior in our day. Maxie Dunnam's *Alive in Christ*[31] is a practical insistence upon the importance of Wesley's doctrine of grace. Bishop Lance Webb, our colleague who is a specialist in this field, wrote splendidly in *The Art of Personal Prayer*,[32] now reprinted by The Upper Room.

I have not even listed such classics as Thomas a' Kempis's *Imitation of Christ*[33] or Blaise Pascal's *Pensees*,[34] assuming that most of us have drunk deeply from these fabled wells.

Dare I conclude this bibliography by suggesting two books outside the purely Christian category, but with remarkable stimulus for the spiritual life? They would be that classic from a Persian pen, *The Rubáiyát of Omar Khayyám*,[35] translated best by Edward Fitzgerald; and Dag Hammarskjöld's magnificent *Markings*.[36] The first, to some, would be pagan; while the second, to all of us, is the tale of an unfinished pilgrimage by an international martyr.

Conclusion

There is a saving simplicity about the adventures that attend the devotional life. As a high school student, I lost a dear friend and classmate, a lad named Pat, who died suddenly from spinal meningitis. Some weeks later I visited his mother and found her quietly serene and eager to offer me, a very young and inexperienced Christian, the comfort she had found in her prayer life and her deep faith in God. As we talked, I found myself gazing upon two old-fashioned samplers hanging on a wall of her living room. One said "God Never Fails" and the other "Prayer Changes Things."

Perhaps such an uncomplicated faith is the ultimate objective of devotional odysseys. Sometimes one reaches such mature spiritual victory only after difficult intellectual and emotional struggle. But to reach it, and then to share it, is life's greatest experience. Even for bishops.

Endnotes

1.   The story about Dr. Harkness appears in my book *A Bishop Speaks His Mind* (Nashville: Abingdon Press, 1987), 25.

2.   Georgia Harkness, *Grace Abounding* (Nashville: Abingdon Press, 1943).

3.   Richard J. Foster, *Celebration of Discipline* (San Francisco: Harper & Row, 1978).

4.   William R. Cannon, *Journeys after St. Paul* (New York: The Macmillan Company, 1963).

5.   St. Augustine, *Confessions of St. Augustine* (London: J. M. Dent & Sons Limited, 1907).

6.   John Henry Jowett, *My Daily Meditation* (New York: Fleming H. Revell Company, 1914).

7.   Oswald Chambers, *My Utmost for His Highest* (New York: Dodd, Mead & Company, 1935).

8.   Mrs. Charles Cowman, *Streams in the Desert: Vol. I* (Minneapolis: World-Wide Publishing, 1965).

9.   S. D. Gordon, *Quiet Talks on Prayer* (New York: Fleming H. Revell Company, 1904).

10.   S. D. Gordon, *Quiet Talks on Power* (New York: Fleming H. Revell Company, 1903).

11.   Evelyn Underhill, *The Spiritual Life* (Wilton, CT: Morehouse, 1984).

12.   E. Stanley Jones, *Abundant Living* (New York: Abingdon Press, 1942).

13.   Robert E. Speer, *Five Minutes a Day* (Philadelphia, The Westminster Press, 1943).

14.   Ralph S. Cushman, *Spiritual Hilltops* (New York: Abingdon Press, 1932).

15.   Ralph S. Cushman, *Practicing the Presence* (New York: Abingdon Press, 1936).

16.   Ralph S. Cushman, *Meditations and Verse on Living in Two Worlds* (New York: Abingdon-Cokesbury Press, 1952).

17.   William Temple, *Daily Readings from William Temple* (New York: Abingdon-Cokesbury Press, 1952).

18.   John Baillie, *A Diary of Private Prayer* (New York: Charles Scribner's Sons, 1949).

19.   John Baillie, *A Diary of Readings* (Nashville: Abingdon Press, 1955).

20.   Thomas R. Kelly, *A Testament of Devotion* (New York: Harper & Brothers, 1941).

21.   Jane Merchant, *In Green Pastures* (Nashville: Abingdon Press, 1959).

22.   Costen J. Harrell, *Walking with God* (New York: Abingdon-Cokesbury Press, 1928).

23.   Costen J. Harrell, *The Wonders of His Grace* (Nashville: Abingdon Press, 1966).

24.   Frances I. Jackson, *The Loneliest Journey* (Philadelphia: The Westminster Press, 1949).

25.   A good example is Henri J. M. Nouwen, *With Open Hands* (Notre Dame, Indiana: Ave Maria Press, 1972).

26.   Morton T. Kelsey, *Caring* (New York: Paulist Press, 1981).

27.   Morton T. Kelsey, *The Other Side of Silence: A Guide to Christian Meditation* (New York: Paulist Press, 1976).

28.   Morton T. Kelsey, *Afterlife: The Other Side of Dying* (New York: Paulist Press, 1980).

29.   Mother Teresa, *A Gift for God* (San Francisco: Harper & Row, 1975).

30.   Malcolm Muggeridge, *A Twentieth-Century Testimony* (Nashville: Thomas Nelson, 1978).

31.   Maxie Dunnam, *Alive in Christ: The Dynamic Process of Spiritual Formation* (Nashville: Abingdon, 1982).

32.   Lance Webb, *The Art of Personal Prayer* (Nashville: The Upper Room, 1977).

33.   Thomas a' Kempis, *The Imitation of Christ* (Milwaukee: Bruce Publishing, 1940).

34.   Blaise Pascal, *Pensees* (London: J. M. Dent & Sons Limited, 1931).

35.   Omar Khayyám, *The Rubáiyát of Omar Khayyám,* Edward Fitzgerald, trans. (Boston: L. E. Page and Company, 1898).

36.   Dag Hammarskjöld, *Markings* (New York: Alfred A. Knopf, 1964).

XII

John Wesley:
Our Historical Contemporary

It was a distinct honor to be invited to address the annual dinner of the Friends of the World Methodist Museum at Lake Junaluska on June 27, 1986. I was aware that I was not competent to follow Dr. Frank Baker, eminent Wesley scholar, who had spoken the year before. Consequently, I prepared with more than ordinary care, reading widely and consulting with two or three authorities, including the late Dr. Albert Outler, who could give me counsel.

If this study has any particular value, it may lie in my effort to deal with John Wesley as a preacher. I have encountered few who have attempted to provide an analysis of our Founding Father from the standpoint of his pulpit work.

My interest in the work of the World Methodist Museum has continued across the years. It houses one of the most outstanding collections of documents and artifacts, especially but not exclusively Wesleyan, in this country. The historical and artistic imagination of Dr. Joe Hale is largely responsible for the recent development of this fascinating treasury.

John Wesley: Our Historical Contemporary

In 1820 Robert Southey, English poet-laureate and Admiral Nelson's biographer, wrote his famous *Life of John Wesley,* offering a rationale for his decision, as a writer from the polite world, to spend time with such a religious figure in these words: "The history of men who have been prime agents in those great moral and intellectual revolutions which from time to time take place among mankind is not less important than that of statesmen and conquerors." Southey went on to predict daringly that the time might come when Wesley's name would be more generally known than that of "Frederic or of Catherine." As Southern Methodist University President Umphrey Lee, another distinguished biographer of the little Oxford don, observed at the close of the preface to his fascinating book *The Lord's Horseman,* "that time came sometime ago."

The contention by the famous British historian William Edward Hartpole Leckey that John Wesley saved England from a fate worse than the French Revolution is well known. Wesley's preeminence is secure, as an evangelist, a practical genius, and a reformer. Few eighteenth-century leaders have left a mark upon history so clear and enduring. Dr. Outler reminds us of a statement by Bishop Warburton, one of Wesley's more malicious critics: "He was formed of the best stuff Nature ever put into a fanatic to make him the successful head and leader of a sect."[1]

Scholars have never been in agreement over his place in the history of Protestant thought. His earliest biographers created the image of an Oxonian who became a pietist and whose signal accomplishment was the founding (quite unintentional) of another denomination in Protestantism. Alexander Knox accused him of being a "major theologian who managed to fuse the best of St. Augustine and St. Chrysostom!" Dr. Outler goes on to say that the people called Methodists have been "more inclined to honor Wesley as their founder than as their mentor."[2] Although Dr. Outler edited his earlier major treatment of Wesley for a library of Protestant thought in a determined effort to establish Methodism's founder as a theologian, and surely with some success, it must still be acknowledged that Mr. Wesley was not, to use Dr. Outler's words, "a contemplative man."[3]

One remembers with a smile Dr. Samuel Johnson's fretful comment after one of his celebrated visits with Wesley at London's Olde Cheshire Inn, "He can talk well on any subject but he is always obliged to go at a certain hour," which was another way of saying that Wesley's entire life was characterized by a sense of ruthless haste and urgency. Thus, one would surely need to affirm that his enormous impact upon the history of the Western world was *a combination of the cognitive and the active.* This Southey surely realized as he offered his own compelling reasons for addressing Wesley as a subject.

Another remarkable discovery which rewards any persistent study of John Wesley has to do with much about his life, thought, and career which is applicable to the problems and opportunities of the Christian community in our own late twentieth century. His neat, usually impeccable attire was different from that of today, and what Dr. Thomas Oden has referred to as his late Augustan style of Hanoverian English was surely far removed from our modern idiom.[4] He did his travel largely by stagecoach and horseback over the narrow turnpikes of old England and spoke to his incredible audiences (sometimes in excess of 20,000) without benefit of the nineteenth-century's improved sounding board or the twentieth-century's public address system.

But there were basic similarities between circumstances in the Britain of Wesley's day and our own world in the late 1980s. The intellectual climate of the mid-eighteenth century was informed by the Age of Reason, and many thoughtful people regarded the organized church and the Christian way of life as being dead. Montesquieu, the French essayist, declared that if anyone discussed religion in eighteenth-century England, he or she was instantly the subject of derisive laughter. Morals were likewise low. The prominent leaders of state were unbelievers and often distinguished by immoral conduct, while the masses were philosophically and culturally ignorant and were visited constantly by a degree of violence which often rivaled the terrorism of our time.

Because Wesley was a practical and pragmatic man, not simply a thinker and a dreamer, he elected to fashion his application of theology to the problems which he experienced in his own day, effecting the kind of happy marriage between religion's vertical and horizontal dimensions which became a hallmark of his Christian legacy to the believing ages. In doing so, he quite unintentionally made himself our historical contemporary and so caused the Methodist movement to be both timely and timeless in every era of history, including this one.

The many-faceted life and career of Susanna Wesley's second son and fifteenth child defies total coverage in any single study. One could approach John Wesley as an evangelist (which he was always), as an educator (which he also was at all times), as a reformer, as a public-spirited citizen, as an organizer and administrator of religious affairs, as an author, as a scholar, as a colporteur, as a gently patrician component, along with Dr. Johnson and Lord Chesterfield, of old England's polite society, as a scientist of sorts, or as a preacher. I have chosen the last role for this particular study, remembering that he wrote on July 28, 1757, in his *Journal,* "About noon I preached at Woodseats, in the evening at Sheffield. I do indeed *live* by preaching!"

I understand, as all of us must, that Wesley was not the most exciting or eloquent preacher of his time. Even a casual survey of the dramatic career of George Whitefield would suggest that Whitefield himself was Wesley's superior in the pulpit. Prominent historians as late as 1755 had not even heard of Wesley, and Seymour in his story of the Evangelical Revival makes him appear as a marginal figure. However, in the perspective of the centuries, his preaching, though not incontestably superior, was undeniably the most significant in its cumulative effect upon human history during his lifetime and throughout the nineteenth century. Also, it is quite clear from any study of his own *Journal,* his letters, and now his diaries that John Wesley himself felt preaching to be the most important of his vocational functions. As Professor Outler says in his provocative introductory essay to the *Wesley Works,* "For Wesley it was *preaching* that defined his vocation preeminently. This was the principal means of gathering converts into Christian fellowship and of nurturing them in it."[5] Moreover, it is this writer's deep conviction that one may discover most readily in Wesley's preaching elements which are, or should be, reproducible in a helpful way where the church's mission in the 1980's, often confused and sometimes unclear, is concerned. Thus I have determined to focus our thought this evening upon his *preaching*.

Wesley's Homiletical Philosophy

In his *Notes,* Mr. Wesley stated clearly his belief that "in the first church, the primary business of apostles, evangelists, and bishops was to preach the Word of God."[6] Even before he left England for Georgia on that ill-fated mission which Outler describes as a fiasco and which ended with Wesley's fleeing the American shores in the face of a formal grand jury indictment on twelve separate counts, he wrote in a letter to John Burton dated October 10, 1735, "My tongue is a devoted thing."

John Wesley gave clear primacy to the role of preaching in the conversion of sinners. Here he accepted the Classical and Protestant view with its urgent insistence on the necessity for the Church to be continually formed by the "event" in which faith is aroused by the true preaching of the Word. While he revised the thirty-nine Articles of the Church of England for the Methodists in America, Wesley kept unchanged the article on the Church, Article XIX (becoming Article XIII):

The visible Church is a congregation of faithful men in which the pure Word of God is preached and the sacraments be duly administered according to Christ's ordinance in all things that of necessity are requisite to the same.

In his *Journal* Wesley makes the claim that his preaching is always faithful to "the fundamental doctrines of the Church, clearly laid down, both in her Prayers, Articles, and Homilies," asserting that *many of the clergy are unfaithful to the Word.*[7] There is no doubt in my mind that Wesley interpreted "the pure Word of God" to imply the presence of a supernatural power, i.e., the Holy Spirit Himself, *in the sermon event,* and that he attributed life-changing results experienced in listening to sermons to the work of the Holy Spirit Himself in the heart and mind of the listeners while the sermon was being preached. He had the same essential view of the Sacraments, but that would need to be the subject of another study.

Edwin Charles Dargan, in his two-volume *History of Preaching,* gave one of the best brief statements about Wesley's homiletical philosophy:

> Wesley's preaching was eminently characteristic of the man. As to contents, it was Arminian in theology, evangelical in doctrine, and full of Scripture; in thought it was rich, logical, clear, and strong; in imagination not deficient, yet not especially marked; in feeling intense but not vehement; in style clear and sweet, without notable eloquence or passion; not so stilted as was the usual manner of his age, and yet to our taste lacking in ease and simplicity... .[8]

Many authorities, including Fant and Pinson in their introductory chapter to the Wesley sermons chosen for their *Twenty Centuries of Great Preaching,* have referred to Wesley's pulpit work as representing *both learning and religion.* This is surely one of the truest appraisals of Wesley's preaching to be found anywhere, as well as one of the simplest. His own learning was massive, embracing an encyclopedic comprehension of the world as he knew it and human knowledge as it existed at that time, far and away beyond the learning of most of his contemporaries. It is true that his sermons were almost overwhelmingly biblical in their base and that he was, as he himself said, *homo unius libri*—a man of one book. All of his knowledge of the Bible was informed by an excellent understanding of its original tongues, and his allusions to Hebrew and Greek are constantly injecting themselves into his exposition of the Scriptures.

However, one must understand that Wesley was totally aware of that *variety of rhetorical traditions* in English preaching which characterized the pulpit of his day. He understood well the tradition of classical learning that had shaped English prose. He could have conversed upon the manner in which eloquence in Greek and Latin is dependent upon rhythms, sonorities, and images, as well as on neologisms and "conceits." He grasped fully how all of this had resulted in a certain ornate style current in English preaching in his day, and strikingly similar to the baroque in art and music, whose well-known proponents were Lancelot Andrews, John Donne, and Jeremy Taylor. Donne, in particular, had delivered the most eloquent sermons in the English language, and it is passing strange that literature has never recognized his homiletical efforts as generously as it has his other writings. But over against all of this approach to sermonizing there had arisen a plainer, more direct style among the great Edwardian preachers like Thomas Cranmer, who strove for *clarity as well as beauty* in his pulpit utterances.

In the same tradition, the Puritans had elevated the sermon to central place in Christian worship, symbolized by a centered pulpit and characterized by careful biblical exposition. To them preaching must be prophecy, never for show, and always clear and plain to the hearer. This was the homiletical philosophy which John Wesley deliberately adopted for his own.

In the implementation of his dedicated commitment to *plain preaching*, learned partly at the feet of his father, Samuel Wesley, John Wesley strove diligently to wear his learning lightly. In his Preface (1746) to his very first collection of *Sermons on Several Occasions*, he goes to extraordinary length to delineate his reasons for practicing a plain style in his preaching, even stressing his intention "to forget all that ever I have read in my life." To be sure, he not only did not accomplish this resolve; he probably never intended to accomplish it. But what he did do was simply to take the vast reading and assimilation of knowledge which remained one of his magnificent obsessions until the end of his life and subject it to a process of intellectual digestion and simplification which enabled him to pass it on, in quite another form, to all to whom he preached across the long years. This surely helps to explain his nearly unbelievable appeal to those who worked in the collieries as well as those who frequented the fashionable clubs of London.

Yet upon many occasions Wesley allowed the vast resources from his own exposure to literature, history, and other eighteenth-century disciplines to creep into his pulpit utterances. In his sermon "Human Life a Dream," he uses *nine* separate poetic quotations, perhaps still an item for the *Guinness Book of Records!* In the same sermon he cites Moultray and relates the story of the shooting of King Charles XII of Sweden at the siege of

Fredrickssten. Never surrendering his preference for Bible allusions in his preaching (there are one hundred and nine quotations from the Scriptures in his sermon "Scriptural Christianity"), he nonetheless drew richly upon other illustrative materials, not the least of which were personal experiences, in his effort to make the gospel understandable and gripping. But never, never did he allow the plain and clear focus of his message to be dimmed by an overabundant display of his own learning.

Another point needs to be made in our consideration of Wesley's homiletical philosophy. Here there is a direct contrast between his approach to the place and use of the sermon in the process of winning human beings to Christ and that of his distinguished contemporary George Whitefield. Wesley preached to win converts, but when they had been won, he gathered them into classes and arranged for them to come under an appropriate discipline to assure their spiritual growth and to enable them to enjoy the encouragement of warmhearted Christian fellowship in the process. Whitefield, by his own admission, never did this. Magnificent preacher that he was, he depended solely upon the power of the sermon and gave little or no thought to what should come afterward. So it was that he said near the end of his life, "My brother Wesley acted wisely. The souls that were awakened under his ministry he joined in class, and thus preserved the fruit of his labors. This I neglected, and my people are a rope of sand."

Part of Wesley's dedication to the plain preaching of plain truth was evidenced in his unapologetic use of congregational singing to draw his crowds, create their moods, and reinforce his message. He always insisted that the singing be *in unison,* and he referred to *part-singing* as being "an intolerable insult on common sense, and utterly incompatible with any devotion." The significant role of singing the gospel in Wesley's plan of proclamation resulted in the Methodists learning much of their theology from hymns, not as dogma to be accepted but as a glowing experience to be enjoyed. It was Bishop Francis J. McConnell, one of our brilliant minds in this century, who observed that Wesley never bothered to refute the skepticism of his famous contemporary David Hume, but rather elected to set England to singing in order that the tides of emotion which poured from thousands of hearts might turn the people from death to newness of life and so sweep away the sophistries of doubt.

I must insert a parenthesis here about the interesting relationship between John Wesley and George Whitefield. Their friendship went far back to the Holy Club and the day when the Wesley brothers were involved in persuading Whitefield to go the first time to America. Whitefield's progressive devotion to the teachings of Jesus Christ and especially Calvin's viewpoint, in spite of the common evangelical bond he and Wesley strongly shared, placed embarrassing, if intermittent, strain upon their friendship for each other, particularly as Wesley embraced more and more the teachings of the seventeenth-century Dutch Reformed theologian Jacobus Arminius. In 1739 Wesley preached in Bristol his famous sermon on "Free Grace," affirming an antipredestination theology, and Whitefield retaliated in 1741 with a pamphlet entitled "A Letter to the Reverend Mr. John Wesley: In Answer to His Sermon, Entitled *Free Grace.*" Thus the rupture was made open and persisted for sometime but was reconciled in the end—and the basic affection between the two never really died.

One wonders, and perhaps has no right to do so, if John Wesley entertained mild jealously for George Whitefield across the years, jealously based upon the extravagant accolades given by a galaxy of distinguished people to the great evangelist called "The Wayfaring Witness" by his biographer Professor Stuart Henry. Wesley's preaching never enjoyed such dramatic approbation, and he was never the charmer of humans which Whitefield was. Yet George Whitefield was a vital force in early Methodism, praising the movement and even declaring just before he died that "Moses was a Methodist!"

On September 30, 1770, at Newbury Port in Massachusetts George Whitefield died, and word reached England that he wished his old friend John Wesley to preach his funeral there in his native land. There was irony in this, and surely John Wesley recognized it—as, indeed, a careful reading of *Sermon 53,* the funeral sermon (preached at least two times and published in five editions over two years), will reveal. Dr. Outler has called it "the epilogue to a complex history of friendly rivalry and open conflict."

Perhaps Heaven is intended for the synthesizing of such strong, if contradictory, friendships. Each, on balance, was a strange mixture of Arminianism and Calvinism; each made the influence of the other greater. A book about this relationship would be an interesting volume to write and a fascinating one to read.[9]

Wesley's Preaching Methods

John Wesley himself tells us that he had *four* objectives for each sermon. The first was to *invite*, or to persuade his hearers in a conciliatory manner to do what was recommended in his message. He frequently achieved this goal by creating a sense of need, a method not unlike that which might be employed by a skillful problem-solving preacher in our own moment of history.

Second, he sought always to *convince* his hearers of the truth of the gospel. Here was the place where he practiced his "plain preaching" to excellent advantage. Bishop Gerald Ensley, himself a Wesleyan scholar of no small ability, made this statement: "He drew a taught logical bow and shot straight at the target without digressions of any sort."[10] His listeners invariably acknowledged that the subject matter which he was presenting was, indeed, the *truth,* and that he was speaking always to *them.* In his first Preface (1746), already referred to, he described his plain style with a Latin phrase: "I now write, as I generally speak, *ad populum,* to the bulk of mankind."[11]

Third, Wesley always endeavored to *"offer Christ,"* never as a purely theological figure but as an answer to a human being's particular plight. He opposed in his day and would surely oppose in ours much of the so-called "gospel preaching" which was abroad: "Let but a pert, self-sufficient animal, that has neither sense nor grace, bawl out something about Christ, or his blood, or justification by faith, and his hearers cry out, 'what a fine Gospel sermon!'"[12] Wesley had a strong Christology, but he never dissipated his sermon time playing with Christological puzzles and rarely even undertook to develop in a systematic way the great traditional doctrines about Jesus Christ. He was more concerned always about establishing Christ as the Solution for human problems, which was ever the question he raised in preaching. His offering of the Savior as One who could meet all issues, from the forgiveness of sin to guidance for life, was constantly his central objective.

Fourth, Wesley undertook to *"build up,"* ever seeking to send men and women away *feeling better*. He was a thousand miles removed from the dyspeptic mood of some of his contemporary evangelists. His was a day when hell-fire preaching was the rule, but he was always conspicuously restrained in his presentation of this idea. He deeply believed, as did Jesus, that more people are brought to repentance by contemplating the beauty of holiness than by dwelling on the ugliness of sin. He had no use for negative preaching, saying upon one occasion, "It cannot be that they should long obey God from fear, who are deaf to the motives of love." Once, following a visit to Edinburgh, he wrote:

> I was sorry to find both the Society and the congregation smaller than when I was here last. I impute this chiefly to the manner of preaching which has been generally used. The people have been told frequently and strongly of their coldness, deadness, heaviness, and littleness of faith, but very rarely of anything that would move thankfulness. Hereby many were driven away and those that remained were kept cold and dead.[13]

As has already been said, Wesley was a biblical preacher of the first order, and all of his sermons were based upon either a text, a chapter, or a book of the Scriptures. He often followed the lectionary's suggestions of his day with regard to a choice from the Gospels and Epistles. He generally announced his theme and text and proceeded to collate all parallel passages from the Scriptures which dealt with the same idea. He tells us upon more than one occasion that he prepared his sermons with only the text of the Scriptures in the original tongues before him. The kind of preparation paraphernalia known to most modern preachers, including concordances, commentaries, ready-to-serve outlines, and compendia of illustrations, would have been anathema to Wesley.

He wrote his sermons in full but preached them extemporaneously. He had learned to preach extempore while at Oxford, where he prepared his own sermons and also (which will surprise many) collected *and preached* the sermons of others, mainly in Christ Church Cathedral and St. Mary's! He was convinced by 1739 that effective preaching is always an interpersonal encounter between the preacher and his hearers and that oral preaching, that is, preaching without manuscript, must be the effective order of the day. But there was *always* a manuscript except on those fairly frequent occasions when he undertook his oral preaching by leaning heavily upon an earlier written document but varying significantly and even radically from it. We have records of many of the texts which he used upon such occasions, but little additional material.

Wesley usually had three points, rarely attempting that most difficult of all sermonic preparation and presentation, the single-point sermon which Phillips Brooks mastered so splendidly. There was little wit or humor in the preaching of Wesley, but those who heard his sermons bore witness to the fact that they were never tedious or dry but always characterized by a lively style which added spark to their solid substance. He himself gave advice to his young preachers at this point:

Let your whole deportment before the congregation be serious, weighty and solemn. Always suit your subject to your audience. Choose the plainest text you can. Take care not to ramble, but keep to your text and make out what you take in hand...Take care of anything awkward or affected, either in your gesture, phrase, or pronunciation. Beware of clownishness, either in speech or dress. Wear no slouched hat.[14]

There are several descriptions of Wesley's preaching given by those who heard him, some of whom were friendly and others not so. One of the students who heard him preach at St. Mary's, Oxford, was Benjamin Kennicott, neither a Methodist nor a friend of Wesley. He wrote as follows:

When he mounted the pulpit, I fixed my eyes on him and his behavior. He is neither tall nor fat; for the latter would ill become a Methodist. His black hair quite smooth, and parted very exactly, added to a peculiar composure in his countenance, showed him to be an uncommon man...

And now he began to exalt his voice .... Under these three heads he expressed himself like a very good scholar, but a rigid zealot; and then he came to what he called his plain, practical conclusion .... And he fired his address with so much zeal and unbounded satire as quite spoiled what otherwise might have been turned to a great advantage.[15]

There is a running debate about Wesley's calmness in delivery. Some, including Fant and Pinson, editors of *Twenty Centuries of Great Preaching,* doubt that he always maintained a delivery which was unexcited and dispassionate. But the majority of those from whom I have read seem to feel that his preaching constantly employed a quiet manner, often enlivened. Horace Walpole once heard him and described him as "an actor," deploring the fact that "toward the end, he exalted his voice, and acted a *very ugly enthusiasm."* His voice, even when not raised above the ordinary conversational level, was piercing, penetrating and capable of carrying *at least one hundred and forty yards.* John Hampson, a close associate, compared his style to "the calm equal flow of a placid stream, gliding gently within its banks, without the least ruffle or agitation upon its surface," at the same time commenting that Whitefield "alternately thundered and lightened upon his audience." Hampson wrote a more complete criticism of Wesley as a preacher in the following paragraphs:

His attitude in the pulpit was graceful and easy; his action calm and natural, yet pleasing and expressive; his voice not loud, but clear and manly; his style neat, simple, perspicuous: and admirably adapted to the capacity of his hearers.

His discourses, in point of composition, were extremely different on different occasions. When he gave himself sufficient time for study, he succeeded; and when he did not, he frequently failed. A clear proof that the employments, in which he was engaged, were too numerous, and the economy, to which he gave himself up, too tedious and minute, for a man who generally appeared in the pulpit *twice or thrice* a day. We have frequently heard him, when he was excellent, acute and ingenious in his observations, accurate in his descriptions, and clear and pointed in his expositions. Not seldom however have we found him the reverse . . . . Many have remarked, that when he fell into anecdote and story-telling, which was not seldom, his discourses were little to the purpose. The remark is true. We have scarcely ever heard from him a tolerable sermon, in which a story was introduced.[16]

It has been said that the late Leslie Weatherhead, striving for clarity and simplicity of expression, often rewrote a sentence *ten* times before using it in a sermon. Wesley could well have been his model. There is a beautiful story from his younger days as a preacher which says that, having noticed a lack of understanding of his discourses by his congregations, he requested an intelligent serving maid to hear him read a sermon and to stop him at every word she did not understand. She did so with annoying frequency, but each time Wesley, increasingly distraught, resolutely substituted an easy word for the hard one. He used as his own style-models the Epistles of John in the New Testament.

The story of preaching in the eighteenth century is replete with extravagant allusions to the dramatic eloquence of George Whitefield. Leckey closes a classic description of Whitefield the preacher with a reference to Garrick's statement that "Whitefield could pronounce the word Mesopotamia in such a way as to move an audience to tears." David Garrick, the great tragedian, was joined by Dr. Johnson, Benjamin Franklin, the fastidious Lord Chesterfield, and Lord Egmont in unrestrained admiration of Whitefield's remarkable preaching ability. Obviously, Wesley did not play in the same league. But, also obviously, his sermons possessed far more thoughtful and philosophical substance than did those of Whitefield; and, because of the marvelous manner in which he followed through with administrative ingenuity the organization of his converts into disciplined groups, his preaching had a permanence of results totally unknown to that of the great "Wayfaring Witness."

Another aspect of Wesley's preaching method needs to be emphasized here. On Monday, April 2, 1739, he took a decisive step which freed him from dependence upon bishops and priests alike. "At four in the afternoon," he wrote, "I submitted to be more vile, and proclaimed in the highways the glad tidings of salvation, speaking from a little eminence in a ground adjoining to the city, to about 3,000 people." Wesley's unwilling adoption of *field preaching,* or preaching in the open air, in the streets of a city, in a church yard, in a park, or at a crossroads, was partially the result of Whitefield's success in this type of venture, which Wesley had observed and of which he may have been slightly jealous. Mainly, however, it was a result of his undeniable compulsion to preach wherever opportunity offered. Lee observes that "the spectacle of a clergyman in full canonicals preaching from a table in the street or from a mound on the common was so unusual in eighteenth-century England as to attract a crowd anywhere."[17] It was the field-preaching approach that finally set Wesley free to publish his unique message to the world. And this freedom he pursued relentlessly until his strength failed him and the end came.

The records reveal that John Wesley preached an average of *eight-hundred sermons per year,* more than fifteen a week. In a day when it was not usually done, he contrived to keep all of his services of worship *within one hour,* and rebuked his preachers who did not follow this course of action.

The Reproducible Wesley

Every honest leader in United Methodism today is compelled to ask himself or herself if the Methodist way of doing things can survive a new era in human thought and action, and perhaps in ecclesiology. For example, it is quite apparent that the Methodist method of *deploying ministry* runs counter to the anti-authoritarian mood of our time. The *sent* ministry represents a process basically inconsonant with the 1980s. To be sure, the consultative process, still unlearned but with much to commend itself to all of us, is an ingenious method of bridging the chasm between the historic polity of our church and what is essentially a freer, more independent era. The problem is one of practicability, or to put it differently, the simple question of whether or not the sent philosophy can be conserved if major elements of the *called* philosophy must be built into it.

Another point at which honest United Methodists must acknowledge a problem is the survival today of Mr. Wesley's view of the place of the sermon in the life of the church. More and more across our annual conferences the popularity of an abbreviated discourse seems to be growing, with an increasing number of ministers confining their homiletical efforts to ten, twelve, or fifteen minutes at the most. Complicating the development is the often commendable and nearly always aesthetically correct effort to provide a carefully worked out worship setting in which the sermon, perhaps not always intentionally, is relegated to a secondary or even a tertiary role in the midst of an elaborate pattern of music and liturgy. This is a far cry from the ancient Puritan insistence upon the sermon as "the chief regular means of grace" with its preference for "a centered pulpit with its great sounding board and red velvet cushion for the pulpit Bible."[18] One might add other points of departure from the Wesleyan position which are evident in the life of the United Methodist Church today, including changes in the ordination service, whose newer version is rooted more in a variety of interpretations of early church thought and custom than in the understandings of Mr. Wesley.

It must be noted in passing that John Wesley had, for his day, a very liberal view about women preachers, based likely on his own experience of the spiritual influence of his mother, Susanna. He, from the first, appointed women as band and class leaders, although early on he exhibited some of his father's reluctance over allowing them actually to preach. However, by 1771, he had matured in his thinking to the point where he wrote to Mary Bosanquet, who later married John Fletcher, as follows:

Londonderry, June 13, 1771

My dear sister,

I think the strength of the cause rests there, on your having an *Extraordinary Call*. So, I am persuaded, has every one of our Lay Preachers: otherwise I could not countenance his preaching at all. It is plain to me that the whole Work of God termed Methodism is an extraordinary dispensation of His Providence. Therefore, I do not wonder if several things occur therein which do not fall under ordinary rules of discipline. St. Paul's ordinary rule was, "I permit not a woman to speak in the congregation." Yet in extraordinary cases he made a few exceptions; at Corinth, in particular.

I am, my dear sister,

Your affectionate brother,
J. Wesley[19]

But the thesis of this particular study is that certain fundamental needs of our modern United Methodist Church can be met more satisfactorily by a contemporary reproduction of some of John Wesley's emphases than by any other means available. The brief development of this idea which I offer here is intended to be merely suggestive of other possibilities not mentioned.

A. *A High Doctrine of the Bible.* It is the studied conviction of this writer that many maladies characteristic of our denomination in the 1980s are traceable to the plain, simple, and extremely unfortunate fact that, gradually across recent years, we have compromised our earlier understanding of the Bible as God's Word. Let me make two things very clear just here: I am opposed to the various theories of scriptural inerrancy, just as I am opposed to anything else that smacks of bibiolatry. Second, I am constantly grateful for the facts and insights which reverent critics have brought to our understanding of the Bible since the end of the nineteenth century. People like Sir George Adam Smith, Professor S. R. Driver, and, in modern days, Dr. James S. Stewart, and Professor Hugh Anderson have been able without intellectual dishonesty to accept the gifts of sound biblical scholarship and still to embrace Scripture as being something infinitely more and higher than mere human writing. An examination of the position of Mr. Wesley at this point would constitute overdue therapy for our Church. Let me quote a single paragraph from him:

I have thought, I am a creature of a day, passing through life, as an arrow through the air... . I want to know one thing, the way to Heaven: how to land safe on that happy shore. God himself has condescended to teach the way; for this very end He came from Heaven. He hath written it down in a book! O give me that book!

At any price, give me the book of God! I have it: here is knowledge enough for me.[20]

Wesley was always, as has been said earlier, *homo unius libri*. Unquestionably, in the mind of this writer, it is time for his church today to become again a church of one Book.

   B.   *Sound Arminian Theology.* John Wesley had no patience with theological aberrations, even when offered in the guise of academic respectability. The great doctrines generally associated with his preaching and teaching include *prevenient grace, repentance* and *justification by faith,* the *atonement,* the *work of the Holy Spirit in new birth and assurance,* the *doctrine of the church, Christian perfection,* and *eschatological redemption.* This is the catalogue of beliefs belonging uniquely in the Wesleyan tradition which former Yale Dean Colin W. Williams proposes in his significant book *John Wesley's Theology Today.* They offer an abundance of preaching material for the lifetime of any faithful Wesleyan pulpiteer, and they constitute the kind of solid theological substance which, served up intelligently and vividly, surely would inform the membership of our denomination with new inspiration and commitment.

   Wesley was not a systematic theologian. Outler refers to him as an *Anglican folk-theologian,* "whose theological competence and creativity were dedicated to popular evangelism, Christian nurture, and reform, so that his theology could be evaluated more directly by his own stated (Anglican) norms: Scripture, reason, and Christian antiquity."[21] The plain fact is that many of our pulpits are offering an unfortunate and indefensible blend of Wesley with Karl Barth, Jürgen Moltmann, and the liberationists of Latin America. While it is always helpful to learn from other theological positions, the blending of these with the Wesleyan perspective only causes that perspective to lose its uniqueness and power. I am suggesting, without apology, that the modern United Methodist Church needs to accept again as the agenda for its theology the components which Dean Williams identified for us.

   C.   *Methodological Flexibility.* One of the thrilling practices of Wesley, already dealt with in this paper, was his adoption of field preaching as a method which, while actually abhorrent to him personally, he discovered to be effective in reaching the multitudes with the gospel. The principle is more than the fact. Wesley was able and willing to bend his own preferences to fit the demonstrated circumstances of his times. I am convinced he would do the same thing were he alive today. And so must we who *are* alive today. New methods, fresh, sometimes daring and bold, must be found to communicate the message of the Christian gospel. Times have changed and the old approaches, successful in other days, often must be honorably retired, and new approaches discovered and implemented.

D. *Preaching*. John Wesley was, indeed, a preacher. This paper has undertaken to make this point and to give it some measure of documentation. His *plain preaching of plain truth* captured the multitudes and resulted in countless conversions to Jesus Christ. It was fundamentally biblical in its construction and depended entirely upon the work of the Holy Spirit to produce miracles of transformation in the lives of those who heard it. I submit, without argument, that contemporary United Methodism needs to recover once again its conviction about the centrality of *the proclamation of the Word* and to realize anew that God's Spirit does indeed work through faithful preaching to bring to pass that which cannot otherwise occur. Our seminaries need to understand this, and graduates of their classrooms need to go forth into annual conferences with a comprehension of what preaching is all about and a commitment to master its *craft* and *art*. The preaching event needs to loom large on the Christian horizon once more and never to be relegated to a ten-to-twelve minute slot in an intricately conceived liturgical pattern.

Strangely enough, John Wesley, in that distant day, seemed to comprehend something of the importance of dialogical preaching as opposed to hortatory preaching. The deep and intense feeling which informed his sermons and moved multitudes was never communicated by elevated voice and irresponsible declamation but rather by impeccable logic, clear exposition, and a conscious effort to bring Divine resources to bear upon specific human problems. As a preacher, he was as modern as tomorrow morning. What a renaissance of vigor and vitality would visit United Methodism today if his quality of preaching could return to our pulpits!

E. *Hope*. Throughout the preaching of Mr. Wesley there resounds a message of *undiminished hope*. "His theology ends as it begins, with the optimism of grace triumphing over the pessimism of nature."[22] He admonished his preachers never to proclaim sanctification in a way to discourage those who had not attained that level of perfection. Moreover, throughout his preaching, there is a clear note about heaven and a clear note about hell. He believed that the quality of life which a Christian may attain upon earth is a foretaste of the reality of another world. Jesus Christ will come again to judge both the quick and the dead, gathering believers into His perfect kingdom and completing the great salvation by His gift of a new heaven and a new earth. The *dimension of eternity* was constantly present in the sermons of Mr. Wesley, and Methodism was literally builded upon the assurance of that dimension and its significance.

In a world of Nicaragua, Chernobyl, Afghanistan, and a terrible catastrophe in space, it is literally inexcusable to enter the pulpit without a message of hope. The moral revolution with its incredible devastation can only be controlled by the recapture of human conviction that life does not end with death and that a human being, in the end, is responsible to Almighty God for his or her deeds in the flesh. Perhaps more than any other of the lost ingredients of the gospel, we need to recover our belief in *the eternal dimension*. The eschatology of hope is a part of our Christian birthright needed to restore glory and spiritual power to the contemporary church. I suggest simply that John Wesley has much to teach us at this point in the dangerous 1980s.

A Concluding Word

Is it any wonder that the prestige of Wesley grows more dazzling with the passing years? He has broken out of the narrow, sectarian confines of a single denomination and has been appropriated by a world view which ranks him with the major prophets, apostles, and saints of all time. Dr. James Joy reminds us that "his tablet is in Westminster Abbey, with the memorials of monarchs, statesmen, empire-builders, philanthropists, and men of letters. The scholars of two continents have begun to recognize him as belonging in the grand succession of Saint Paul, Saint Augustine,

Martin Luther, *and John Wesley*—the great awakeners of the human soul—themselves awakened by the touch of God."[23]

Southey said it before Joy, and with his words we began our study.

When Wesley died in 1791, he had arranged for six poor men to carry him to his grave in the unconsecrated ground behind City Chapel in London, and soon thereafter a well-intentioned but innocently thoughtless preacher named John Pawson burned a great portion of the Wesley papers in the fireplace of Mr. Wesley's home. The smoke that curled out of the chimney bore with it treasures of knowledge the world will never have about the little Oxford don who flung his leg across the back of a horse and rode out to save Old England. But more important than this, we may only conjecture what he would say about all that we who are his followers have done to the movement which he began.

Endnotes

1.   *John Wesley*, Albert C. Outler, ed. (New York: Oxford University Press, 1964), vii.

2.   Ibid., vii.

3.   Ibid., viii.

4.   Thomas C. Oden, *The New Birth: John Wesley* (San Francisco: Harper & Row, 1984), xiii.

5.   *The Works of John Wesley: Vol. I,* Albert C. Outler, ed. (Nashville: Abingdon Press, 1984), 13.

6.   John Wesley, *Explanatory Notes upon the New Testament* (London: Bowyer, 1755), Acts 6:2.

7.   *The Journal of John Wesley.* Standard Edition, Vol. II, Nehemiah Curnock, ed. (London: the Epworth Press, 1938), 274-76.

8.   Edwin Charles Dargan, *A History of Preaching: Vol. II* (Grand Rapids, MI: Baker Book House, 1954), 323.

9.   *The Works of John Wesley: Vol. II,* Albert C. Outler, ed. (Nashville: Abingdon Press, 1985), 325.

10.   Francis Gerald Ensley, *John Wesley Evangelist* (Nashville: Methodist Evangelistic Materials, 1958), 42.

11.   *The Works of John Wesley, Vol. I,* Albert C. Outler, ed. Sections 2 and 5, 103, Wesley's own Preface to his published sermons.

12.   I have been unable to find the primary source for this quotation. However it is used by Bishop Ensley, *John Wesley Evangelist,* 42.

13.   Again, I cannot locate the primary source, but have quoted from Bishop Ensley, *John Wesley Evangelist,* p. 43.

14.   *The Works of John Wesley: Vol. III* (Grand Rapids: Zondervan, 1958), 224-225.

15.   *Standard Sermons of John Wesley,* Edward H. Sudgan, ed. (London: Epworth Press, 1951), 89.

16.   I have been unable to trace the primary source for this quotation, but it is included in Umphrey Lee, *The Lord's Horseman* (Nashville: Abingdon Press, 1954), 80.

17.   Ibid., 81-82.

18.   *The Works of John Wesley: Vol. I,* Albert C. Outler, ed., 21-22.

19.   Frank Baker, *John Wesley and the Church of England* (Nashville: Abingdon Press, 1970), 204.

20.   *The Works of the Reverend John Wesley, A.M.: Vol. I* (New York: B. Waugh and T. Mason, 1835), xix.

21.   *The Works of John Wesley, Vol. I,* Albert C. Outler, ed., xi.

22.   Colin W. Williams, *John Wesley's Theology Today* (Nashville: Abingdon Press, 1960), 199.

23.   James Richard Joy, *John Wesley's Awakening* (Nashville: Methodist Publishing House, 1937), 7.

XIII

On Being Leaders
and Selecting Battle Lines

The one-year tenure granted the president of the United Methodist Council of Bishops presents a perplexing problem as to how to make maximum use of such a short time. Some in recent years, myself included, have chosen to bring a presidential message about areas of concern which seem important. Since my term was the year before the 1988 General Conference, I chose two issues: racism and human sexuality. The second, I knew, was destined for prominence on the agenda in St. Louis.

I shall always remember the morning of November 17, 1987, at Lake Junaluska when I gave this address. At its close, the great majority of my colleagues stood and applauded. But some did neither. I fully understood, for I knew that there were members of the Council, some my dear friends, who could not agree with my perspectives on the second matter.

The address was widely publicized in the church press, and a great flood of letters reached my office in Lakeland, Florida, making it necessary to involve extra secretarial assistance in acknowledging them. As far as I am aware, I was the only leader among bishops and general secretaries who elected to speak in a public forum on the complex sexuality issues prior to the 1988 General Conference.

On Being Leaders and Selecting Battle Lines

To speak at this moment from the position in which you, my dear and honored colleagues, have placed me imposes a frightening responsibility. I must utter the truth in love about the church *as I see it,* but I must recall constantly that I speak as one member of this Council of Bishops, albeit your president, *to* the Council and the Church, and not *for* either. With these parameters of authority clearly established in my own mind, I offer some serious and deeply felt observations about the subject "On Being Leaders and Selecting Battle Lines."

The diary of a French soldier in the days of the First World War told an interesting story. It was the twilight hour of the first Armistice Day, November 11, 1918. A group of Allied officers were laughing and drinking in their headquarters, celebrating with glad abandon the cessation of hostilities. The last gun had been fired; the last soldier had died. The rivers of blood would run no more. The officers were in a mad frenzy of reckless joy as they let the truth of the armistice dawn fully upon their minds. It was release—blessed release. They joked, they laughed, they wept, they shouted in a bedlam of wild exultation. Then, suddenly and solemnly, another man came into their midst. A swift silence of profound respect hushed the raucous noise in the lounge. The newcomer did not smile, but noting the hilarity of the men, he addressed a simple sentence to them: "You may lay aside your weapons," he said, *"for the war has been postponed twenty years."* It was a strange utterance that fell like a shroud over the men of the Allied command. How absurd, how ridiculous, how pessimistic! The speaker was Marshal Ferdinand Foch, Generalissimo of the Allied Armies. And his words—seemingly so out of place in that hour of celebration—were the grim prophecy of a reality, timed almost precisely. The war indeed was postponed only twenty years.

So the Church's warfare with evil is never over—occasionally postponed, perhaps, but never over. Many years ago in the Advent season I stood as a young preacher in the rear of the old sanctuary in State Street Church, Bristol, Virginia, while a great choir moved thrillingly into the Hallelujah Chorus from Handel's *Messiah,* only to have my deeply felt response to the stirring music interrupted by the jarring, shrill ringing of a telephone somewhere outside the nave, a telephone nobody was answering. Heavenly celebration is always accompanied by the clamor of earthly noises. *C'est la vie!* For a United Methodist bishop this is especially true: his or her engagement with evil is constant, predicated always upon timeless principles of biblical insights and understanding as well as the pronouncements of General Conference.

The bishops must lead the church. They must exercise their constitutional authority to guide United Methodism's spiritual and temporal affairs, particularly when there are crises and when contrary winds of doctrine threaten the church's basic health. United Methodists everywhere, lay and clerical, have a right to expect and demand such leadership. Our pastoral letter "In Defense of Creation" proved to be an auspicious beginning of what I join you in hoping will be an era of bold episcopal leading. I propose that we need now to build additionally upon that foundation of commendable initiative.

I mention two arenas where I am convinced our strong influence is needed terribly today; there could be just as well ten, but the two chosen will be suggestive of others not mentioned. One of these I shall treat more briefly because it is so familiar to us; however, the brevity employed is not intended to diminish the significance of the issue.

Racism

Sadly, and with shame, we must acknowledge that racism is still the most disgraceful scandal in United Methodism. A perceptive article in the July/August (1987) issue of *New World Outlook,* featuring comments by several members of this Council, reviews the subject well.

There has been progress in the placement of ethnics in leadership positions on all levels of the church's structure, even though this has been achieved at heavy cost to local congregations in pastoral care and pulpit power. But progress in the delicate area of open itinerancy, particularly in some sections of the church, has been minimal, and this has handicapped greatly the recruitment of able, brilliant young ethnic ministers. There has been a mixture of blame, a major portion, to be sure, lodged in the white community but with some responsibility belonging to ethnics, especially blacks, because of certain attitudes ultimately harmful to their own interests.

The most regrettable aspect of the present situation is that, to many of us who have struggled with the issue for decades, dangerous retrogression seems to have set in. The cause is old, and the dramatic ardor of many of its bold earlier champions has experienced "the destruction that wasteth at noonday" (Psalm 91:6b). Weariness and apathy have slowed down procedures which, because of persistent zeal, used to register steady, sometimes painful, but always visible gains each year. Beyond activistic achievements the slower but evermore significant educational process continued its relentless campaign to produce attitudinal changes until even gloomy souls could glimpse faint light at the end of the tunnel. But to many keen observers the long trains of change seem to be lumbering to a halt, in the North as well as the South, and perhaps even more so there. The latent, inbred racism of my generation of whites, present in spite of sincere efforts on our part to exorcise it, has begun to move in upon our moral exhaustion and bring once more the discouraging specter of satisfaction with the status quo. This ominous development must be arrested *now,* a task belonging inescapably to the church's spiritual leadership. The battle lines are open itinerancy and ministerial recruitment, with an intense corollary concern for stronger clergy leadership in the predominantly ethnic church. The latter need, actually basic to the other two, must be addressed forthrightly and the continuing exit from local church ministry to more glamorous, often better paid, general church positions reevaluated honestly in terms of the long-range health of the United Methodist ethnic community. Satisfying quotas at the expense of the very constituency such quotas were designed to protect is grotesquely self-defeating.

Occupying these battle lines will not be an easy task and will require intentional courage, initiative and perseverance on the parts of bishops and cabinets. In many instances in this country it will need to happen in spite of widespread political, cultural, and social reactionism at this moment in time. To allow the current lethargy to continue without substantial challenge will be to lose precious territory already taken and to risk returning to the social insensitivity of the 1950s and earlier.

It is doubly tragic (and sometimes incomprehensible) that issues like racism and sexism still exist as *chronic* maladies in the life of our church in spite of decades of moral and spiritual enlightenment, strong denominational programs, and precise General Conference directives. Their clear solutions are both implicit and explicit in the basic mandates of the Christian gospel. We as a church ought long since to have implemented them and be ready now to address a plethora of other critical concerns that throng the horizons of the contemporary human situation.

Human Sexuality

Actions by several of the general agencies of our church proposing serious and sometimes far-reaching changes in United Methodism's current positions on various issues related to human sexuality have been reported and headlined in different news releases by our church press. Stories related to occurrences and the adoption of positions in *unofficial* groups have also been communicated to our church by the same press. In some instances, complications from the dissemination of such news have been exacerbated by predictable distortions accomplished through the secular press. Widespread popular reaction, the overwhelming part of it negative, has resulted across United Methodism. Because of this, one very important truth needs to be reiterated for the sake of our people: the *only* body ever authorized to speak *for* United Methodism is its General Conference, and the presently existing positions taken by the General Conferences of our Church on these issues are clear and unequivocal. However, the actions featured in recent news articles are targeted upon the next General Conference.

Parenthetically, perhaps it is time to scrutinize the ethic which permits an *official* agency of the church to expend large amounts of energy, time, and funds attempting to effect change in the laws of United Methodism instead of seeking better ways to implement those laws as they have been enacted by General Conference.

There will be many agenda items in St. Louis next spring, but none more carefully monitored by United Methodists, clerical and lay, across this and other lands than those having to do with human sexuality. I believe the intercession of episcopal leadership on this issue is warranted because of the involvement of basic principles of historic Christian teaching. I also raise the matter in this setting because I believe the church's response to serious overtures for *radical* change could affect substantively the *unity of United Methodism* in the next quadrennium.

Let me pose some simple questions that trouble me greatly as I ponder the spiritual health of our church in late 1987 and our seeming silence on certain issues.

Have we left an impression on our people that we no longer believe in the critical significance of traditional Christian morality as we summarized it in our own episcopal address in 1980: "In singleness, celibacy; in marriage, fidelity"? Do people assume, however falsely, that we are in *de facto* agreement with authors like Father John McNeill and Dr. Karen Lebacqz, who wrote articles in *The Christian Century* in March and May, respectively, in 1987 pleading for new and radical perspectives on human sexuality within the church? Are we perceived as being hesitant to affirm with fresh emphasis the integrity, sanctity, and importance of traditional marriage and the family in our time?

We know well that religion without morality is a mockery before God. Is it time for us to declare openly our conviction that the crumbling of character in a people is the sure prelude to the disintegration of a nation, a lesson which Edward Gibbon, writing in the eighteenth century, taught us when he analyzed the causes for the decline and fall of the Roman Empire? Do we need to assure our church that we will never surrender to the pressures of articulate and persistent groups who purpose to write a new charter for Christian sexual ethics quite apart from the total impact of Scripture and ecclesiastical history, and clearly alien to the convictions of successive General Conferences, when these people represent only a small contingent in United Methodism and yet have seen fit to challenge the whole church? Have we faced the grim fact that the unity of United Methodism, won at so dear a price in the 1930s and again in the 1960s, could be imperiled if such a fundamental change in our church's understanding of human sexuality should occur?

Our ecclesiastical response to the terrifying AIDS crisis, the worst affliction to visit the human family since the plagues of the Middle Ages, has been to call for additional funds for research, more hospital space, and the elimination of homophobia and discrimination—all good. But we seem to have stopped short, up until now, of pleading vigorously for an end to those sexually permissive lifestyles which surely play a material role in the continued spread of AIDS. Our collegiality with friends and coworkers who favor a more liberal perspective on human sexuality has often made us reluctant to voice convictions which might offend them; and so we have risked becoming unintentional accomplices in the perpetration of a monstrous and fatal compromise. Mere endorsement of safe sex is an incalculably weak position to be assumed by a church dedicated to the promulgation of high moral principles and fundamental Christian values. Our worldwide community of Christian believers has a right to expect far more of us.

The liberal Protestant community, I fear, has been guilty of sanctified stillness on many of the urgent questions identified with men and women as sexual beings. Anthony Robinson, writing in *The Christian Century* in June 1987, reminds us of Stanley Hauerwas's accusation that the liberal churches are "public legalists and private antinomians." To quote Robinson: "We pronounce on issues of national policy with great certainty but when it comes to bedroom policy we seem to have little to say."

Pertinent to ministerial responsibility in this general arena is the provocative and perhaps controversial essay by President Leonard I. Sweet of United Theological Seminary entitled "The Plover Report" (the title invokes an interesting use of Kierkegaard's well-known Middle English rainbird metaphor). Dr. Sweet records evidence of a widening gap between pulpit and pew becoming, in his words, "as big as the Grand Canyon." In another and earlier writing he indicts the modern seminary for "repotting homegrown Christian piety" in such manner as to structure a new kind of faith among ministers which is not easily shared with laity. His conclusions are based upon extensive interviews with bishops and district superintendents (the United Methodist community's rainbirds or "plovers") largely in the northern part of our church.

My point is this: if we as episcopal leaders of United Methodism do not assess correctly the reasonable concerns of the overwhelming majority of lay people in our local congregations and offer to our church the quality and vigor of moral and spiritual leadership they have a right to expect from us, we ourselves shall be guilty of widening the gap between clergy and laity in our day; and there surely will come a time when long-suffering lay patience finally is exhausted and both the vitality and the unity of our denomination threatened. Our attractively rationalized acquiescence to subtle intimidation by zealous pressure groups within our connection, themselves often wholly insensitive to General Conference actions, can in the end become a tragic betrayal of multiplied thousands, perhaps millions, of loyal United Methodist lay people (and often ministers as well) who constitute the indispensable support base for our far-flung mission in today's world.

A disgruntled member of this Council of Bishops said to me in recent weeks, "If our United Methodist Church could vote on the human sexuality issue, we all know what that vote would be." Even though our total reasoning in favor of our present positions is based properly upon far more defensible arguments, are we not obligated to pay attention to the very obvious will of our people in this matter?

It is a plain fact that any substantive revision in our church's present official view of human sexuality, in my considered judgment, would provoke literally unmanageable circumstances in United Methodist congregations across this country and throughout the world. Because we are a global church, it is only right for us to give particular attention to the effect of our actions upon members of our denomination in countries other than the United States. In the event of a clear change in our positions, it is not inconceivable that the major unannounced item on the agenda at the St. Louis General Conference could become the unity of the church.

Any legislation by the General Conference that opens the way for the acceptance of homosexuality as an alternate, normal lifestyle within the Christian community would be impossible for vast numbers of United Methodists all over the world to accept, would violate their understanding of the principles of biblical religion, and would precipitate an angry exodus of unpredictable proportions from our church. I am quite aware that there are sincere people (many of whom are my friends) who regard the practice of homosexuality and the living of the Christian life as being totally compatible with each other and who see no moral issue involved. I doubt that they understand fully the depth of the convictions held by those of us who feel otherwise, or that these convictions in very many dedicated United Methodists are not products of homophobic emotion or fundamentalist religion. Such people—most of us would not deny that they constitute at least a considerable majority in United Methodism and the larger Christian community—accept simply and naturally the Judeo-Christian tradition as the principal fountainhead for belief that homosexuality is out of harmony with the gracious intentions of God for relations between the two sexes. They are adamantly unwilling to embrace those reinterpretations of the Bible which, since the 1970s, have sought to legitimatize homosexuality. This is United Methodism's dangerous dilemma today, terribly complicated by the dramatically rising incidence of AIDS. Its potential for divisiveness is monumental. Methodism in the 1840s was ruptured by differing views about human slavery; it could be that our church in the 1980s must decide if radically differing views on human sexuality will be allowed to rupture it again.

My plea, speaking as your president, is for the retention of United Methodism's *present positions* with regard to human sexuality, including homosexuality. The carefully crafted phraseology presently contained in the *Book of Discipline* has conveyed its clear meaning to our entire church. To attempt even subtle and adroit changes in existing language, I fear, could point the church in the direction of an *altered basic position* and unquestionably would be interpreted in this way by our membership. Present wording provides contrapuntal balance between the articulation of clear, historic Christian principle and insistence upon all-embracing Christian pastoral compassion and love.

This may be interpreted by some as a plea urged upon the president of the Council of Bishops by the so-called "evangelical" contingent of United Methodism, a highly respectable and loyal group of committed people to whom we would do well to listen more carefully than we do. *But I deny the charge.* The initiative for this address is wholly my own, and I speak as a minister trained in the liberal tradition of Methodist seminaries in the 1940s. If the moment has come when liberals cannot speak out for moral rectitude and traditional family integrity in the Christian community, then we dwell in a tragic twilight of impending religious doom. I insist that liberal Christians should never surrender to their more conservative sisters and brothers those understandings of personal and social morality which belong proudly to the long history of Christendom.

What I have said may also be interpreted as being insensitive to the deep needs of the homosexual community and to our church's correct insistence that this community's men and women are "people of sacred worth" for whom a Savior died. *I also deny this charge.* A lifelong friend, dear to my heart, has been homosexual since our college days together; and I have learned from him the poignant agonies through which homosexuals pass in our time. I have ministered to gay people across forty-five years, always, I trust, with understanding and Christian love, and I shall continue to do so.

Let it be said emphatically that the problem of homophobia, morally reprehensible and pragmatically serious, must be addressed far more effectively by the Christian community than has been done up until now. *Positive* efforts to offer pastoral care to homosexual people and to make clear to them the unqualified love and concern promised in the *Book of Discipline* must become an intentional part of United Methodism's program and ministry on all levels. However, the acceptance of homosexuality as a lifestyle compatible with Christianity is *not* required in order to oppose homophobia.

Actually these are not the primary matters at issue in this address. We are dealing with what, to many of us, is still very much a biblical and moral question. We are talking about the rightness or wrongness of placing an ecclesiastical imprimatur upon lifestyles undeniably related to the instability of the family and the growing peril of AIDS. We are speaking also about qualifications for Christian ministry in our United Methodist Church.

Summary Statement

I have intended that *racism* and *human sexuality* should be suggestive of many other problems in whose solutions I believe the Council of Bishops must assume vigorous leadership. If the *Book of Discipline* is taken seriously, the United Methodist Church will not rise far above the integrity and courage of its Episcopacy, to which it has committed "carrying into effect the rules, regulations and responsibilities prescribed and enjoined by the General Conference ...." We have sacred and inescapable obligations.

Effective leadership seems in short supply today, both nationally and ecclesiastically. One prominent university president in the United States, speaking caustically of the church's leaders in a recent address, used these shattering words: "Having lost their faith in God, they are trying to determine who should hold the keys to the wine cellar." The British author Harry Blamires, whose sobering book *The Christian Mind* I encountered more than five years ago and keep near me still, says, "As a thinking being the modern Christian has succumbed to secularization. He accepts religion—its morality, its worship, its spiritual culture; but he rejects the religious view of life, the view which sets all earthly issues within the context of the eternal."[1]

The effort to convert embraces the concept of the transformation of the mind. So we bishops, in my judgment, must lead vigorously in converting, or "turning around," the mind of United Methodism to a fully Christian view on the issue of race and to a creative use of the principle of open itinerancy. Likewise, we must not fear to try to sway the mind of the modern world powerfully toward a philosophy of human sexuality which will honor Scripture and civilized tradition as well as safeguard the integrity of the family and the health of the human race. To fail here would be to betray not only our great church, but God as well.

I do not believe for a moment that we have lost our faith in God; and I devoutly hope we are not concerned about worldly issues like wine cellar keys. But I know the problems with which the church wrestles today are of vast concern to God as well as to us, and that "the stars in their courses [will fight] against Sisera" (Judges 5:20*b*) when we endeavor to do what is everlastingly right in the sovereign name of our Redeemer.

My sister and brother bishops, let us dare to lead the United Methodist people in our time even when the issues are complex and difficult, and there are those who do not understand.

"Unto him be glory in the church by Christ Jesus throughout all ages, world without end. Amen" (Ephesians 3:21).

Endnote

1.   Harry Blamires, *The Christian Mind* (London: S.P.C.K., 1963), 3-4.

XIV

In the House of the Lord Forever

This was the sermon preached at the opening worship service of the General Conference in St. Louis, Missouri, on April 26, 1988, while I was still president of the Council of Bishops. It combined the memorial *and* communion *themes, and sought, not too subtly, to establish a mood for the sessions which were to follow.*

The sermon appeared later in Best Sermons II, *edited by Dr. James W. Cox and published by HarperCollins Publishers, copyright 1989. It is used here with permission.*

In the House of the Lord Forever

The Lord is my shepherd, I shall not want;
    he makes me lie down in green pastures.
He leads me beside still waters;
    he restores my soul.
He leads me in paths of righteousness
    for his name's sake.
Even though I walk through the valley of
    the shadow of death,
I fear no evil; for thou art with me;
    thy rod and thy staff, they comfort me.
Thou preparest a table before me
    in the presence of my enemies;
thou anointest my head with oil,
    my cup overflows.
Surely goodness and mercy shall follow me
    all the days of my life;
and I shall dwell in the house of the Lord
    for ever.

                    --Psalm 23 (RSV)

Henry Ward Beecher called this the "nightingale" of the psalms. Its musical cadences translated into seventeenth-century English have been a part of the lives of millions of educated men and women since childhood. The charm and power of these simple sentences haunt our hearts. They easily suggest a blending of the *memorial* and *communion* themes. The psalm portrays the pilgrimage of a man or woman of faith and climaxes with a ringing affirmation that such a person, at the end of life's earthly journey, will "dwell in the house of the Lord forever." It also speaks about a table which is prepared, a Host who presides over that table with unfailing care for His guests, and ample food for the famished pilgrim. Implicit in these beautiful verses is the idea of love undivided, the kind of love that produces, beyond earthly differences, the priceless treasure of *unity* among God's people.

Let us, then, attempt to bring together the concepts of memorial moments and holy communion against the backdrop of a great phrase from the final verse of the Shepherd Psalm, "in the house of the Lord forever."

Memorial Moments

It is appropriate to begin this General Conference by remembering those bishops, episcopal spouses, a Judicial Council member, and General Conference delegates who have completed their journey into Christian immortality. We do this reverently and with heartfelt gratitude for their lives, remembering that all of God's leaders, ourselves included, are sinners saved by grace before they are anything else. Because the gospel is forever true, God gives us, in spite of our human frailty, the privilege of telling its wonder and power. We pay our affectionate tribute of Christian love to all those memorialized today, into whose mighty labors we have entered.

Basic to all other Christian doctrines is the biblical faith in life beyond death. The great Russian novelist Dostoevsky, filled always with the Resurrection certainty of his Eastern Orthodox Church, declared that without confidence in immortality one actually believes nothing. Often in recent decades this particular Christian tenet has seemed to be the "lost chord" of theology.

Somewhere, long ago, I heard Bishop Edwin Holt Hughes, the unforgettable sage of an earlier episcopacy, tell about an evening stroll he took on an ocean beach and a casual encounter with a man who complained that he hadn't heard a sermon on heaven since childhood. Walking on, gazing into the lovely tints of a sunset sky, Bishop Hughes pondered the man's statement and recalled his own predictable preoccupation with the valid claims of the social gospel across the years. Then, remembering the Savior's perfect blending of time and eternity, he resolved to provide at least a partial answer to that man's problem. Returning to his hotel, he sat down and wrote a sermon on heaven, giving this story as its introduction.

We correctly deplored the use of the old "pie in the sky" emphasis to sanctify the idea of religion as an escape from the brutal realities of this world. We struggled to make our United Methodism one of God's viable vehicles for applying the gospel to the open, bleeding wounds of suffering society. But somewhere in the process, unintentionally I think, we came close to abandoning Christianity's historic use of the *eternal dimension* to complete its portrait of human life. The price we have paid for this omission is startling, complex, and devastating. It amounts to neglect of the Resurrection itself, although the first Christians never saw the Resurrection primarily as the means of Jesus' escape from the grave but rather as the living God in omnipotent action. As we remember today our beloved Christian dead, it is appropriate, to borrow the title of a great sermon by Michael Ramsey, that we should be "thinking about Heaven"[1]—and, more importantly, about the power of the Resurrection. Otherwise, those of us gathered here in St. Louis, to paraphrase Thomas Carlyle's words about Samuel Taylor Coleridge, will be addressing our massive tasks with looks "of anxious impotence" in our eyes.

Because of the awful heaviness of decisions to be made here, we would do well to remember that in Wesleyan religion social conscience and courage must spring from a saving awareness of God in Jesus Christ, otherwise they are impermanent and dangerous. Our passion to help the poor, the oppressed, and the wronged results from the revolutionary liberation which has come to us through personal encounter with the Resurrection God. Not to recognize this is to invite *missional disaster:* we cannot, we dare not erect a constantly expanding superstructure of social activism upon a steadily diminishing foundation of religious faith. Great enterprises for God grow in the rich soil of vital belief, intentional spiritual discipline, and steadily renewed exposure to the whole treasury of Christian doctrine, especially the Resurrection.

The Shepherd Psalm closes with the statement, "I will dwell in the house of the Lord forever." The foundation of the Christian's confidence that life continues beyond the grave is his or her unshakable faith in the *supernatural power of God,* the same power which was at work dramatically in the lives of those whom we remember in this hour and which has prepared for them places in another and better world where, beyond these shadows, there are new tasks, new dreams, new goals.

Celebrating their fidelity, we must take candid inventory of our own faithfulness as this General Conference begins. If, indeed, the Lord is truly our shepherd, it should matter to us most that God's own will be done here. Not what we seek, but *what God wishes* should be the guideline for each day's work. Our motivation and our toil must please the heart of the Eternal One. Through this simple commitment, in a way quite beyond our knowing, the great, inexplicable energies of creation will be released both in and through this General Conference. Because there are spiritual laws quite as operative as physical laws, United Methodism can never reclaim its historic power in our day until it affirms again that the eager discovery of Almighty God's will is the one diapason note of real religion. There is no purer way to remember those who have died in Christ and who dwell now in the house of the Lord forever than to think, speak, and act in such a manner that the Holy Spirit may find it easy to dwell in this place during these sessions. When such occurs, this vast headquarters for General Conference will become, indeed, the house of the Lord!

Holy Communion

"Thou preparest a table before me in the presence of my enemies; thou anointest my head with oil, my cup overflows." In this beautiful poem we encounter the hospitality of a gracious and generous host along with a quaint, curious characteristic of ancient Eastern culture. Those of vastly different convictions could eat at the same table without prejudice or danger, for the place of eating had all the privileges of a city of refuge. In these beloved verses a faithful shepherd has brought his flock safely home. Allowing here for the picture of the flock to shift abruptly to one of people, the image of home is made alluring by mention of a lavishly spread table and a watchful, kind host ready to meet his guest's every need.

Nestled in the midst of the Old Testament, this passage lends itself gracefully to Christian application. What a portrait of the meaning of Holy Communion! Surely there are here today hundreds of strong, independent, committed Christian thinkers and leaders, representing vastly different opinions and judgments on vital matters but belonging gratefully to one Lord, the Lord whose love and concern have prepared the supper. We have come from our many places and lands with our personal needs, our doubts and fears, our weariness, our resentment of wrongs, our anxieties and uncertainties. Yet we are one in our devotion to what we understand to be our church's best interests. Our Lord Jesus knows all of this, and hovers near to bring us renewal and restored faith and to share with us His own mind, if we will allow it. Too, in a dear and intimate way, the very ones whom we have sought to memorialize in these solemn moments are also with us. It is a time for the communion of saints. We are about to enter into the greatest privilege a child of God has on earth, that of taking for ourselves the symbols of the broken body and the shed blood of our Lord.

The Lord's table represents always *unity of spirit,* even when there is disagreement in viewpoint. Unity is never achieved easily, and not at all until those who go in its quest have it as their magnificent obsession. Even then it is hard to come by. Many years ago Mr. Justice Oliver Wendell Holmes said that he would not give a fig for the simplicity *this* side of complexity but that he would give his very life for the simplicity on *the other* side of complexity. I speak of the unity of our church which lies on the other side of complexity and I exalt it in these opening moments of General Conference as a precious treasure which must be sought relentlessly, even painfully by all of us.

The Lord's table also symbolizes a common faith and, for us, the historic content of the Wesleyan tradition. We are both liberated and restrained by this realization, liberated to experience new insights of truth within the rich repertoire of our special heritage, restrained lest we violate the time-honored parameters of our knowledge of the gospel. By our commitment to the clear, historic interpretation of the Scriptures left to us by the little Oxford don, we avoid the tempting *privatization* of religious beliefs and practices which has become such a deadly peril in our time. Thank God, we are never free to design our own understanding of Jesus' message, except within those guidelines which generations of devout scholars have developed for us. This was never intended to stifle creativity or to discourage new and valid insights. It was meant to lend necessary spiritual and historical discipline to our contemporary ventures across fresh frontiers. We are the church, not a sect or a cult, and there *are* standards that must always apply.

We take Holy Communion in gratitude for those whom we memorialize and in humble hope that their mantles of effectiveness may fall upon us as we seek wisdom and sound judgment for the labors ahead. We know we must have this if we are to discharge well our responsibility here in St. Louis.

I sat as a delegate to the General Conference in 1964 in Pittsburgh and listened to Bishop Herbert Welch, age 102, preach the sermon at the beginning of that great conclave. I can still hear his vibrant voice as it rang out with these words:

> There is no room here for self-assertion, or suspicion, for contempt or hatred. There is no room for bitterness, for parties and slogans.... For here, in the house of the Lord, belong peace and good will, understanding and patience, humility and compassion.... We shall be united in the confidence that "our times are in his hand"; that He will fight our battles for us, and the peace of God will keep our minds and hearts.[2]

Ah, Herbert Welch, prince of the church, prophet of the faith, may we hear your voice again here in St. Louis as it was heard nearly a quarter of a century ago in Pittsburgh!

Memorial moments and Holy Communion *do* go together: they unite the church triumphant and the church militant in a common effort to know the mind of Christ and to do the will of God. Because love is one and undivided, the Christian's hope for heaven is never far from his or her hope that the Kingdom will come here on earth. So it is that we have invoked this nightingale of the psalms to build a bridge for our minds and hearts between the memory of heroic disciples and the memory of a suffering Savior. The haunting beauty of this ancient poem thrills each of us. It pleads for the unity of the people of God, living and dead, and, more importantly, the unity of The United Methodist Church, whose very life is in our hands during these sessions. Our challenge is to respond that we may dwell in the house of the Lord forever.

Nels Ferré once told about a missionary to a leper colony who visited the Vanderbilt Divinity School and said to the students and faculty, "I have come to the seminary here to learn how to pray." Then Professor Ferré wrote, "Deep in the pew I felt very small, knowing that we seminary professors could teach other things far better than we could teach that."[3]

Members of this General Conference, some have feared, may be able to do other things far better than to lead United Methodism toward the fuller implementation of God's will and the discovery of a stronger unity in Christ. They may be right. God grant that they are not. So it is that we come now *in the house of the Lord* to His table, remembering His own prayer in a long-ago garden: *"that they all may be one"* (John 17:21*a*).

Amen.

Endnotes

1.   *Best Sermons, Volume X,* G. Paul Butler, ed. (New York: Trident Press, 1968). A sermon entitled "Thinking about Heaven" by His Grace, the Archbishop of Canterbury Arthur Michael Ramsey, pp. 200-203.

2.   Ibid., a sermon entitled "Communion" by Bishop Herbert Welch, p. 134.

3.   Nels F. S. Ferré, *Strengthening the Spiritual Life* (New York: Harper & Brothers, 1951), 13.

XV

The Excellency of Carmel

This address, given at the National Convocation on World Mission and Evangelism in Louisville, Kentucky, on July 11, 1990, followed within a few days Mrs. Hunt's and my return from an extended trip to Turkey and Greece and the islands of the Aegean Sea. In fact, the final alterations in the manuscript were accomplished on shipboard as our vessel cruised the ancient waters so closely identified with the journeyings of St. Paul.

It was a costly address for me. I had acquired an open sore on my left foot while striding over the rough stone streets of old Ephesus in Turkey, and an infection had already developed at the time of our return to the United States. I went on to Louisville knowing that additional walking was unwise but convinced that I must try to keep my engagement there. When I returned to Lake Junaluska, a streptococcal infection had set in, and I faced a week of hospitalization and two months of slow convalescence.

This address has been included in an anthology containing the papers presented at the National Convocation on World Mission and Evangelism, entitled The World Forever Our Parish *and published by Bristol House, Ltd., Lexington, Kentucky. It is reprinted here by permission.*

The Excellency of Carmel

It shall blossom abundantly and rejoice, Even with joy and singing. The glory of Lebanon shall be given to it, The excellence of Carmel and Sharon. They shall see the glory of the Lord, The excellency of our God.

—Isaiah 35:2 (NKJV)

Introductory Words

Vivid childhood memories are persistent. When I was a little boy, my father took me one Sunday to hear Bishop Horace Mellard Dubose, listed in the 1988 *Book of Discipline* as the one-hundred eighty-first bishop elected by our denomination. His startling rotundity impressed my childish mind: he was almost literally a "Mr. five-by-five." If he had played golf, he would have had to address the ball without ever seeing it. He was the first and only preacher I ever heard who divided his prayer into an introduction, three points, and a conclusion!

Bishop Dubose was also an amateur archeologist, and it was announced that he would give an archeological lecture at three o'clock that afternoon in Munsey Memorial Methodist Church. My father insisted that we should go, and we did. The one thing I remember from that lecture is that Bishop Dubose had been to Mount Carmel, which, as you know, is a prominent mountain at the head of a range on the eastern coast of the Mediterranean Sea, dividing the coastal plain of Palestine into two parts. It was the scene of the contest between the prophets of Baal and the prophet Elijah, as recorded in the books of Joshua, 1 Kings and Jeremiah. I shall never forget Bishop Dubose telling that little Sunday afternoon audience that he had found at the very summit of this bald, blistered mountain a wide variety of lovely, colorful flowers. In the crevices of this broad expanse of rock, unrelieved by any presence of soil, some unseen power had arranged for these incredibly beautiful flowers to appear and bloom. This, he said, was "the excellency of Carmel."

I never forgot that mysterious, picturesque allusion, and years later, with that memory, I came to appreciate the rich suggestiveness of this Old Testament phrase. Mount Carmel had its forbidding surface of rounded rock, but it also had its gallant array of brilliant hues worn by brave and defiant little flowers emerging miraculously from thousands of tiny breaks in the stone. I thought of other beautiful Old Testament phrases such as beauty for ashes, joy for mourning. All of them make clear that the business of the God whom we Christians worship is forever to turn midnight into dawning, or, as Bishop Arthur J. Moore hauntingly said, to make an old world young again.

Therefore, I have chosen to speak today about this perennial paradox of our Heavenly Father's creation. The Mount Carmels of human history have always had both their rocks and their flowers. It is the duty of a Christian man or woman to recognize the sobering message of the rocks but ever to look for the ravishing beauty of the flowers. Which is to say that, because God is who He is, with mercy and power, there is, for the likes of you and me, always that light which in the end is able to overcome all darkness.

The exciting drama of the eighteenth chapter of 1 Kings is rich in the materials it provides for the Christian preacher determined to wrest hope out of despair. Elijah, demonstrating incredible courage, pits himself against four-hundred fifty priests of Baal; and, in an event which changed the course of Israel's religious history, demonstrates the superiority of the Hebrew God Yahweh to Baal. The terrible destruction of the drought was broken and the refreshing rains came. Since it all took place on Mt. Carmel, this enriches the meaning of the phrase "the excellency of Carmel."

Against the backdrop of this Old Testament story and the meaningful allusion offered so many years ago by Bishop Dubose, let me speak a little while about our own United Methodism in terms of its rocks and its flowers.

First, the Rocks

Our low doctrine of the Bible. I begin with this, because it may be responsible for all our other ills. But how very careful we who belong in the classical tradition of evangelical Christianity need to be at this point!

Modern evangelicalism's most divisive controversy has centered on whether or not the scriptures are without error. Inerrancy has become, for many, the litmus test of authenticity. Historically, this doctrine, never a part of classical evangelicalism, is a hangover from the old fundamentalism of post-World War I days. Strictly speaking, this is simply not part of the Wesleyan perspective. As Dr. William J. Abraham, McCreless Professor of Evangelism at Southern Methodist University, has put it, "It is not based on scripture itself, it is ultimately irreconcilable with the actual phenomena of the Bible, and it is not required for construing scripture as normative for Christian faith and practice."[1]

I agree with Professor Abraham. I am puzzled, even alarmed, because contemporary evangelicalism in our own United Methodist ranks seems to be flirting dangerously with an insistence upon an inerrant Bible which endangers the real rebirth of the Wesleyan movement in our time and among thoughtful, intelligent people.

I am not an inerrantist and certainly not a bibliolator. But I do believe deeply in the inspiration and the authority of the Bible. I believe that the Holy Scriptures hold in them everything required for Christian faith and practice. I believe that the Bible brings the Word of God to us.

It seems to me that our careless, if not willful, disregard for the Bible's authority has brought us to a point where the Christian community has been unduly and improperly infiltrated by contemporary humanism and the moral and sexual revolutions of recent decades. This has been particularly true in the instance of the subtle but tragic deterioration of the family. The compromise of purity and the dilution of principles and standards related to human sexuality are surely integrally related to a new and humanistic perception of the Christian scriptures. Too, our doctrinal impoverishment, a characteristic of the church during the last half-century and longer, could not have occurred without a drastically changed attitude toward the Bible.

The Bible is a human book, a mirror in which we see ourselves; but it is also a divine book, the historical self-revelation of God himself, as through the rushing centuries He has sought to woo and win the souls of human beings. The Bible prophesies and reveals the Christian God Incarnate—Jesus Christ our Lord.

In the diamond fields of South Africa, a rare and wonderful stone was found, later to be known as the flystone diamond. Placed under a magnifying glass, one is able to see enclosed in all its brilliancy a little fly with body, wings and eyes in the most perfect state of preservation. How it came there no one knows, but no human skill can take it out. So in Holy Scripture, the Spirit of God is found in a place from which no human power can ever extricate it.

I believe the Bible. A deliberate, reverent return to a high doctrine of Holy Scripture would be a giant step in the direction of reclaiming the soul of our beloved church. This, more than anything else, would render us teachable where the indispensable leadership of the Holy Spirit is concerned.

Our departure, consciously or unconsciously, from Mr. Wesley. Despite a nearly 95 percent affirmation of our new theological statement by the General Conference of 1988, certain difficult-to-believe developments appear to be surfacing in our church, developments patently opposed to United Methodism's declared faith. For example, a special committee studying our understanding of baptism is said to be considering proposing to the 1992 General Conference that baptism, at any age, "initiates full participation into the body of Christ," requiring no subsequent vows or act of confirmation. An infant, for example, would be listed as a full member of the Church. Furthermore, baptism "ordains" the baptized person into the general ministry of the Church to embody the gospel and the Church in the world.

The second matter may simply represent an updating of an understanding which we have articulated more gently for a number of years, namely that all baptized believers are members of the general ministry of the Church, with certain persons being set aside for a representative ministry of preaching, administration of the sacraments, and other forms of worship. The important difference to note is that it is being suggested now that we employ the term "ordain" in connection with the *general* ministry as well as the *representative* ministry.

It has seemed to me that much of our thinking with regard to the ministry today and the ordinals which deal with it reflects more the ideas of Martin Luther than those of John Wesley. The Methodist Ordinal, as Bishop Cannon has said, is

> . . . an adaptation, or rather to be more exact, a slight abridgement of the Anglican Ordinal of 1661. Cranmer's original was based on a medieval prototype, the Sarum Text in Latin. These reflect a basic concept of ministry as separate, distinct, and to a degree different from the laity of the Church. Martin Luther, in contrast, teaches the priesthood of all believers and delineates the ministry as representative, a designated segment of the faithful chosen by them to perform publicly . . . .[2]

It could be that we have not examined carefully what our unconscious(?) adoption of Lutheran thought about ministry may imply for our total situation. For example, if we follow the Lutheran position, as we seem to be doing now, and if we grant the practicing homosexual a right to be a baptized member of the Church, we have in effect already granted him or her the right of general ministry. Particularly would this become a dangerous situation if we should attach the term *ordain* to the idea of general ministry. The question then is reduced to whether we wish to grant the homosexual the additional right of representative ministry. This is a point which I have not encountered up to now in arguments for or against the ordination of homosexuals, but I believe it may be a factor to be borne in mind as this difficult question continues to be addressed.

May I suggest that it is already quite late in the day for United Methodists to analyze where certain study groups involving the ministry of our Church may be leading us. It seems ironic for us to boast a new theological statement dedicated to a return to Wesleyan principles, when important collateral statements now under development appear ready to lead us in opposite directions. In a certain setting some months ago, I questioned a member of one of our study committees as to whether or not the committee had measured its proposals against the content of the new theological statement, and this person replied that the matter had not even been mentioned!

Turning to quite another issue, let me refer you to a short essay in the February 7-14, 1990, issue of *The Christian Century,* written by a United Methodist minister on the West Coast named Robert Morley. Morley's thesis is that evangelism cannot possibly work in modern United Methodism because we have become a church, consciously or unconsciously, committed to *universalism.* As he puts it, "We no longer believe a decision for Christ matters much either in this life or the next....We believe or hope that God is going to find a way to save everybody." He goes on to point out that "we don't talk about saving the lost or converting the sinners or reconciling to God those who are separated from Him; we speak of churching the unchurched."[3]

I submit to you that Morley's point is well taken and very timely. There is nothing new about universalism; it goes back at least as far as the time of Clement of Alexandria in the late second century and his pupil Origen in the third century. But it was categorically repudiated by Wesley, and by Bishops Coke and Asbury in their *1798 Disciplinary Notes,* in which they called for resistance toward "heretical doctrines," noting especially Arianism, universalism, socialism, and other views contrary to Wesley's teaching *(Discipline 1798,* p. 113).

Our views about hell and eternal punishment undoubtedly have undergone change, much of it for the better. But our quiet, gradual, almost imperceptible adoption of the idea that God's love rules out His judgment destroys the deepest meanings in the plan of salvation by which the Church has grown through the centuries. Imagine talking about early Methodism without speaking of the *lostness* of humanity! The first followers of Wesley believed profoundly that a man or a woman without God is a lost being. I suggest that a basic need of United Methodism today, to use Thomas Carlyle's unforgettable expression, is "to see the infinite beauty of holiness and the infinite damnability of sin." Only then will our people feel again an irrepressible impulse to win others to Jesus Christ as Lord and Savior.

Universalism, even when espoused by a man as distinguished as William Barclay, must surely be a denial of the fundamental framework of a righteous creation and a radical readjustment in God's agelong design for the redemption of His children. Pierce Harris, the colorful Atlanta preacher, used to remind his hearers bluntly about the fact of accountability in our holy religion. "Someday," he would say, "you will look up and see the Divine Storekeeper coming down the long stairway of the stars, rattling his keys and calling out, 'It's closing time, folks!'" This undeniable biblical truth is not easily dismissed.

A leadership of avoidance. I must be brief here and blunt. Leadership in our United Methodism, and I say this reluctantly and with a consciousness that the indictment applies first of all to myself, has failed in recent years. There have been exceptions, dramatic exceptions, of course; and for these we are deeply thankful to Almighty God. But these have simply helped to establish the bottom-line fact, which is that the real problems confronting our church and responsible in large measure for its diminishing membership have not been addressed by responsible denominational leaders. This does not mean that many of their efforts and activities have not been good and necessary. I myself believe that United Methodism must, in every generation, focus its resources upon those great social issues which deeply affect the welfare of the human family; and I would propose no retreat from such missional enterprises. I am confident that they are in harmony with the will of God. But this in no way alters the conclusion that the principal issues threatening the survival of the church in our time, knowingly or unknowingly, have been avoided.

We have been confronted with wave upon wave of new and insidiously perilous socio-cultural developments attacking the ideals and value structures of the centuries and bringing with them intellectual perspectives frequently unfriendly to the Christian religion. We have made little effort to stimulate the maturing of a new Christian mind equipped to do battle against these alien influences in our common life. I said I would be blunt. Our well-intentioned efforts to deal with the nuclear threat and injustices toward racial minorities and women have consumed so much of our time and energy and resources that we have seemed to be virtually unaware that a new and deadly paganism has come on stage in our moment of history. Too little of our reading and study has been focused upon what actually has been happening to the soul of our world.

One illustration is our indefensible ambivalence about homosexuality. The voices of successive General Conferences have been clear and strong on this issue, calling for faithful, caring ministry to the homosexual but declaring homosexual practice to be contrary to the Creator's plan and "incompatible with Christian teaching." In spite of this fact, pleas for the acceptance of the homosexual into ministry and homosexuality as an approved lifestyle within the Christian community have been persistent. The struggle is far from over, and unless responsible current leadership in United Methodism is able to find the motivation and the courage required to support steadily and vigorously the official position of our church on this pivotal matter of Christian ethics and conduct, we may surely expect at least a partial reversal of our present stance in 1992.

Another example may be appropriate. I was in a Detroit bookstore three or four months ago and noticed to my surprise that practically one entire wall was devoted to a display of books and literature related to the New Age Movement. Three shelves were given entirely to writing by and about Shirley MacLaine, whom I knew vaguely for her earlier work as an actress and her later involvement with teachings about reincarnation and other singularly anti-Christian doctrines. The New Age, which some describe as "a return of the counterculture artifacts of the Hippie period," seems to the casual observer to be a conglomeration of intriguing ideas about good vibes, organic foods, karma, acupuncture, extraterrestrials, crystals, psychics, channeling, extrasensory perception, and witchcraft. Actually, it is composed of components greater than all of these, the meanings of which strike at the very roots of classical Christianity. Critics and those knowledgeable about the New Age promise us that it will not go away and that it can be expected to effect a change in life on this planet more drastic than any we have dared to contemplate. I am convinced that New Age poses a frightening threat to all the teachings which we as Christians hold precious.

Persistent homosexual pleas for respectability and the New Age movement are simply two items among a plethora of issues and movements which our contemporary ecclesiastical leadership has seemed to avoid. Another would be an honest inquiry into the reasons for the dissatisfaction about modern United Methodism on the part of so many loyal, thoughtful followers of John Wesley. Such an inquiry could prove to be important and informative. Humanly speaking, I have regretted the appearance of individuals, groups, and organizations critical of our church and those of us who work in it; but I have realized again and again that these parties sometimes constitute *amici curiae,* friends of the court. They have sought to call our attention to things terribly wrong within our own structures and to lead us back into the kind of responsible operational integrity which can cure many of our ills. However, our strategy, time after time, has been to *criticize our critics* instead of listening openly to their words of counsel. Thus, pride has wed stupidity in a union of disaster. We have been precinct politicians instead of intelligent statespeople!

When I was elected bishop in 1964, my dear friend, the late Bishop Ferdinard Sigg of the Geneva Area in Europe, scholar, linguist, saint, wrote from Zurich a letter with this sentence: "You have entered into a hall of magnificent opportunity, and into a room of very great temptation." Across twenty-six years as a bishop of the church, I have comprehended, fully but sadly, his meaning.

These examples which I have given are all part of the *rocks* of our Mount Carmel, these and many, many more.

The sky over our church in these destiny-laden moments is dark with ominous clouds that tell the story of our unfaithfulness as United Methodist ministers and people. We stand at the summit of the mountain, our feet on the hard, unrelenting stone. But Elijah will come, the awful drought end, and refreshing rains bring once more colorful legions of flowers.

And, Second, the Flowers . . .

Many times, since that faraway Sunday afternoon when I heard Bishop Dubose lecture about his journey to Carmel, I have wished I might have been with him. I can envision the exciting miracle of those beautiful flowers growing out of the crevices of the stony mount, the riot of colors carpeting the rock. Were they mountain heather, vetch, buttercups, goldenrod, the snowy white of Queen Anne's lace, or a startling variety of all of these and more?

The important thing is that someone with the courage of Elijah came, and, in our memory of the Carmel of history, the beauty of the flowers replaces the repulsiveness of the rocks. Night becomes dawn.

The people known as United Methodists. I believe unswervingly in the spiritual integrity of the lay members of the United Methodist Church and am proud that during the twenty-four years of my active episcopacy I was frequently described as the layperson's bishop. My indebtedness is incalculable to the laypeople who, across nearly fifty years of my own ministry, have supported my efforts, borne with my failures in and out of the pulpit, gently corrected my many mistakes, loved me and believed in me, surrounded my family with innumerable kindnesses, and prayed for me nearly without ceasing. If there were some who were cantankerous and even mean, and there were, there were many, many more who were helpful, sympathetic, and loved the Church and the Lord Jesus Christ with committed integrity.

I read somewhere recently how Mother Teresa, when she made a decision to permit the BBC to film her ministry among Calcutta's dying multitudes, said to Malcolm Muggeridge, "Let's do it! Let's do something beautiful for God!" How many *wonderful* laypeople God has permitted me to know through the years who joyfully have dedicated their lives to doing something beautiful for Him!

But the laity of the church have deep, agonizing concerns, and many of these focus upon what we as ministers have failed to do or to do well. They have been disturbed over certain directions that United Methodism has taken in recent years. They are more than ready for the kind of revival of Bible-centered faith which will set right many of the unfortunate circumstances to which I have alluded. There is a long-suffering wistfulness about them. God has already performed His miracle of prevenient grace in their midst, and they are strong in their hope that they may yet see bright flowers springing from the rocky crevices of Mount Carmel. They cling boldly to their jubilant expectancy of a better day in the life of United Methodism. I said these words at the conclusion of my chapter "Only a Layperson" in a book I wrote five years ago:

The church does not exist for its ministry. It exists for the laypeople, those who are in it now and those who will be in it in days and years ahead.... When they have an authentic experience of Jesus Christ and information about United Methodism which we who are their ministers are able to provide, our church will be safe in their hands. *Even if they change some things!*[4]

Theological currents. I grew up in a day of unapologetic theological liberalism and was trained in one of the great liberal seminaries of our church. But now the pendulum has swung. For a number of years, an evangelical renaissance, both international and ecumenical, has been developing and growing within the Christian community. Its impact has been far-reaching and enduring and is now taking on characteristics of maturity. It is too bad that there are still elements within the Christian Church (often among its leadership) which have not realized or acknowledged the reality of this development or its controlling role in the decline or growth of churches. It is *not* a return to the fundamentalism of the twenties and thirties, although there has been an ongoing struggle within new evangelical ranks to plant seeds from this now outdated movement. It is, instead, a well-informed, often scholarly, socially aware, culturally contemporary, intellectually respectable phenomenon, Bible-based and characterized by a late-twentieth-century recovery of the classical theology of Christian history. At its best, it is hypersensitive to the complex needs and problems of modern men and women. And, despite cleavages within itself, it continues to grow dramatically, fed by vigorous minds like Lesslie Newbigin and our own William Ragsdale Cannon, whose remarkable lives and ministries bridge the time-span between the era of Stewart, Thielicke, Outler, and Niles and the present.

One of the most obvious reasons for the decline of our church's membership in recent decades, I am convinced, is the persistent but puzzling failure of our own leadership to comprehend the reality of this evangelical renaissance and its far-reaching implications. What I am endeavoring to say is that the theological signs of our times constitute a strong and vibrant ally in our effort to achieve the spiritual renewal of United Methodism. Our problem has been that we have continued to insist upon programmatic directions contrary to the major theological trends of our time. When we find the insight and courage to fix our sails to coincide with those strong currents prevailing in this final decade of the present century, we shall witness a sudden, dramatic righting of the vessel we call United Methodism.

The Holy Spirit. I referred earlier in this address to *The Christian Century* essay by Robert Morley. Let me quote now its final paragraph:

> These are my confessions, yet I confess also to a certain amount of hope. All I have said would instantly be rendered moot if the Holy Spirit decided to blow through our church again. If the fire and the energy of the Holy Spirit animated The United Methodist Church again, the spirit would send all of us organizers, doubters and semi-ineffectual article writers scurrying for cover. Perhaps, if the history of the church is any guide, evangelism must always be seen as the prerogative of the Holy Spirit—more a happening than a program, less a procedure than a surprise. Let those of us who wait in this in-between time, rather than planning program procedures, examine ourselves and our faith to see if there is anything at all that will not be burned up and blown away if the Holy Spirit comes.[5]

As I have grown older, I have thought increasingly about what God wants in my own life and in His world. Too often, I fear, we preside over the creation of elaborate and extravagant program designs, invest untold hours and huge amounts of money in their implementation, only to discover at the end of a year or quadrennium that they have accomplished little, if any, toward the achievement of Kingdom objectives. Any good business woman or man would rule them out on the basis of extremely poor cost effectiveness. *The simple explanation may be that these designs were not what God wanted after all.* We built a house upon the shifting sands of human dreams and ambitions, and the heavy winds of contemporary culture blew the house down. Any house which we project, if it is to last, *must* be built upon the solid rock of Almighty God's will and desire.

Like Robert Morley, I have come deeply to believe that the brightest flower blooming on our Mount Carmel, and the strongest hope facing our church, is the exciting probability of some grand initiative on the part of the Holy Spirit. We must realize anew that the United Methodist Church belongs to Almighty God and that He is infinitely more concerned about its future in the world and in the Christian community than any one of us, or all of us put together, could ever be. I believe in miracles, and I *know* that God, in His infinite power and mercy, stands ready to become part once again of the compelling Wesleyan task of spreading scriptural holiness over the earth. I know that He wills a solution to the problems that torture United Methodism. I know also that He wills the church's unity, the recovery of its deep doctrinal conviction, and the rebirth of a magnificent evangelistic obsession to capture the twenty-first century for Jesus Christ. Then shall all of those things which presently hinder and frustrate us fall like the terrible tyrannies of history.

Have you ever stood in the yard of Trinity Church in Boston and gazed upon that magnificent statue by Saint Gaudens, where the figure of Christ hovers broodingly behind Phillips Brooks? The Holy Spirit *will* come. G. K. Chesterton, writing in his memorable way about the darkness which enveloped medieval Europe when the Franciscan movement was born, described that new invasion of the living, redeeming God into human history:

> While it was twilight, a figure appeared silently and suddenly on a little hill above the city dark against the fading darkness. For it was the end of a long and stern night, a night of vigil...He stood with his hands lifted as in so many statues and pictures, about him was a burst of birds singing; and behind him was the break of day.[6]

That was Saint Francis of Assisi, bringing back to a weary earth Heaven's dawning. Let us recover our own confidence in the power of God to put down His opposition, to remake His church, and let us expect His Holy Spirit! Where is our faith? Have we prayed, actually agonized in prayer, for the intervention of Heaven at this time of concern for our church?

A Concluding Word

Dare we believe that the flowers of our Mount Carmel, in the end, will triumph over its rocks? The rocks are real and we dare not deny their importance. We must face them and deal with them. But, I am convinced, the promise and hope of the flowers are more formidable than all our problems and failures.

My gravest apprehension is that, humanly speaking, time may be running out on those of us who are eager to translate our "lover's quarrel" with the church into positive change. Former Dean and Research Professor Emeritus of Systematic Theology at the Divinity School, Duke University, Dr. Robert E. Cushman published a book last year entitled *John Wesley's Experimental Divinity,* whose closing paragraph states clearly the urgency of this entire matter:

> ...the spectacular decline of membership in The United Methodist Church during the past decade and more may suggest that very many have wearied beyond endurance with the church that manages mainly "the form of Godliness," on the one hand, and seems doctrinally shapeless on the other.[7]

It is so easy for those of us who have experienced little encouragement in our sincere efforts to turn United Methodism's vessel around in the troubled, turbulent waters of today's world to become disillusioned, even bitter and cynical. Thus it is that the sound of our voices is softened, if not silenced, and our efforts lose their influence and impact. You may remember the familiar story of Lucifer, the Prince of Darkness, after he had been expelled from Heaven. Being asked what he missed most from that life which now lay behind him, he replied, "I miss the trumpets in the morning." We who love our church more ardently than some can understand, in our sheer weariness, have lost the music of the trumpets of the morning out of our declarations and strategies. We need desperately to recover what Professor Stewart once called "the kindling contact of the flame of Heaven."

Marcus Dods was fascinated in his closing months by a chemical metaphor that helped him vastly. Discouraged and out-of-heart, he felt that his life was ebbing. Yet his spirit rallied and held on. "For," said he, "I have seen a scientist, with a phial in either hand, drop one drop from the one into the other fluid and nothing happened; a second drop and nothing happened, a third, a fourth, a fifth, too many drops to number, and still nothing happened; and then one more, exactly like the others, but in an instant everything had changed." And so it may be with our own faithfulness, our own courageous, sacrificial efforts. Perhaps the great tide has been turning now for longer than we know, and tomorrow we shall see the breaking of that day for which our hearts have longed and our spirits struggled!

It is His church, not ours. Once again, as long, long ago on Carmel, the God of Israel, Elijah's God and ours, surely will demonstrate His power and His grace. The drought will end, the refreshing rains come, and the exquisite color of myriads of flowers will appear miraculously in the rocky crevices of the mount. Behold, even again, "the excellency of Carmel"! Amen and amen.

Endnotes

1.   William J. Abraham, *The Coming Great Revival* (San Francisco: Harper & Row, 1984), 85.

2.   This significant quotation from Bishop Cannon does not appear in any of his published works. Both he and I have searched for it diligently. He believes it was part of some article he wrote for a church periodical but cannot identify it more precisely. He has verified its accuracy.

3.   Robert Morley, "Confessions of a Naysayer," *The Christian Century* (February 7-14, 1990): 117-118.

4.   Earl G. Hunt, Jr., *A Bishop Speaks His Mind* (Nashville: Abingdon, 1987), 61.

5.   Robert Morley, 118.

6.   Dudley Barker, *G. K. Chesterton: A Biography* (New York: Stein and Day Publishers, 1973), 256.

7.   Robert E. Cushman, *John Wesley's Experimental Divinity: Studies for Methodist Doctrinal Standards* (Nashville: Kingswood Books, an imprint of Abingdon Press, 1989), 189.

XVI

The Old Story in a New Day

This is a sermon preached at Wesley Theological Seminary, Washington, D.C., upon the occasion of the installation of Dr. James Cecil Logan as the E. Stanley Jones Professor of Evangelism. The date was October 17, 1990, and the event part of an extraordinary week devoted to Christian evangelism and planned brilliantly by the seminary's President Douglass Lewis. Dr. Logan, to whom I had given his first teaching position at Emory & Henry College during my presidency, moved from a distinguished career in systematic theology over into evangelism at his own request. The professorship is sponsored by the Foundation for Evangelism. Mr. and Mrs. B. B. Lane, prominent United Methodists of Alta Vista, Virginia, supply one-half of the required support and other friends of the Foundation the second half.

A few summers ago I was invited to teach an abbreviated course in preaching at Wesley, and the fulfillment which this experience brought created a special place in my heart and mind for this strategically located and important seminary in our nation's capital.

The Old Story in a New Day

...that utterance may be given me in opening my mouth boldly to proclaim the mystery of the gospel ... that I may declare it boldly, as I ought to speak.

—Ephesians 6:19-20 (RSV)

In early July of this year, my wife and I walked the fabled streets of old Ephesus. The night before, on board the Greek ship Pegasus in the Aegean Sea, I had read again the inspired words of the writer of Ephesians and found myself joining him in asking the church for prayer that all of us who are ministers might be enabled to tell the old, old story effectively in a new and indescribably different day.

Against the backdrop of a summer memory, I recall the words of that remarkable Jesuit teacher Gustave Weigel: "The church is the one institution on earth which exists for the sake of those who are not yet in it." It is with this in mind that I invite you to think with me about Christian evangelism in our moment of history.

Evangelism Must Be Intellectually Respectable

The two foremost American evangelists in the earlier years of the New World were Jonathan Edwards, early president of Princeton University, often described as the most creative thinker in the history of this hemisphere, and Charles Grandison Finney, New York lawyer, professor, and later president of Oberlin College. Edwards is remembered historically in association with the Great Awakening. Although famous for his sermon "Sinners in the Hands of an Angry God," he preached far more often about the love of God and the joy implicit in the knowledge of Jesus Christ. Finney, initially untrained in theology and a critic of all seminary education, is credited with being the father of American revivalism.

The fact that the genesis of evangelism in this country is indissolubly associated with these two men and their work in successive centuries constitutes a vigorous argument against the unfortunate dichotomy which has persisted between evangelism and education. The two were joined happily in their lives and careers. Our evangelistic beginnings under Edwards and Finney also document for us the important fact that there is no valid contradiction between faith and reason, or between zealous soul-winning and unapologetic intellectual integrity.

Years ago Paul Elmer More, a Harvard graduate with a brilliant and inquisitive mind, went off to the New England town of Shelburne, Massachusetts, with his dog and a collection of books representing the masterpieces of the ages. With no religious convictions at all, he started a long trek through the Greek, Latin, German, French, and English classics. His first series of Shelburne Essays, eleven thoughtful volumes, told the story of his high but thoroughly humanistic thinking. Then came a baffling change in the structure of his outlook, revealed in his book *Christ the Word*. It could be accounted for only through some great fresh influence on his mind. A friend discovered that the transformation had been inaugurated when he began seriously to study the New Testament and Greek philosophy up to the time of Nicaea and Chalcedon. What happened was one of the utterly wonderful intellectual conversions of the centuries. He moved from Platonism to a radiant belief in the Christian Incarnation and then, just at the time of his death, to the concept of the Saviorhood of God.[1] What a memorable and timeless example of the revolutionary influence of the Christian evangel upon the informed mind! It is still true that educated people, facing the issues of human destiny, often find themselves inevitably confronting Jesus Christ and the Christian gospel. Do you remember the Pope's line in Browning's "Ring and the Book": "Life's business is just *the terrible choice*"?

The practice of Christian evangelism at its best has always rested back upon the foundation of sound biblical interpretation and theological understanding. In his Fondren Lectures a generation ago, Bishop Edwin Holt Hughes, after commenting about Jonathan Edwards and Charles Finney, asked if it can be possible that "someday we shall see that conjunction again—the mighty evangelist represented in the eminent educator?" Hughes went on to point out, using the illustrations of John Wesley and Saint Paul, that "the real scholar and the flaming preacher have more than once dwelt in a single personality."[2]

There may be historical significance in United Methodism pioneering in the acceptance of evangelism as an academic discipline in the curricula of modern seminaries. From that long-ago day when Charles Wesley spoke about uniting knowledge and vital piety, our church has undertaken, often with desperate sincerity, to effect a marriage between the study desk and the altar, the library and the sanctuary, the mind and the soul. We have struggled consistently to offer Jesus Christ within a context of intellectual integrity.

The intellectual respectability of evangelism always must be kept current. A devastating criticism of contemporary efforts to win people to the gospel and the church, articulated well by my longtime friend Dr. Haskell M. Miller, emeritus member of this faculty, refers to the difficulty which thoughtful people of the 1990s suffer in attempting to reconcile the perspectives and emphases of Christian traditions with the dynamics of their own social and cultural experiences and their consequent inability to respond to an evangelism which fails to take into account the contemporary crisis in thought invoked by the new science and technology.[3] This observation suggests a major tragedy of mid-twentieth-century religious liberalism, namely its failure to discover either the motivation or the technique for an adequate evangelism, and thus its loss of the power to reproduce itself.

Evangelism can and must offer the gospel in a manner that is intellectually respectable in this year of our Lord, 1990. When it does, as was true in earlier years, the results for God and His church will be both positive and startling.

Dean Hough of Drew once said, "True evangelicalism is intelligence on fire." Such an understanding, in this speaker's judgment, must be the *magna charta* of any effective evangelism in the nineties.

Evangelism Must Recognize and Adapt to Change

The only dependable constant in the contemporary picture of reality is change itself. This is unsettling to all of us who have become reasonably comfortable in our present perspectives and prejudices. The most difficult task in ecclesiastical acrobatics is that of comprehending fully the staggering dimensions of change in the world today, then constructing an acceptable Christian response without altering or abandoning those aspects of the church's beliefs and practices which constitute, properly, the *sine qua non* of a believer's commitment to Jesus Christ. A part of this complex process is the ability to evaluate accurately heretofore unknown developments which are appearing on today's horizon, such as the New Age movement. The casual observer may associate it with a conglomeration of intriguing ideas about good vibes, organic food, karma, acupuncture, extraterrestrials, crystals, psychics, channeling, extrasensory perception, and witchcraft. But the New Age is composed of components greater than all of these, the meanings of which strike at the very root of classical Christianity.

Another illustration of the anatomy of change with which we are required to deal perceptively is the reality of the evangelical renaissance, a sweeping ecumenical and international phenomenon, deeply troubled within itself, which, for puzzling reasons, has not been acknowledged fully by the leadership of the mainline Christian community. In an article in *The Christian Century* for January 17, 1990, David Stoll, author of an important new book *Is Latin America Turning Protestant?* asks why the amazing growth of evangelical churches in Latin America is so largely ignored by North American scholars and then responds with a disturbing sentence: "The reason I suspect, is that evangelical gains contradict our agenda."[4]

The current evangelical resurgence is a far cry from the old-time fundamentalism of the twenties and thirties. It boasts its own impressive brand of intellectual depth and integrity and has birthed a small galaxy of pedagogical stars, brilliant by any standard, who teach in a startling variety of institutions, including mainline seminaries like Yale and Duke. It has acquired a keen and demanding social conscience, fresher by far than its counterpart in the liberal sector. This conscience deals principally with the more traditional issues of racism, war, poverty and ecology. It handles sexism, abortion and homosexuality with a predictable sensitivity to evangelical principles. Its apocalypticism is muted, if present at all; and its comprehension of modern secular culture is realistic.

Today's evangelical packaging of the Christian faith may be more marketable than the product offered by some of the mainline denominations.

The cultural changes which surround us this afternoon, curiously enough, can be suggested by a series of catchy acronyms which have invaded the current vernacular of urban society in our land. *Yuppies,* young urban professionals, first appeared around 1984, leading to *Buppies* (black urban professionals), *Huppies* (Hispanic, etc.), *Guppies* (gay) and *Puppies* (pregnant). All of these, I am informed by sophisticated friends, have become more or less passe. Today we have *Grumps* (grim, ruthless, upwardly mobile professionals), *Dinks* (those with dual-income, no kids), *Sitcoms* (those with single-income, two children, outrageous mortgages); and, just to recognize the graying populace in this country, *Opals* (older people with active lifestyles) and *Suppies* (senior yuppies)! Someone mentioned to me a few days ago a final category named *Oinks* (those with one-income and no kids)! Clustered around all of these semi-ludicrous acronyms, and suggested by them, are many details about contemporary styles of living which help to dramatize in a frightening way the drastically altered human situation with which the person dedicated to winning human beings to the Christian way must deal in our time.

But I am reminded of a letter that Pierre Teilhard wrote to Henri Termier on November 11, 1954, in which the great Catholic scientist and priest had this sentence: "They were so busy counting the waves that they did not notice the tide!"[5] So it is with us. Wade Clarke Roof of the University of California at Santa Barbara, writing in *The Christian Century* a year ago, referred to Francis Fitzgerald's description of American society in the late twentieth century as a centrifuge. He went on to remind us that a centrifuge "is an apparatus that operates at high-speed and sorts out substances at differing densities."[6] Under the impetus of centrifugal force, centers collapse and their elements re-form themselves in different and more fragmented groupings. One impact of Professor Roof's discerning article is that it may be time, once again, for liberal Christianity to formulate in language and program its concerns about personal faith, rather than leave such a critical matter to New Age and human-potential therapies.

A new book by the respected guru of the evangelical world, Carl F. H. Henry, is entitled *Twilight of a Great Civilization*,[7] the caption betraying the message of the text. What Dr. Henry seems to be seeing, beyond Pierre Teilhard's waves, is the whole terrible tide of an increasingly pluralistic, secularized cultural revolution. For many, the very idea of God smacks of massive irrelevance. This is the *milieu* in the midst of which evangelism must be done now, in the years before the turn of the new century, and then surely on into the 2000s.

There are, to be sure, concomitant developments in the realms of theology and religious thought. We turn to them next.

Evangelism Must Recover Confidence In Its Message

Walking into a local Chinese restaurant for lunch a week or so ago, accompanied by a friend, we suddenly noticed two automobiles side-by-side in the restaurant's parking lot. The first car boasted a bumper sticker with this inelegant wording: "Life is a bitch, and then you die." The second vehicle had a bumper sticker with these words: "First United Methodist Church Cares for You." What a shocking contrast in life philosophies and perspectives! What a dramatic microcosm of the human situation in the midst of which the evangel of Christ must be offered in today's world! Sadly but quite obviously the second bumper sticker announcing the Christian concern represented a minority, while the first bumper sticker with its strident pagan vulgarism stood for a shockingly large number of people today.

What is the message which evangelism is to proclaim, the content of the concern expressed in the wording on the second bumper sticker? The substance of the Christian evangel is stated quite simply: "For God so loved the world that He gave His only begotten Son, that whoever believes in Him should not perish but have everlasting life" (John 3:16, NKJV); and then: "But seek first the Kingdom of God and His righteousness, and all these things will be added to you" (Matthew 6:33, NKJV). The message is always both personal and social, but it is personal before it is social. At its heart there is the idea of a transformed life made possible by divine forgiveness and grace, whose new directions point the believer toward sacrificial involvement in righting the wrongs of the world for Jesus' sake. This is the gospel, and it is this word of redeeming hope which negates the bitter cynicism of the first bumper sticker we saw.

There are some new difficulties in the way of the Christian who seeks to believe the church's historic evangel and share it with others. These problems are essentially theological and one of them at least is very recent. In preparing this message, I reviewed the last two years' issues of *The Christian Century* and *Christianity Today* (I have read them both for thirty-five years). I was amazed to note the emergence of two dominant themes, about equally present in each publication, both of which seem to threaten the very principle of evangelism. The first is the proposal to abandon the *uniqueness of Jesus Christ* as a concession to the growing presence in our world today of other religions like Islam, Hinduism, and Buddhism and a further concession to the startling fact that there are now more Moslems than Methodists in the United States! This kind of thinking would make Jesus Christ no longer the *only* way to salvation but rather *one of several* ways.

As far as I know, this sort of radically syncretistic effort to reconcile differences between Christianity and other religions constitutes a fresh development in theology. To be sure, the problem is not new, but the solution is—to me at least. It is a plea for the surrender of the most important territory we have ever held. A corollary principle, already voiced in many settings, is the absence of any ethical right on the part of Christians to urge men and women of other religions to accept Jesus Christ as Savior and Lord.

The second issue dealt with so prominently in these two Christian periodicals during the last half-quadrennium is the idea of *universal salvation*. Oversimplified, this is the doctrine that in the end God will work it out so that every person will be saved. This is not a new viewpoint, but its open prominence in Christian thought *is* new. A major book *God Does Not Foreclose* by Dr. David Lowes Watson, a prominent United Methodist scholar related to the General Board of Discipleship, articulates this idea brilliantly.[8] In a sense these two concepts complement each other. They seem to fit together comfortably. Both swiftly will become urgent, if controversial, issues within the contemporary Christian community. Some of us feel that they threaten, among other things, both the necessity and legitimacy of evangelism. They are being advanced on many fronts by sincere and thoughtful Christian scholars, and the resolution of the problems they present may eventuate in what one editor has called "the theological showdown of the decade."

Many developments in contemporary Christian dialogue, of which the foregoing are but two, seem to militate against the kind of confidence in the Christian message that is totally essential as a basis for vigorous and effective evangelism. Unless the message is crystal clear in our own minds and hearts, we cannot communicate it thrillingly to other human beings. In fact, unless we are ourselves fundamentally convinced that human life without Jesus Christ is lost, and unless this lostness produces in us, to use Puritan language, the "gift of tears," we *shall not* be productive sharers of the gospel. The trumpet will give an uncertain sound!

Related to the necessity for confidence in the message of evangelism are two other matters. First, we must recognize our dismal failure in attempting to influence successfully in our own culture members of the various ethnic groups, particularly Blacks; youth and young adults; citizens and craftspeople in the community of arts and letters; and, assuming we are to have the ethical privilege of evangelizing them, members of Islam and other non-Christian religious groups. The second matter is our equally dismal failure to proclaim the gospel from our pulpits in a way which urgently invites and produces decision.

One has only to read again the stirring sermons of Harry Emerson Fosdick from the great Riverside pulpit in New York City to sense the tragic truth of the point I am making. Dr. Fosdick, quite clearly, was the most effective pastoral evangelist of his day, and we have not identified his comparable successor since he retired forty years ago. May God send us and seminaries equip for us *pulpit virtuosos* who so deeply believe in the truth of their message that, without apology, they seek to implement the timeless advice of Phillips Brooks in his great Yale Lectures: "Preach doctrine! Preach all the doctrine you know and learn forevermore; but preach it not that people may believe, but preach it that people may be saved by believing it!"

Evangelism Must Hear the Voice of God

How often must we remind ourselves that the implementation of the church's mission, particularly evangelism, is essentially a spiritual enterprise? It was Karl Barth who said, "To clasp hands in prayer is the beginning of an uprising against the disorder of the world." Perhaps an appropriate commentary on Professor Barth's observation comes from Martin Luther in his *Table Talk*. Luther had a pet dog which always stood by the table while his master ate, looking for some morsel which might fall from Luther's plate or hand. The dog watched with open mouth and motionless eyes, prompting Luther to comment, "Oh, if I could only pray the way this dog watches the meat! All his thoughts are concentrated on the piece of meat. Otherwise, he has no thought, wish, or hope."[9]

Sometimes I find myself wondering if the mortal malady afflicting the church in our time is not the Christian's tragic failure to go beyond the necessary intellectual analysis of faith's entities and structures, to comprehend that doing God's will is an adventure far more transcendent in its nature than any mere human transactions. It has to do with the Almighty, with eternity, and with the human spirit in revolutionary communion with its Savior. Many years ago, as a young preacher, I heard the picturesque British evangelist Gipsy Smith, Sr., assert that "a Christian is someone who always makes you think of Jesus." After many years of studying, preaching, and living, I cannot find it in myself to question these words. However, now I know that it is not possible for a mere woman or man effectively to cause another human being to think of Jesus without a miracle of spiritual transformation having occurred first in the life of that person! The voice of God has to be heard.

It is just here, I am persuaded, that the noblest programs and projects of the Church so often falter and fail. Unless we pause in the midst of the shrill cacophony of worldly noises to hear the voice of God, it simply is not possible for us to bring our emotions, minds, and wills into compelling focus upon the spiritual tasks we have undertaken. In Robert Moats Miller's monumental biography of Harry Emerson Fosdick, mention is made of the great Riverside preacher's practice of listening to student sermons in his classes at

Union Seminary in New York. One day he heard a young Methodist minister. After praising this young man's outline and content, Dr. Fosdick continued, "You are a Methodist, aren't you? Then where, where is your *passion?*"[10] It was a proper question, for unless there is that intense interior motivation which comes from deep conviction and feeling, it is highly unlikely that a Christian's words, in or out of the pulpit, will move others to meaningful response. It is the valid experience of God's redeeming grace in Jesus Christ which leads a man or woman to confront the *lostness* of a fellow human being and to offer that person, in God's name, the priceless gift of salvation.

Let me return now to Gustave Weigel's words with which I began this message. If the great Jesuit was right in contending that the church exists "for the sake of those who are not yet in it," then the bottom-line objective of the new professorship which James Cecil Logan will fill with great distinction here at Wesley Seminary is to equip generations of United Methodist ministers, in these neo-pagan days of modern history, to deal with that numerous and diverse company of people who are outside the church and have no conscious desire to enter it or the life for which it stands.

Joseph Conrad said years ago that the role of the artist in human civilization is to offer for tired, distracted, bemused people "that glimpse of truth for which they have forgotten to ask." This, I submit, is also the task of the minister of the gospel who would be an evangelist.

Endnotes

1.   Lynn Harold Hough, *The Great Evangel* (Nashville: Cokesbury Press, 1936), 65-69.

2.   Edwin Holt Hughes, *Evangelism and Change* (New York: The Methodist Book Concern, 1938), 41.

3.   Haskell M. Miller, "United Methodist Church's Membership Loss: What the Experts Are Missing," *Circuit Rider* (March 1989): 8-9.

4.   David Stoll, "A Protestant Reformation in Latin America" *The Christian Century* (Jan. 17, 1990): 44-48.

5.   Robert Speaight, *Pierre Teilhard de Chardin* (New York and Evanston: Harper & Row, 1967), 313.

6.   Wade Clarke Roof, "The Church in the Centrifuge," *The Christian Century* (Nov. 8, 1989): 1012-1014.

7.   Carl F. H. Henry, *Twilight of a Great Civilization* (Westchester, IL: Crossway Books, a division of Good News Publishers, 1988).

8.   David Lowes Watson, *God Does Not Foreclose* (Nashville: Abingdon Press, 1991).

9.   Martin Luther, *Table Talk*. Quoted in "Reflections: Classic and Contemporary Excerpts," *Christianity Today* (March 3, 1989): 23.

10.   Robert Moats Miller, *Harry Emerson Fosdick* (New York: Oxford University Press, 1985), 324.